Visit classzone
and get connected

Online resources for students and parents

ClassZone resources provide instruction, practice, and learning support.

eEdition Plus ONLINE

This interactive version of the text encourages students to explore science.

Content Review Online

Interactive review reinforces the big idea and key concepts of each chapter.

SciLinks

NSTA-selected links provide relevant Web resources correlated to the text.

Chapter-Based Support

Math tutorials, news, resources, test practice, and a misconceptions database help students succeed.

Now it all clicks!™

CLASSZONE.COM

McDougal Littell

McDougal Littell Science

Waves, Sound, and Light

transfer of
energy

EM wave

MECHANICAL WAVE

PHYSICAL SCIENCE

A ▶ Matter and Energy
B ▶ Chemical Interactions
C ▶ Motion and Forces
D ▶ Waves, Sound, and Light
E ▶ Electricity and Magnetism

LIFE SCIENCE

A ▶ Cells and Heredity
B ▶ Life Over Time
C ▶ Diversity of Living Things
D ▶ Ecology
E ▶ Human Biology

EARTH SCIENCE

A ▶ Earth's Surface
B ▶ The Changing Earth
C ▶ Earth's Waters
D ▶ Earth's Atmosphere
E ▶ Space Science

Acknowledgments: Excerpts and adaptations from *National Science Education Standards* by the National Academy of Sciences. Copyright © 1996 by the National Academy of Sciences. Reprinted with permission from the National Academies Press, Washington, D.C.

Excerpts and adaptations from *Benchmarks for Science Literacy: Project 2061*. Copyright © 1993 by the American Association for the Advancement of Science. Reprinted with permission.

ISBN-13: 978-0-618-84255-1

ISBN-10: 0-618-84255-1   2 3 4 5 VJM 10 09 08 07

Internet Web Site: http://www.mcdougallittell.com

Science Consultants

Chief Science Consultant

James Trefil, Ph.D. is the Clarence J. Robinson Professor of Physics at George Mason University. He is the author or co-author of more than 25 books, including *Science Matters* and *The Nature of Science*. Dr. Trefil is a member of the American Association for the Advancement of Science's Committee on the Public Understanding of Science and Technology. He is also a fellow of the World Economic Forum and a frequent contributor to *Smithsonian* magazine.

Rita Ann Calvo, Ph.D. is Senior Lecturer in Molecular Biology and Genetics at Cornell University, where for 12 years she also directed the Cornell Institute for Biology Teachers. Dr. Calvo is the 1999 recipient of the College and University Teaching Award from the National Association of Biology Teachers.

Kenneth Cutler, M.S. is the Education Coordinator for the Julius L. Chambers Biomedical Biotechnology Research Institute at North Carolina Central University. A former middle school and high school science teacher, he received a 1999 Presidential Award for Excellence in Science Teaching.

Instructional Design Consultants

Douglas Carnine, Ph.D. is Professor of Education and Director of the National Center for Improving the Tools of Educators at the University of Oregon. He is the author of seven books and over 100 other scholarly publications, primarily in the areas of instructional design and effective instructional strategies and tools for diverse learners. Dr. Carnine also serves as a member of the National Institute for Literacy Advisory Board.

Linda Carnine, Ph.D. consults with school districts on curriculum development and effective instruction for students struggling academically. A former teacher and school administrator, Dr. Carnine also co-authored a popular remedial reading program.

Donald Steely, Ph.D. serves as principal investigator at the Oregon Center for Applied Science (ORCAS) on federal grants for science and language arts programs. His background also includes teaching and authoring of print and multimedia programs in science, mathematics, history, and spelling.

Sam Miller, Ph.D. is a middle school science teacher and the Teacher Development Liaison for the Eugene, Oregon, Public Schools. He is the author of curricula for teaching science, mathematics, computer skills, and language arts.

Vicky Vachon, Ph.D. consults with school districts throughout the United States and Canada on improving overall academic achievement with a focus on literacy. She is also co-author of a widely used program for remedial readers.

Content Reviewers

John Beaver, Ph.D.
Ecology
Professor, Director of Science Education Center
College of Education and Human Services
Western Illinois University
Macomb, IL

Donald J. DeCoste, Ph.D.
Matter and Energy, Chemical Interactions
Chemistry Instructor
University of Illinois
Urbana-Champaign, IL

Dorothy Ann Fallows, Ph.D., MSc
Diversity of Living Things, Microbiology
Partners in Health
Boston, MA

Michael Foote, Ph.D.
The Changing Earth, Life Over Time
Associate Professor
Department of the Geophysical Sciences
The University of Chicago
Chicago, IL

Lucy Fortson, Ph.D.
Space Science
Director of Astronomy
Adler Planetarium and Astronomy Museum
Chicago, IL

Elizabeth Godrick, Ph.D.
Human Biology
Professor, CAS Biology
Boston University
Boston, MA

Isabelle Sacramento Grilo, M.S.
The Changing Earth
Lecturer, Department of the Geological Sciences
San Diego State University
San Diego, CA

David Harbster, MSc
Diversity of Living Things
Professor of Biology
Paradise Valley Community College
Phoenix, AZ

Richard D. Norris, Ph.D.
Earth's Waters
Professor of Paleobiology
Scripps Institution of Oceanography
University of California, San Diego
La Jolla, CA

Donald B. Peck, M.S.
*Motion and Forces; Waves, Sound, and Light;
  Electricity and Magnetism*
Director of the Center for Science Education (retired)
Fairleigh Dickinson University
Madison, NJ

Javier Penalosa, Ph.D.
Diversity of Living Things, Plants
Associate Professor, Biology Department
Buffalo State College
Buffalo, NY

Raymond T. Pierrehumbert, Ph.D.
Earth's Atmosphere
Professor in Geophysical Sciences (Atmospheric Science)
The University of Chicago
Chicago, IL

Brian J. Skinner, Ph.D.
Earth's Surface
Eugene Higgins Professor of Geology and Geophysics
Yale University
New Haven, CT

Nancy E. Spaulding, M.S.
Earth's Surface, The Changing Earth, Earth's Waters
Earth Science Teacher (retired)
Elmira Free Academy
Elmira, NY

Steven S. Zumdahl, Ph.D.
Matter and Energy, Chemical Interactions
Professor Emeritus of Chemistry
University of Illinois
Urbana-Champaign, IL

Susan L. Zumdahl, M.S.
Matter and Energy, Chemical Interactions
Chemistry Education Specialist
University of Illinois
Urbana-Champaign, IL

Safety Consultant

Juliana Texley, Ph.D.
Former K–12 Science Teacher and School Superintendent
Boca Raton, FL

English Language Advisor

Judy Lewis, M.A.
Director, State and Federal Programs for reading proficiency
and high risk populations
Rancho Cordova, CA

Teacher Panel Members

Carol Arbour
Tallmadge Middle School,
Tallmadge, OH

Patty Belcher
Goodrich Middle School,
Akron, OH

Gwen Broestl
Luis Munoz Marin Middle School,
Cleveland, OH

Al Brofman
Tehipite Middle School,
Fresno, CA

John Cockrell
Clinton Middle School,
Columbus, OH

Jenifer Cox
Sylvan Middle School,
Citrus Heights, CA

Linda Culpepper
Martin Middle School,
Charlotte, NC

Kathleen Ann DeMatteo
Margate Middle School,
Margate, FL

Melvin Figueroa
New River Middle School,
Ft. Lauderdale, FL

Doretha Grier
Kannapolis Middle School,
Kannapolis, NC

Robert Hood
Alexander Hamilton Middle School,
Cleveland, OH

Scott Hudson
Covedale Elementary School,
Cincinnati, OH

Loretta Langdon
Princeton Middle School,
Princeton, NC

Carlyn Little
Glades Middle School,
Miami, FL

Ann Marie Lynn
Amelia Earhart Middle School,
Riverside, CA

James Minogue
Lowe's Grove Middle School,
Durham, NC

Joann Myers
Buchanan Middle School,
Tampa, FL

Barbara Newell
Charles Evans Hughes Middle School,
Long Beach, CA

Anita Parker
Kannapolis Middle School,
Kannapolis, NC

Greg Pirolo
Golden Valley Middle School,
San Bernardino, CA

Laura Pottmyer
Apex Middle School,
Apex, NC

Lynn Prichard
Booker T. Washington Middle Magnet
School, Tampa, FL

Jacque Quick
Walter Williams High School,
Burlington, NC

Robert Glenn Reynolds
Hillman Middle School,
Youngstown, OH

Stacy Rinehart
Lufkin Road Middle School,
Apex, NC

Theresa Short
Abbott Middle School,
Fayetteville, NC

Rita Slivka
Alexander Hamilton Middle School,
Cleveland, OH

Marie Sofsak
B F Stanton Middle School,
Alliance, OH

Nancy Stubbs
Sweetwater Union Unified School District,
Chula Vista, CA

Sharon Stull
Quail Hollow Middle School,
Charlotte, NC

Donna Taylor
Okeeheelee Middle School,
West Palm Beach, FL

Sandi Thompson
Harding Middle School,
Lakewood, OH

Lori Walker
Audubon Middle School & Magnet Center,
Los Angeles, CA

Teacher Lab Evaluators

Andrew Boy
W.E.B. DuBois Academy,
Cincinnati, OH

Jill Brimm-Byrne
Albany Park Academy,
Chicago, IL

Gwen Broestl
Luis Munoz Marin Middle School,
Cleveland, OH

Al Brofman
Tehipite Middle School,
Fresno, CA

Michael A. Burstein
The Rashi School,
Newton, MA

Trudi Coutts
Madison Middle School,
Naperville, IL

Jenifer Cox
Sylvan Middle School,
Citrus Heights, CA

Larry Cwik
Madison Middle School,
Naperville, IL

Jennifer Donatelli
Kennedy Junior High School,
Lisle, IL

Melissa Dupree
Lakeside Middle School,
Evans, GA

Carl Fechko
Luis Munoz Marin Middle School,
Cleveland, OH

Paige Fullhart
Highland Middle School,
Libertyville, IL

Sue Hood
Glen Crest Middle School,
Glen Ellyn, IL

William Luzader
Plymouth Community Intermediate School,
Plymouth, MA

Ann Min
Beardsley Middle School,
Crystal Lake, IL

Aileen Mueller
Kennedy Junior High School,
Lisle, IL

Nancy Nega
Churchville Middle School,
Elmhurst, IL

Oscar Newman
Sumner Math and Science Academy,
Chicago, IL

Lynn Prichard
Booker T. Washington Middle Magnet
School, Tampa, FL

Jacque Quick
Walter Williams High School,
Burlington, NC

Stacy Rinehart
Lufkin Road Middle School,
Apex, NC

Seth Robey
Gwendolyn Brooks Middle School,
Oak Park, IL

Kevin Steele
Grissom Middle School,
Tinley Park, IL

Waves, Sound, and Light

Unit Features

1 Waves 6

the **BIG** idea

Waves transfer energy and interact in predictable ways.

2 Sound 34

the **BIG** idea

Sound waves transfer energy through vibrations.

How is this guitar player producing sound? page 34

How does this phone stay connected? page 70

Features

Visual Highlights

Internet Resources @ ClassZone.com

INVESTIGATIONS AND ACTIVITIES

EXPLORE THE BIG IDEA

Chapter Opening Inquiry

CHAPTER INVESTIGATION

Full-Period Labs

EXPLORE

Introductory Inquiry Activities

INVESTIGATE

Skill Labs

Standards and Benchmarks

Each chapter in **Waves, Sound, and Light** covers some of the learning goals that are described in the *National Science Education Standards* (NSES) and the Project 2061 *Benchmarks for Science Literacy*. Selected content and skill standards are shown below in shortened form. The following National Science Education Standards are covered on pages xii–xxvii, in Frontiers in Science, and in Timelines in Science, as well as in chapter features and laboratory investigations: Understandings About Scientific Inquiry (A.9), Understandings About Science and Technology (E.6), Science and Technology in Society (F.5), Science as a Human Endeavor (G.1), Nature of Science (G.2), and History of Science (G.3).

Content Standards

1 Waves

	National Science Education Standards
B.3.a	Energy is transferred in many ways. Energy is often associated with • sound • light • mechanical motion

	Project 2061 Benchmarks
4.F.4	Vibrations in materials set up wavelike disturbances that spread away from the source. Sound and earthquake waves are examples. These and other waves move at different speeds through different materials.

2 Sound

	Project 2061 Benchmarks
4.F.4	Vibrations start waves. Waves move at different speeds in different materials.

3 Electromagnetic Waves

	National Science Education Standards
B.3.c	Light interacts with matter by • transmission • absorption • scattering
B.3.f	Energy from the Sun is transferred to Earth in the form of • visible light • infrared light • ultraviolet light

	Project 2061 Benchmarks
4.F.1	Light from the sun is made up of a mixture of many different colors of light, even though to the eye the light looks almost white. Other things that give off or reflect light have a different mix of colors.
4.F.4	Waves move at different speeds through different materials.
4.F.5	Human eyes detect only a small range of waves in the electromagnetic spectrum. Different wavelengths of visible light are perceived as different colors.

4 Light and Optics

	National Science Education Standards
B.3.c	To see an object, light from that object must enter the eye.
	Project 2061 Benchmarks
4.F.2	Something can be "seen" when light waves emitted or reflected by it enter the eye—just as something can be "heard" when sound waves from it enter the ear.
4.F.5	Human eyes respond to only a narrow range of wavelengths of electromagnetic radiation—visible light. Differences of wavelength within that range are perceived as differences in color.

Process and Skill Standards

	National Science Education Standards		**Project 2061 Benchmarks**
A.1	Identify questions that can be answered through investigation.	1.A.3	Some knowledge in science is very old and yet is still used today.
A.2	Design and conduct a scientific investigation.	1.C.1	Contributions to science and technology have been made by different people, in different cultures, at different times.
A.3	Use appropriate tools and techniques to gather and interpret data.	6.A.5	People use technology to match or go beyond the abilities of other species.
A.4	Use evidence to describe, predict, explain, and model.	9.B.3	Graphs can show the relationship between two variables.
A.5	Use critical thinking to find relationships between results and interpretations.	9.C.4	Graphs show patterns and can be used to make predictions.
A.6	Consider alternative explanations and predictions.	9.D.3	The mean, median, and mode are different ways of finding the middle of a set of data.
A.7	Communicate procedures, results, and conclusions.	11.C.4	Use equations to summarize observed changes.
A.8	Use mathematics in scientific investigations.	12.B.4	Find the mean and median of a set of data.
E.1	Identify a problem to be solved.	12.C.3	Use appropriate units, use and read instruments that measure quantities such as length, volume, weight, time, rate, and temperature.
E.2	Design a solution or product.		
E.3	Implement the proposed solution.	12.D.1	Use tables and graphs to organize information and identify relationships.
E.4	Evaluate the solution or design.	12.D.2	Read, interpret, and describe tables and graphs.
F.4.c	Use systematic thinking to estimate risks.	12.D.4	Understand information that includes different types of charts and graphs, including circle charts, bar graphs, line graphs, data tables, diagrams, and symbols.
F.4.d	Decisions are made based on estimated risks and benefits.	12.E.4	There may be more than one good way to interpret scientific findings.

Introducing Physical Science

Scientists are curious. Since ancient times, they have been asking and answering questions about the world around them. Scientists are also very suspicious of the answers they get. They carefully collect evidence and test their answers many times before accepting an idea as correct.

In this book you will see how scientific knowledge keeps growing and changing as scientists ask new questions and rethink what was known before. The following sections will help get you started.

What Is Physical Science?

In the simplest terms, physical science is the study of what things are made of and how they change. It combines the studies of both physics and chemistry. Physics is the science of matter, energy, and forces. It includes the study of topics such as motion, light, and electricity and magnetism. Chemistry is the study of the structure and properties of matter, and it especially focuses on how substances change into different substances.

The text and pictures in this book will help you learn key concepts and important facts about physical science. A variety of activities will help you investigate these concepts. As you learn, it helps to have a big picture of physical science as a framework for this new information. The four unifying principles listed below will give you this big picture. Read the next few pages to get an overview of each of these principles and a sense of why they are so important.

- **Matter is made of particles too small to see.**

- **Matter changes form and moves from place to place.**

- **Energy changes from one form to another, but it cannot be created or destroyed.**

- **Physical forces affect the movement of all matter on Earth and throughout the universe.**

the BIG idea

Each chapter begins with a big idea. Keep in mind that each big idea relates to one or more of the unifying principles.

Matter is made of particles too small to see.

This simple statement is the basis for explaining an amazing variety of things about the world. For example, it explains why substances can exist as solids, liquids, and gases, and why wood burns but iron does not. Like the tiles that make up this mosaic picture, the particles that make up all substances combine to make patterns and structures that can be seen. Unlike these tiles, the individual particles themselves are far too small to see.

What It Means

To understand this principle better, let's take a closer look at the two key words: *matter* and *particles.*

Matter

Objects you can see and touch are all around you. The materials that these objects are made of are called **matter.** All living things—even you—are also matter. Even though you can't see it, the air around you is matter too. Scientists often say that matter is anything that has mass and takes up space. **Mass** is a measure of the amount of matter in an object. We use the word **volume** to refer to the amount of space an object or a substance takes up.

Particles

The tiny particles that make up all matter are called **atoms.** Just how tiny are atoms? They are far too small to see, even through a powerful microscope. In fact, an atom is more than a million times smaller than the period at the end of this sentence.

There are more than 100 basic kinds of matter called **elements.** For example, iron, gold, and oxygen are three common elements. Each element has its own unique kind of atom. The atoms of any element are all alike but different from the atoms of any other element.

Many familiar materials are made of particles called molecules. In a **molecule,** two or more atoms stick together to form a larger particle. For example, a water molecule is made of two atoms of hydrogen and one atom of oxygen.

Why It's Important

Understanding atoms and molecules makes it possible to explain and predict the behavior of matter. Among other things, this knowledge allows scientists to

• explain why different materials have different characteristics
• predict how a material will change when heated or cooled
• figure out how to combine atoms and molecules to make new and useful materials

Matter changes form and moves from place to place.

You see matter change form every day. You see the ice in your glass of juice disappear without a trace. You see a black metal gate slowly develop a flaky, orange coating. Matter is constantly changing and moving.

What It Means

Remember that matter is made of tiny particles called atoms. Atoms are constantly moving and combining with one another. All changes in matter are the result of atoms moving and combining in different ways.

Matter Changes and Moves

You can look at water to see how matter changes and moves. A block of ice is hard like a rock. Leave the ice out in sunlight, however, and it changes into a puddle of water. That puddle of water can eventually change into water vapor and disappear into the air. The water vapor in the air can become raindrops, which may fall on rocks, causing them to weather and wear away. The water that flows in rivers and streams picks up tiny bits of rock and carries them from one shore to another. Understanding how the world works requires an understanding of how matter changes and moves.

Matter Is Conserved

No matter was lost in any of the changes described above. The ice turned to water because its molecules began to move more quickly as they got warmer. The bits of rock carried away by the flowing river were not gone forever. They simply ended up farther down the river. The puddles of rainwater didn't really disappear; their molecules slowly mixed with molecules in the air.

Under ordinary conditions, when matter changes form, no matter is created or destroyed. The water created by melting ice has the same mass as the ice did. If you could measure the water vapor that mixes with the air, you would find it had the same mass as the water in the puddle did.

Why It's Important

Understanding how mass is conserved when matter changes form has helped scientists to

• describe changes they see in the world
• predict what will happen when two substances are mixed
• explain where matter goes when it seems to disappear

Energy changes from one form to another, but it cannot be created or destroyed.

When you use energy to warm your food or to turn on a flashlight, you may think that you "use up" the energy. Even though the camp-stove fuel is gone and the flashlight battery no longer functions, the energy they provided has not disappeared. It has been changed into a form you can no longer use. Understanding how energy changes forms is the basis for understanding how heat, light, and motion are produced.

What It Means

Changes that you see around you depend on energy. **Energy,** in fact, means the ability to cause change. The electrical energy from an outlet changes into light and heat in a light bulb. Plants change the light energy from the Sun into chemical energy, which animals use to power their muscles.

Energy Changes Forms

Using energy means changing energy. You probably have seen electric energy changing into light, heat, sound, and mechanical energy in household appliances. Fuels like wood, coal, and oil contain chemical energy that produces heat when burned. Electric power plants make electrical energy from a variety of energy sources, including falling water, nuclear energy, and fossil fuels.

Energy Is Conserved

Energy can be converted into forms that can be used for specific purposes. During the conversion, some of the original energy is converted into unwanted forms. For instance, when a power plant converts the energy of falling water into electrical energy, some of the energy is lost to friction and sound.

Similarly, when electrical energy is used to run an appliance, some of the energy is converted into forms that are not useful. Only a small percentage of the energy used in a light bulb, for instance, produces light; most of the energy becomes heat. Nonetheless, the total amount of energy remains the same through all these conversions.

The fact that energy does not disappear is a law of physical science. The **law of conservation of energy** states that energy cannot be created or destroyed. It can only change form.

Why It's Important

Understanding that energy changes form but does not disappear has helped scientists to

• predict how energy will change form
• manage energy conversions in useful ways
• build and improve machines

Physical forces affect the movement of all matter on Earth and throughout the universe.

What makes the world go around? The answer is simple: forces. Forces allow you to walk across the room, and forces keep the stars together in galaxies. Consider the forces acting on the rafts below. The rushing water is pushing the rafts forward. The force from the people paddling helps to steer the rafts.

What It Means

A **force** is a push or a pull. Every time you push or pull an object, you're applying a force to that object, whether or not the object moves. There are several forces—several pushes and pulls—acting on you right now. All these forces are necessary for you to do the things you do, even sitting and reading.

• You are already familiar with the force of gravity. **Gravity** is the force of attraction between two objects. Right now gravity is at work pulling you to Earth and Earth to you. The Moon stays in orbit around Earth because gravity holds it close.

• A contact force occurs when one object pushes or pulls another object by touching it. If you kick a soccer ball, for instance, you apply a contact force to the ball. You apply a contact force to a shopping cart that you push down a grocery aisle or a sled that you pull up a hill.

• **Friction** is the force that resists motion between two surfaces pressed together. If you've ever tried to walk on an icy sidewalk, you know how important friction can be. If you lightly rub your finger across a smooth page in a book and then across a piece of sandpaper, you can feel how the different surfaces produce different frictional forces. Which is easier to do?

• There are other forces at work in the world too. For example, a compass needle responds to the magnetic force exerted by Earth's magnetic field, and objects made of certain metals are attracted by magnets. In addition to magnetic forces, there are electrical forces operating between particles and between objects. For example, you can demonstrate electrical forces by rubbing an inflated balloon on your hair. The balloon will then stick to your head or to a wall without additional means of support.

Why It's Important

Although some of these forces are more obvious than others, physical forces at work in the world are necessary for you to do the things you do. Understanding forces allows scientists to

• predict how objects will move
• design machines that perform complex tasks
• predict where planets and stars will be in the sky from one night to the next

The Nature of Science

You may think of science as a body of knowledge or a collection of facts. More important, however, science is an active process that involves certain ways of looking at the world.

Scientific Habits of Mind

Scientists are curious. They are always asking questions. Scientists have asked questions such as, "What is the smallest form of matter?" and "How do the smallest particles behave?" These and other important questions are being investigated by scientists around the world.

Scientists are observant. They are always looking closely at the world around them. Scientists once thought the smallest parts of atoms were protons, neutrons, and electrons. Later, protons and neutrons were found to be made of even smaller particles called quarks.

Scientists are creative. They draw on what they know to form possible explanations for a pattern, an event, or an interesting phenomenon that they have observed. Then scientists create a plan for testing their ideas.

Scientists are skeptical. Scientists don't accept an explanation or answer unless it is based on evidence and logical reasoning. They continually question their own conclusions and the conclusions suggested by other scientists. Scientists trust only evidence that is confirmed by other people or methods.

Scientists cannot always make observations with their own eyes. They have developed technology, such as this particle detector, to help them gather information about the smallest particles of matter.

Scientists ask questions about the physical world and seek answers through carefully controlled procedures. Here a researcher works with supercooled magnets.

Science Processes at Work

You can think of science as a continuous cycle of asking and seeking answers to questions about the world. Although there are many processes that scientists use, scientists typically do each of the following:

- Observe and ask a question
- Determine what is known
- Investigate
- Interpret results
- Share results

Observe and Ask a Question

It may surprise you that asking questions is an important skill. A scientific process may start when a scientist asks a question. Perhaps scientists observe an event or a process that they don't understand, or perhaps answering one question leads to another.

Determine What Is Known

When beginning an inquiry, scientists find out what is already known about a question. They study results from other scientific investigations, read journals, and talk with other scientists. A scientist working on subatomic particles is most likely a member of a large team using sophisticated equipment. Before beginning original research, the team analyzes results from previous studies.

Investigate

Investigating is the process of collecting evidence. Two important ways of investigating are observing and experimenting.

Observing is the act of noting and recording an event, a characteristic, or anything else detected with an instrument or with the senses. A researcher may study the properties of a substance by handling it, finding its mass, warming or cooling it, stretching it, and so on. For information about the behavior of subatomic particles, however, a researcher may rely on technology such as scanning tunneling microscopes, which produce images of structures that cannot be seen with the eye.

An **experiment** is an organized procedure to study something under controlled conditions. In order to study the effect of wing shape on the motion of a glider, for instance, a researcher would need to conduct controlled studies in which gliders made of the same materials and with the same masses differed only in the shape of their wings.

Scanning tunneling microscopes create images that allow scientists to observe molecular structure.

Physical chemists have found a way to observe chemical reactions at the atomic level. Using lasers, they can watch bonds breaking and new bonds forming.

Forming hypotheses and making predictions are two of the skills involved in scientific investigations. A **hypothesis** is a tentative explanation for an observation, a phenomenon, or a scientific problem that can be tested by further investigation. For example, in the mid-1800s astronomers noticed that the planet Uranus departed slightly from its expected orbit. One astronomer hypothesized that the irregularities in the planet's orbit were due to the gravitational effect of another planet—one that had not yet been detected. A **prediction** is an expectation of what will be observed or what will happen. A prediction can be used to test a hypothesis. The astronomers predicted that they would discover a new planet in the position calculated, and their prediction was confirmed with the discovery of the planet Neptune.

Interpret Results

As scientists investigate, they analyze their evidence, or data, and begin to draw conclusions. **Analyzing data** involves looking at the evidence gathered through observations or experiments and trying to identify any patterns that might exist in the data. Scientists often need to make additional observations or perform more experiments before they are sure of their conclusions. Many times scientists make new predictions or revise their hypotheses.

Often scientists use computers to help them analyze data. Computers reveal patterns that might otherwise be missed.

Scientists use computers to create models of objects or processes they are studying. This model shows carbon atoms forming a sphere.

Share Results

An important part of scientific investigation is sharing results of experiments. Scientists read and publish in journals and attend conferences to communicate with other scientists around the world. Sharing data and procedures gives them a way to test one another's results. They also share results with the public through newspapers, television, and other media.

The Nature of Technology

When you think of technology, you may think of cars, computers, and cell phones, as well as refrigerators, radios, and bicycles. Technology is not only the machines and devices that make modern lives easier, however. It is also a process in which new methods and devices are created. Technology makes use of scientific knowledge to design solutions to real-world problems.

Science and Technology

Science and technology go hand in hand. Each depends upon the other. Even designing a device as simple as a toaster requires knowledge of how heat flows and which materials are the best conductors of heat. Just as technology based on scientific knowledge makes our lives easier, some technology is used to advance scientific inquiry itself. For example, researchers use a number of specialized instruments to help them collect data. Microscopes, telescopes, spectrographs, and computers are just a few of the tools that help scientists learn more about the world. The more information these tools provide, the more devices can be developed to aid scientific research and to improve modern lives.

The Process of Technological Design

The process of technology involves many choices. For example, how does an automobile engineer design a better car? Is a better car faster? safer? cheaper? Before designing any new machine, the engineer must decide exactly what he or she wants the machine to do as well as what may be given up for the machine to do it. A faster car may get people to their destinations more quickly, but it may cost more and be less safe. As you study the technological process, think about all the choices that were made to build the technologies you use.

Identify a Need

Successful technology fills a need; it helps us perform a task we need or want to do. For example, as more cars appear on the road, noise and air pollution become serious threats to the environment and to people's health. Gas consumption also depletes precious petroleum resources. There is a need to find a fuel source for a car that will not pollute the air and that will never run out.

Design and Develop

Hydrogen fuel cells are a potential solution to this need. These cells combine hydrogen and oxygen into water, producing electricity in the process. Engineers have found a way to make fuel cells small enough to fit into a car, yet able to produce enough electricity to power an electric motor. Before arriving at this final design, engineers tried many others.

Test and Improve

Just because a technology works doesn't mean it cannot be improved. A fuel-cell-powered car has been driven from San Francisco to Washington, D.C., but it probably will be a while before it's in dealer showrooms. Engineers won't know how these cars will perform until they're driven in real-world conditions. Engineers also won't know if the average driver will be able to handle the necessary maintenance on the car until the car is made available to ordinary drivers. Improvements in the future may well bring cars powered by fuel cells into garages everywhere.

Using McDougal Littell Science

Reading Text and Visuals

This book is organized to help you learn. Use these boxed pointers as a path to help you learn and remember the **Big Ideas** and **Key Concepts**.

Read the Big Idea.

As you read **Key Concepts** for the chapter, relate them to **the Big Idea**.

Take notes.

Use the strategies on the **Getting Ready to Learn** page.

CHAPTER

2 Soun

the **BIG** idea

Sound waves transfer energy through vibrations.

Key Concepts

SECTION 2.1 Sound is a wave.
Learn how sound waves are produced and detected.

SECTION 2.2 Frequency determines pitch.
Learn about the relationship between the frequency of a sound wave and its pitch.

SECTION 2.3 Intensity determines loudness.
Learn how the energy of a sound wave relates to its loudness.

SECTION 2.4 Sound has many uses.
Learn how sound waves are used to detect objects and to make music.

 Internet Preview

CLASSZONE.COM
Chapter 2 online resources: Content Review, two Visualizations, three Resource Centers, Math Tutorial, Test Practice

---

CHAPTER 2
Getting Ready to Learn

◄ CONCEPT REVIEW

- A wave is a disturbance that transfers energy from one place to another.
- Mechanical waves are waves that travel through matter.

◄ VOCABULARY REVIEW

medium p. 11
longitudinal wave p. 14
amplitude p. 17
wavelength p. 17
frequency p. 17

CONTENT REVIEW
CLASSZONE.COM
Review concepts and vocabulary.

► TAKING NOTES

OUTLINE

As you read, copy the headings on your paper in the form of an outline. Then add notes in your own words that summarize what you have read.

VOCABULARY STRATEGY

Place each vocabulary term at the center of a **description wheel** diagram. Write some words on the spokes describing it.

See the Note-Taking Handbook on pages R45–R51.

SCIENCE NOTEBOOK

I. Sound is a type of mechanical wave
  A. How sound waves are produced
    1.
    2.
    3.
  B. How sound waves are detected
    1.
    2.
    3.

rapid back-and-forth motion — can produce a sound — **VIBRATION** — usually too small to see — can make with vocal cords

KEY CONCEPT
2.1 Sound is a wave.

◄ **BEFORE, you learned**

• Waves transfer energy
• Waves have wavelength, amplitude, and frequency

▶ **NOW, you will learn**

• How sound waves are produced and detected
• How sound waves transfer energy
• What affects the speed of sound waves

VOCABULARY

sound p. 37
vibration p. 37
vacuum p. 41

EXPLORE Sound

What is sound?

PROCEDURE

① Tie the middle of the string to the spoon handle.

② Wrap the string ends around your left and right index fingers. Put the tips of these fingers gently in your ears and hold them there.

③ Stand over your desk so that the spoon dangles without touching your body or the desk. Then move a little to make the spoon tap the desk lightly. Listen to the sound.

MATERIALS

• piece of string
• large metal spoon

WHAT DO YOU THINK?

• What did you hear when the spoon tapped the desk?
• How did sound travel from the spoon to your ears?

Sound is a type of mechanical wave.

OUTLINE
Start an outline for this heading. Remember to leave room for details.

I. Main idea
  A. Supporting idea
    1. Detail
    2. Detail
  B. Supporting idea

In the last chapter, you read that a mechanical wave travels through a material medium. Such mediums include air, water, and solid materials. Sound is an example of a mechanical wave. **Sound** is a wave that is produced by a vibrating object and travels through matter.

The disturbances that travel in a sound wave are vibrations. A **vibration** is a rapid, back-and-forth motion. Because the medium vibrates back and forth in the same direction as the wave travels, sound is a longitudinal wave. Like all mechanical waves, sound waves transfer energy through a medium.

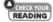 **CHECK YOUR READING** What do sound waves have in common with other mechanical waves? Your answer should include the word *energy*.

Reading Text and Visuals

A Wave Model

When these fans do "the wave" in a stadium, they are modeling the way a disturbance travels through a medium.

Each person only moves up and down.

The wave can move all the way around the stadium.

READING VISUALS In which direction do people move when doing the stadium wave? In which direction does the wave move?

Study the visuals.

• Read the title.

• Read all labels and captions.

• Figure out what the picture is showing. Notice colors, arrows, and lines.

Look at the illustration of people modeling a wave in a stadium. In this model, the crowd of people represents a wave medium. The people moving up and down represent the disturbance. The transfer of the disturbance around the stadium represents a wave. Each person only moves up and down, while the disturbance can move all the way around the stadium.

Ocean waves are another good example of energy transfer. Ocean waves travel to the shore, one after another. Instead of piling up all the ocean water on the shore, however, the waves transfer energy. A big ocean wave transfers enough kinetic energy to knock someone down.

CHECK YOUR READING How does the stadium wave differ from a real ocean wave?

Read one paragraph at a time.

Look for a topic sentence that explains the main idea of the paragraph. Figure out how the details relate to that idea. One paragraph might have several important ideas; you may have to reread to understand.

Waves can be classified by how they move.

As you have seen, one way to classify waves is according to the medium through which they travel. Another way to classify waves is by how they move. You have read that some waves transfer an up-and-down or a side-to-side motion. Other waves transfer a forward-and-backward motion.

Answer the questions.

Check Your Reading questions will help you remember what you read.

2 Unit: Waves, Sound, and Light

Doing Labs

To understand science, you have to see it in action. Doing labs helps you understand how things really work.

① Read the entire lab first.

② Form a hypothesis.

③ Follow the procedure.

④ Record the data.

CHAPTER INVESTIGATION

Wavelength

OVERVIEW AND PURPOSE The pendulum on a grandfather clock keeps time as it swings back and forth at a steady rate. The swings of a pendulum can be recorded as a wave with measurable properties. How do the properties of the pendulum affect the properties of the waves it produces? In this investigation you will use your understanding of wave properties to
- construct a pendulum and measure the waves it produces, and
- determine how the length of the pendulum affects the wavelength of the waves.

MATERIALS
- 1/2 sheet white paper
- tape
- scissors
- string
- meter stick
- fine sand
- graduated cylinder
- 2 sheets colored construction paper

▶ Problem   Write it Up

How does changing the length of a pendulum affect the wavelength?

▶ Hypothesize   Write it Up

Write a hypothesis in "If . . . , then . . . , because . . ." form to answer the problem question.

▶ Procedure

1. Make a data table like the one shown on the sample notebook page.

2. Make a cone with the half-sheet of paper by rolling it and taping it as shown. The hole in the bottom of the cone should be no larger than a pea.

3. Cut a hole in each side of the cone and tie the ends of the string to the cone to make a pendulum.

4. Hold the string on the pendulum so that the distance from your fingers holding the string to the bottom of the cone is 20 cm.

5. Cover the bottom of the cone with your fingertip. While you hold the cone, have your partner pour about 40 ml of sand into the cone.

6. Hold the pendulum about 5 cm above the construction paper as shown. Pull the pendulum from the bottom to one side of the construction paper. Be careful not to move the pendulum at the top, or to pull the pendulum over the edge of the paper.

7. Let the pendulum go while your partner gently pulls the paper forward so that the sand makes waves on the paper. Be sure to pull the paper at a steady rate. Let the remaining sand pile up on the end of the paper.

8. Measure the wavelength from crest to crest or trough to trough. Record the wavelength in your table.

9. Run two more trials, repeating steps 5–8. Be sure to pull the paper at the same speed for each trial. Calculate the average wavelength over all three trials, and record it in your table.

10. Repeat steps 4–8, changing the length of the pendulum to 30 cm and then to 40 cm.

▶ Observe and Analyze   Write it Up

1. **RECORD OBSERVATIONS** Draw the setup of your procedure. Be sure your data table is complete.

2. **IDENTIFY VARIABLES AND CONSTANTS** Identify the variables and constants that affected the wave produced by the moving pendulum. List them in your notebook.

3. **ANALYZE** What patterns can you find in your data? For example, do the numbers increase or decrease as you read down each column?

▶ Conclude   Write it Up

1. **INFER** Answer your problem question.

2. **INTERPRET** Compare your results with your hypothesis. Do your data support your hypothesis?

3. **IDENTIFY LIMITS** What possible limitations or sources of error could have affected your results?

4. **APPLY** Suppose you were examining the tracing made by a seismograph, a machine that records an earthquake wave. What would happen if you increased the speed at which the paper ran through the machine? What do you think the amplitude of the tracing represents?

▶ INVESTIGATE Further

CHALLENGE Revise your experiment to change one variable other than the length of the pendulum. Run a new trial, changing the variable you choose but keeping everything else constant. How did changing the variable affect the wave produced?

Wavelength

Problem How does changing the length of a pendulum affect the wavelength?

Hypothesize

Observe and Analyze

Table 1. Wavelengths Produced by Pendulums

Pendulum Length (cm)	Trial 1	Trial 2	Trial 3	Average Wavelength (cm)
20				
30				
40				

Conclude

⑤ Analyze your results.

⑥ Write your lab report.

Using Technology

The Internet is a great source of up-to-date science. The ClassZone Website and SciLinks have exciting sites for you to explore. Video clips and simulations can make science come alive.

Look for red banners.

Go to **classzone.com** to see simulations, visualizations, and content review.

Watch the video.

See science at work in the **Scientific American Frontiers video.**

Look up SciLinks.

Go to **scilinks.org** to explore the topic.

Atmospheric Pressure and Winds **CODE: MDL010**

Waves, Sound, and Light
Contents Overview

Unit Features

SOUND
Medicine

How will sound waves be used in the future of medicine?

SCIENTIFIC AMERICAN FRONTIERS

View the video segment "Each Sound Is a Present" to learn how advances in medicine are restoring people's hearing.

With traditional ultrasound (top), technicians interpret the image of the fetus. With the newer three-dimensional ultrasound (right), the image is much clearer.

Seeing Inside the Body

Have you ever wondered what the inside of your body looks like? Doctors have tried for many years to find ways of seeing what goes on inside a person's body that makes that person sick. Around 100 years ago, scientists found that a kind of wave called x-rays could be used to make images of the bones inside a person. This common method of seeing inside a body, is used mainly to show bones and teeth. However, repeated exposure to x-rays can be damaging to body cells. In the 1960s doctors started using a different kind of wave called ultrasound to make images of the organs inside the body.

Waves are now used in many medical applications. For example, cochlear implants use radio waves to help people hear. Ultrasound now has many new medical applications, from breaking up kidney stones to monitoring the flow of blood in the body.

Sound and Ultrasound

Sound is a type of wave, a vibration in the air. Humans can hear a wide range of different sounds, from very low pitches to very high. Sounds that are higher in pitch than humans can hear are referred to as ultrasound. They are no different from sounds we can hear, except they vibrate much faster than human ears can detect. Many animals can detect ultrasound; for example, dog whistles are in the ultrasound range.

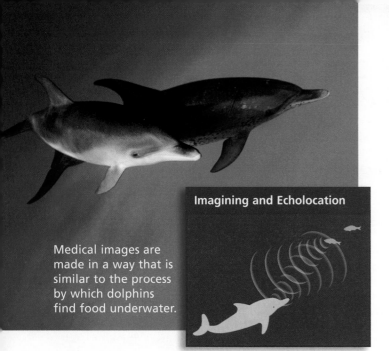

Imagining and Echolocation

Medical images are made in a way that is similar to the process by which dolphins find food underwater.

for the sound to travel to the object and return. Echolocation enables bats to capture flying insects at night and dolphins to catch fish in the ocean depths, where light doesn't penetrate.

Similarly, in ultrasound imaging, a machine sends a beam of ultrasound into a person's body and detects any echoes. The waves reflect whenever they strike a boundary between two objects with different densities. A computer measures the time required for the wave to travel to the boundary and reflect back; this information is used to determine the location and shape of the organ. The computer can then generate a live image of the organ inside the body.

The technology of ultrasound in medicine is based upon a process similar to that used by bats and dolphins to find food, a process called echolocation. The animal emits an ultrasound click or chirp and then listens for an echo. The echo indicates that an object has reflected the sound back to the animal. Over time, these animals have evolved the ability to judge the distance of the object by noting the time required

Ultrasound imaging has been used most often to monitor the development of a fetus inside its mother and to observe the valves of the heart. Blood flow can be color coded with faster flow in one color and slower flow in another color. The colors make it easier to see the location of blockages affecting the rate of flow in the blood vessels. This helps doctors detect blockages and diagnose heart problems.

SCIENTIFIC AMERICAN FRONTIERS

View the "Each Sound Is a Present" segment of your *Scientific American Frontiers* video to learn how a cochlear implant restores hearing to a young girl.

IN THIS SCENE FROM THE VIDEO ▶
A young girl's cochlear implant is turned on for the first time.

HEARING IS A GIFT A recent development in technology is about to give seven-year-old Kelley Flynn something she has always wanted —better hearing. Kelley has been almost completely deaf since she was two years old, and now she is losing the little hearing she does have. The development is a device called

a cochlear implant. Cochlear implants work inside the ear, stimulating the brain when a sound is detected.

Normally, sound travels as vibrations from the outer ear, through the middle ear to the inner ear, where thousands of tiny cells—called hair cells— register the quality of the sound and send a signal to the brain. In a cochlear implant, tiny electrical sensors, or electrodes, mimic the hair cells by registering the sound and sending a signal to the brain. The signals get to the electrodes through a system including a computer, microphone, and radio transmitter and receiver. Using this system, people with little or no hearing are able to sense sounds.

Recent advances in ultrasound technology include the development of portable devices that display images of the body, such as this hand-held device.

Advances in Ultrasound

Waves, including ultrasound, transfer energy. Physical therapists often use this fact when applying ultrasound to sore joints, heating the muscles and ligaments so they can move more freely. If the ultrasound waves are given stronger intensity and sharper focus, they can transfer enough energy to break up kidney stones in the body. The use of focused sound waves is now being tested for its ability to treat other problems, such as foot injuries.

Other recent advances in medical ultrasound include the development of devices that produce clearer images and use equipment that is smaller in size. In the late 1990's portable ultrasound devices were developed that allow the technology to be brought to the patient.

❓ UNANSWERED Questions

As scientists learn more about the use of sound and other types of waves, new questions will arise.

- Will new methods of imaging the body change the way diseases are diagnosed?
- How closely do sounds heard using a cochlear implant resemble sounds heard by the ear?

UNIT PROJECTS

As you study this unit, work alone or with a group on one of these projects.

Magazine Article

Write a magazine article about the medical uses of ultrasound.

- Collect information about medical ultrasound and take notes about applications that interest you.
- If possible, conduct an interview with a medical practitioner who uses ultrasound.
- Read over all your notes and decide what information to include in your article.

Make a Music Video

Make a music video for a song of your choice, and explain how the video uses sound waves and light waves.

- Plan the sound portion of the video, including how the music will be played and amplified.
- For the lighting, use colored cellophane or gels to mix different colors of light. Explain your choices.
- Rehearse the video. Record the video and present it to the class.

Design a Demonstration

Design a hands-on demonstration of echolocation.

- Research the use of echolocation by animals.
- Design a demonstration of echolocation using a tennis ball and an obstacle.
- Present your demonstration to the class.

CAREER CENTER
CLASSZONE.COM

Learn more about careers in audiology.

Waves

the **BIG** idea

Waves transfer energy and interact in predictable ways.

Key Concepts

SECTION

1.1 **Waves transfer energy.**
Learn about forces and energy in wave motion.

SECTION

1.2 **Waves have measurable properties.**
Learn how the amplitude, wavelength, and frequency of a wave are measured.

SECTION

1.3 **Waves behave in predictable ways.**
Learn about reflection, refraction, diffraction, and interference.

Internet Preview

CLASSZONE.COM

Chapter 1 online resources: Content Review, Simulation, Visualization, two Resource Centers, Math Tutorial, Test Practice

What is moving these surfers?

How Can Energy Be Passed Along?

Stand several videos up in a line. Knock over the first video, and notice the motion of the other videos.

Observe and Think Write down your observations. How far did each video move? What traveled from the beginning to the end of the line? Where did the energy to move the last video come from?

How Can You Change a Wave?

Fill a large bowl half-full of water. Dip a pencil into the water and pull it out quickly. Observe the wave that forms. Now try tapping the bowl with the eraser end of your pencil. What will happen if you use more energy to make the waves? Less energy?

Observe and Think What happened to the size of the waves? The speed? Why do you think that is so?

Internet Activity: Waves

Go to **ClassZone.com** to simulate the effect that different degrees of force have on a wave.

Observe and Think What do you think would happen to the wave if you increased the number of times the flapper moved? What other ways could you affect the wave in the pool?

NSTA
scilinks.org

SCiLINKS

Seismic Waves **Code: MDL027**

Getting Ready to Learn

◀ CONCEPT REVIEW

- Forces change the motion of objects in predictable ways.
- Energy can be transferred from one place to another.

◀ VOCABULARY REVIEW

See Glossary for definitions.

force

kinetic energy

potential energy

 CONTENT REVIEW
CLASSZONE.COM
Review concepts and vocabulary.

▶ TAKING NOTES

COMBINATION NOTES

To take notes about a new concept, write an explanation of the concept in a table. Then make a sketch of the concept and label it so you can study it later.

VOCABULARY STRATEGY

Write each new vocabulary term in the center of a **four square** diagram. Write notes in the squares around each term. Include a definition, some characteristics, and some examples of the term. If possible, write some things that are not examples of the term.

See the Note-Taking Handbook on pages R45–R51.

SCIENCE NOTEBOOK

Concept	Explanation	Sketch
Forces and waves	Forces move a medium up and down or back and forth. A wave moves forward.	direction of force / direction of wave

Definition	Characteristics
A disturbance that transfers energy from one place to another	Matter moves in place. Energy travels entire distance.

WAVE

Examples	Nonexamples
Water wave Sound wave	Ball rolling Water rushing downstream

1.1

Waves transfer energy.

◀ **BEFORE,** you learned

- Forces can change an object's motion
- Energy can be kinetic or potential

▶ **NOW,** you will learn

- How forces cause waves
- How waves transfer energy
- How waves are classified

VOCABULARY

wave p. 9
medium p. 11
mechanical wave p. 11
transverse wave p. 13
longitudinal wave p. 14

EXPLORE Waves

How will the rope move?

PROCEDURE

① Tie a ribbon in the middle of a rope. Then tie one end of the rope to a chair.

② Holding the loose end of the rope in your hand, stand far enough away from the chair that the rope is fairly straight.

③ Flick the rope by moving your hand up and down quickly. Observe what happens.

MATERIALS
- ribbon
- rope
- chair

WHAT DO YOU THINK?
- How did the rope move? How did the ribbon move?
- What do you think starts a wave, and what keeps it going?

A wave is a disturbance.

You experience the effects of waves every day. Every sound you hear depends on sound waves. Every sight you see depends on light waves. A tiny wave can travel across the water in a glass, and a huge wave can travel across the ocean. Sound waves, light waves, and water waves seem very different from one another. So what, exactly, is a wave?

A **wave** is a disturbance that transfers energy from one place to another. Waves can transfer energy over distance without moving matter the entire distance. For example, an ocean wave can travel many kilometers without the water itself moving many kilometers. The water moves up and down—a motion known as a disturbance. It is the disturbance that travels in a wave, transferring energy.

READING TiP

To *disturb* means to agitate or unsettle.

○ **CHECK YOUR READING** How does an ocean wave transfer energy across the ocean?

Forces and Waves

READING TiP

As you read each example, think of how it is similar to and different from the other examples.

You know that a force is required to change the motion of an object. Forces can also start a disturbance, sending a wave through a material. The following examples describe how forces cause waves.

Example 1 Rope Wave Think of a rope that is tied to a doorknob. You apply one force to the rope by flicking it upward and an opposite force when you snap it back down. This sends a wave through the rope. Both forces—the one that moves the rope up and the one that moves the rope down—are required to start a wave.

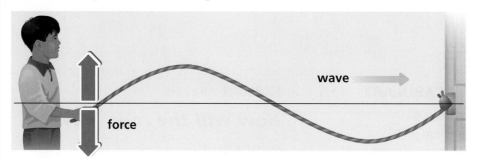

Example 2 Water Wave Forces are also required to start a wave in water. Think of a calm pool of water. What happens if you apply a force to the water by dipping your finger into it? The water rushes back after you remove your finger. The force of your finger and the force of the water rushing back send waves across the pool.

Example 3 Earthquake Wave An earthquake is a sudden release of energy that has built up in rock as a result of the surrounding rock pushing and pulling on it. When these two forces cause the rock to suddenly break away and move, the energy is transferred as a wave through the ground.

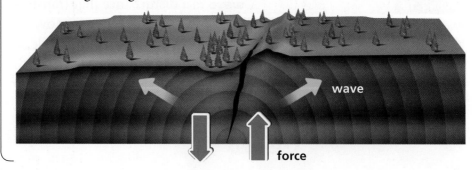

Materials and Waves

A rope tied to a doorknob, water, and the ground all have something in common. They are all materials through which waves move. A **medium** is any substance that a wave moves through. Water is the medium for an ocean wave; the ground is the medium for an earthquake wave; the rope is the medium for the rope wave. In the next chapter, you will learn that sound waves can move through many mediums, including air.

Waves that transfer energy through matter are known as **mechanical waves.** All of the waves you have read about so far, even sound waves, are mechanical waves. Water, the ground, a rope, and the air are all made up of matter. Later, you will learn about waves that can transfer energy through empty space. Light is an example of a wave that transfers energy through empty space.

VOCABULARY
Add a four square for *medium* to your notebook.

 CHECK YOUR READING How are all mechanical waves similar?

Energy and Waves

The waves caused by an earthquake are good examples of energy transfer. The disturbed ground shakes from side to side and up and down as the waves move through it. Such waves can travel kilometers away from their source. The ground does not travel kilometers away from where it began; it is the energy that travels in a wave. In the case of an earthquake, it is kinetic energy, or the energy of motion, that is transferred.

This photograph was taken after a 1995 earthquake in Japan. A seismic wave transferred enough energy through the ground to bend the railroad tracks, leaving them in the shape of a wave.

A Wave Model

When these fans do "the wave" in a stadium, they are modeling the way a disturbance travels through a medium.

Each person only moves up and down.

The wave can move all the way around the stadium.

READING VISUALS In which direction do people move when doing the stadium wave? In which direction does the wave move?

Look at the illustration of people modeling a wave in a stadium. In this model, the crowd of people represents a wave medium. The people moving up and down represent the disturbance. The transfer of the disturbance around the stadium represents a wave. Each person only moves up and down, while the disturbance can move all the way around the stadium.

Ocean waves are another good example of energy transfer. Ocean waves travel to the shore, one after another. Instead of piling up all the ocean water on the shore, however, the waves transfer energy. A big ocean wave transfers enough kinetic energy to knock someone down.

CHECK YOUR READING How does the stadium wave differ from a real ocean wave?

Waves can be classified by how they move.

As you have seen, one way to classify waves is according to the medium through which they travel. Another way to classify waves is by how they move. You have read that some waves transfer an up-and-down or a side-to-side motion. Other waves transfer a forward-and-backward motion.

Transverse Waves

Think again about snapping the rope with your hand. The action of your hand causes a vertical, or up-and-down, disturbance in the rope. However, the wave it sets off is horizontal, or forward. This type of wave is known as a transverse wave. In a **transverse wave,** the direction in which the wave travels is perpendicular, or at right angles, to the direction of the disturbance. *Transverse* means "across" or "crosswise." The wave itself moves crosswise as compared with the vertical motion of the medium.

Transverse Wave

direction of disturbance   direction of wave

Water waves are also transverse. The up-and-down motion of the water is the disturbance. The wave travels in a direction that is perpendicular to the direction of the disturbance. The medium is the water, and energy is transferred outward in all directions from the source.

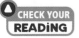 **CHECK YOUR READING** What is a transverse wave? Find two examples in the paragraphs above.

INVESTIGATE Wave Types

How do waves compare?

PROCEDURE

1. Place the spring toy on the floor on its side. Stretch out the spring. To start a disturbance in the spring, take one end and move it from side to side. Observe the movement in the spring. Remember that a transverse wave travels at right angles to the disturbance.

2. Put the spring toy on the floor in the same position as before. Think about how you could make a different kind of disturbance to produce a different kind of wave. (**Hint:** Suppose you push the spring in the direction of the wave you expect to make.) Observe the movement in the spring.

WHAT DO YOU THINK?

- Compare the waves you made. How are they alike? How are they different?
- What kind of wave did you produce by moving the spring from side to side?

CHALLENGE Can you think of a third way to make a wave travel through a spring?

SKILL FOCUS
Comparing

MATERIALS
spring toy

TIME
10 minutes

Longitudinal Waves

READING TiP

The word *long* can help you remember longitudinal waves. The disturbance moves along the length of the spring.

Another type of wave is a longitudinal wave. In a **longitudinal wave** (LAHN-jih-TOOD-n-uhl), the wave travels in the same direction as the disturbance. A longitudinal wave can be started in a spring by moving it forward and backward. The coils of the spring move forward and bunch up and then move backward and spread out. This forward and backward motion is the disturbance. Longitudinal waves are sometimes called compressional waves because the bunched-up area is known as a compression. How is a longitudinal wave similar to a transverse wave? How is it different?

Longitudinal Wave

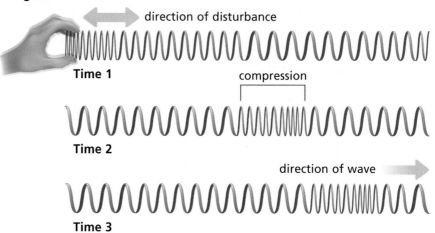

direction of disturbance

Time 1

compression

Time 2

direction of wave

Time 3

RESOURCE CENTER
CLASSZONE.COM

Learn more about waves.

Sound waves are examples of longitudinal waves. Imagine a bell ringing. The clapper inside the bell strikes the side and makes it vibrate, or move back and forth rapidly. The vibrating bell pushes and pulls on nearby air molecules, causing them to move forward and backward. These air molecules, in turn, set more air molecules into motion. A sound wave pushes forward. In sound waves, the vibrations of the air molecules are in the same direction as the movement of the wave.

1.1 Review

KEY CONCEPTS

1. Describe how forces start waves.

2. Explain how a wave can travel through a medium and yet the medium stays in place. Use the term *energy* in your answer.

3. Describe two ways in which waves travel, and give an example of each.

CRITICAL THINKING

4. **Analyze** Does water moving through a hose qualify as a wave? Explain why or why not.

5. **Classify** Suppose you drop a cookie crumb in your milk. At once, you see ripples spreading across the surface of the milk. What type of waves are these? What is the disturbance?

CHALLENGE

6. **Predict** Suppose you had a rope long enough to extend several blocks down the street. If you were to start a wave in the rope, do you think it would continue all the way to the other end of the street? Explain why or why not.

MATH TUTORIAL
CLASSZONE.COM

Click on Math Tutorial for more help with finding the mean, median, and mode.

Wave Heights

Tracking stations throughout the world's oceans measure and record the height of water waves that pass beneath them. The data recorded by the stations can be summarized as average wave heights over one hour or one day.

How would you summarize the typical wave heights over one week? There are a few different ways in which data can be summarized. Three common ways are finding the mean, median, and mode.

Example

Wave height data for one week are shown below.

| 1.2 m | 1.5 m | 1.4 m | 1.7 m | 2.0 m | 1.4 m | 1.3 m |

(1) Mean To find the mean of the data, divide the sum of the values by the number of values.

$$\text{Mean} = \frac{1.2 + 1.5 + 1.4 + 1.7 + 2.0 + 1.4 + 1.3}{7} = 1.5 \text{ m}$$

ANSWER The mean wave height is 1.5 m.

(2) Median To find the median of the data, write the values in order from least to greatest. The value in the middle is the median.

1.2 m   1.3 m   1.4 m   (1.4 m)   1.5 m   1.7 m   2.0 m

ANSWER The median wave height is 1.4 m.

(3) Mode The mode is the number that occurs most often.

ANSWER The mode for the data is also 1.4 m.

Use the data to answer the following questions.

The data below show wave heights taken from a station off the coast of Florida over two weeks.

| Wk 1 | 1.2 m | 1.1 m | 1.1 m | 1.5 m | 4.7 m | 1.2 m | 1.1 m |
| Wk 2 | 0.7 m | 0.8 m | 0.9 m | 0.8 m | 1.0 m | 1.1 m | 0.8 m |

1. Find the mean, median, and mode of the data for Week 1.

2. Find the mean, median, and mode of the data for Week 2.

CHALLENGE A storm carrying strong winds caused high waves on the fifth day of the data shown above for Week 1. Which of the following was most affected by the high value—the mean, median, or mode?

Before going out on the water, boaters can check reports on wave conditions in their area.

1.2 Waves have measurable properties.

▶ **BEFORE, you learned**

- Forces cause waves
- Waves transfer energy
- Waves can be transverse or longitudinal

▶ **NOW, you will learn**

- How amplitude, wavelength, and frequency are measured
- How to find a wave's speed

VOCABULARY

crest p. 17
trough p. 17
amplitude p. 17
wavelength p. 17
frequency p. 17

THINK ABOUT

How can a wave be measured?

This enormous wave moves the water high above sea level as it comes crashing through. How could you find out how high a water wave actually goes? How could you find out how fast it is traveling? In what other ways do you think a wave can be measured? Read on to find out.

Waves have amplitude, wavelength, and frequency.

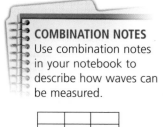

COMBINATION NOTES
Use combination notes in your notebook to describe how waves can be measured.

The tallest ocean wave ever recorded was measured from the deck of a ship during a storm. An officer on the ship saw a wave reach a height that was level with a point high on the ship, more than 30 meters (100 ft)! Height is a property of all waves—from ripples in a glass of water to gigantic waves at surfing beaches—and it can be measured.

The speed of a water wave is another property that can be measured—by finding the time it takes for one wave peak to travel a set distance. Other properties of a wave that can be measured include the time between waves and the length of a single wave. Scientists use the terms *amplitude*, *wavelength*, and *frequency* to refer to some commonly measured properties of waves.

CHECK YOUR READING What are three properties of a wave that can be measured?

Measuring Wave Properties

A **crest** is the highest point, or peak, of a wave. A **trough** is the lowest point, or valley, of a wave. Suppose you are riding on a boat in rough water. When the boat points upward and rises, it is climbing to the crest of a wave. When it points downward and sinks, the boat is falling to the trough of the wave.

crest

trough

❶ Amplitude for a transverse wave is the distance between a line through the middle of a wave and a crest or trough. In an ocean wave, amplitude measures how far the wave rises above, or dips below, its original position, or rest position.

Amplitude is an important measurement, because it indicates how much energy a wave is carrying. The bigger the amplitude, the more energy the wave has. Find amplitude on the diagram below.

❷ The distance from one wave crest to the very next crest is called the **wavelength.** Wavelength can also be measured from trough to trough. Find wavelength on the diagram below.

❸ The number of waves passing a fixed point in a certain amount of time is called the **frequency.** The word *frequent* means "often," so frequency measures how often a wave occurs. Frequency is often measured by counting the number of crests or troughs that pass by a given point in one second. Find frequency on the diagram below.

VOCABULARY
Remember to add a four square to your notebook for each new term on this page.

CHECK YOUR READING How is amplitude related to energy?

Wave Properties

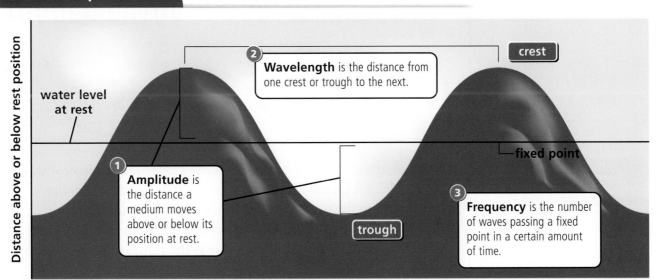

Distance above or below rest position

water level at rest

❷ Wavelength is the distance from one crest or trough to the next.

crest

❶ Amplitude is the distance a medium moves above or below its position at rest.

trough

fixed point

❸ Frequency is the number of waves passing a fixed point in a certain amount of time.

READING VISUALS How many wavelengths are shown in this diagram? How do you know?

How Frequency and Wavelength Are Related

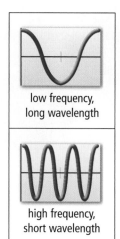

low frequency, long wavelength

high frequency, short wavelength

The frequency and wavelength of a wave are related. When frequency increases more wave crests pass a fixed point each second. That means the wavelength shortens. So, as frequency increases, wavelength decreases. The opposite is also true—as frequency decreases, wavelength increases.

Suppose you are making waves in a rope. If you make one wave crest every second, the frequency is one wave per second (1/s). Now suppose you want to increase the frequency to more than one wave per second. You flick the rope up and down faster. The wave crests are now closer together. In other words, their wavelengths have decreased.

Graphing Wave Properties

The graph of a transverse wave looks much like a wave itself. The illustration on page 19 shows the graph of an ocean wave. The measurements for the graph come from a float, or buoy (BOO-ee), that keeps track of how high or low the water goes. The graph shows the position of the buoy at three different points in time. These points are numbered. Since the graph shows what happens over time, you can see the frequency of the waves.

Unlike transverse waves, longitudinal waves look different from their graphs. The graph of a longitudinal wave in a spring is drawn below. The coils of the spring get closer and then farther apart as the wave moves through them.

REMINDER

Frequency is the number of waves that pass a given point in a certain amount of time.

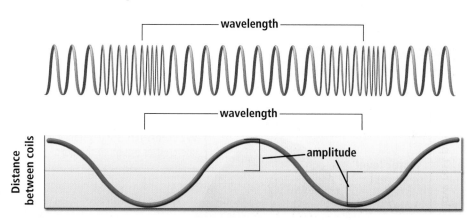

The shape of the graph resembles the shape of a transverse wave. The wavelength on a longitudinal wave is the distance from one compression to the next. The amplitude of a longitudinal wave measures how compressed the medium gets. Just as in a transverse wave, frequency in a longitudinal wave is the number of waves passing a fixed point in a certain amount of time.

VISUALIZATION
CLASSZONE.COM
Watch the graph of a wave form.

CHECK YOUR READING How are longitudinal waves measured?

Graphing a Wave

The graph of a transverse wave looks like a wave itself. The graph shows what happens over time.

The buoy moves up and down as the waves pass.

1 **Time: 0 s** The buoy is below the rest position.

2 **Time: 1 s** The buoy is equal with the rest position.

3 **Time: 2 s** The buoy is above the rest position.

water level at rest

amplitude = 0.2 m

frequency = 0.25/s

READING VISUALS How many seconds does it take for one wave to pass? How much of the wave passes in one second?

INVESTIGATE Frequency

How can you change frequency?

PROCEDURE

1. Tie 3 washers to a string. Tape the string to the side of your desk so that it can swing freely. The swinging washers can model wave action.

2. Pull the washers slightly to the side and let go. Find the frequency by counting the number of complete swings that occur in 1 minute.

3. Make a table in your notebook to record both the length of the string and the frequency.

4. Shorten the string by moving and retaping it. Repeat for 5 different lengths. Keep the distance you pull the washers the same each time.

WHAT DO YOU THINK?

• How did changing the length of the string affect the frequency?

• How does this model represent a wave? How does it differ from a wave?

CHALLENGE How could you vary the amplitude of this model? Predict how changing the amplitude would affect the frequency.

SKILL FOCUS
Collecting data

MATERIALS
• 3 metal washers
• piece of string
• tape
• stopwatch
• meter stick

TIME
30 minutes

Wave speed can be measured.

In addition to amplitude, wavelength, and frequency, a wave's speed can be measured. One way to find the speed of a wave is to time how long it takes for a wave to get from one point to another. Another way to find the speed of a wave is to calculate it. The speed of any wave can be determined when both the frequency and the wavelength are known, using the following formula:

REMINDER
The symbol λ represents wavelength.

$$\text{Speed} = \text{wavelength} \cdot \text{frequency}$$
$$S = \lambda f$$

Different types of waves travel at very different speeds. For example, light waves travel through air almost a million times faster than sound waves travel through air. You have experienced the difference in wave speeds if you have ever seen lightning and heard the thunder that comes with it in a thunderstorm. When lightning strikes far away, you see the light seconds before you hear the clap of its thunder. The light waves reach you while the sound waves are still on their way.

How fast do you think water waves can travel? Water waves travel at different speeds. You can calculate the speed using wavelength and frequency.

Suppose you wish to calculate the speed of an ocean wave with a wavelength of 16 meters and a frequency of 0.31 (wave) per second. When working through the problem in the example below, it is helpful to think of the frequency as

$$f = 0.31 \text{ (wave)/s}$$

even though the units for frequency are just 1/second. You can think of wavelengths as "meters per wave," or

$$\lambda = 16 \text{ m/(wave)}$$

RESOURCE CENTER
CLASSZONE.COM

Find out more about wave speed.

Calculating Wave Speed

▶ **Sample Problem**

An ocean wave has a wavelength of 16 meters and a frequency of 0.31 wave per second. What is the speed of the wave?

What do you know?   wavelength = 16 m,

frequency = $0.31 \dfrac{\text{(wave)}}{\text{s}}$

What do you want to find out?   Speed

Write the formula: $S = \lambda f$

Substitute into the formula: $S = 16 \dfrac{\text{m}}{\text{(wave)}} \cdot 0.31 \dfrac{\text{(wave)}}{\text{s}}$

Calculate and simplify: $16 \dfrac{\text{m}}{\cancel{\text{(wave)}}} \cdot 0.31 \dfrac{\cancel{\text{(wave)}}}{\text{s}} = 5 \dfrac{\text{m}}{\text{s}}$

Check that your units agree: Unit is m/s. Unit for speed is m/s. Units agree.

Answer: $S = 5$ m/s

▶ **Practice the Math**

1. In a stormy sea, 2 waves pass a fixed point every second, and the waves are 10 m apart. What is the speed of the waves?

2. In a ripple tank, the wavelength is 0.1 cm, and 10 waves occur each second. What is the speed of the waves (in cm/s)?

1.2 Review

KEY CONCEPTS

1. Make a simple diagram of a wave, labeling amplitude, frequency, and wavelength. For frequency, you will need to indicate a span of time, such as one second.

2. What two measurements of a wave do you need to calculate its speed?

CRITICAL THINKING

3. **Observe** Suppose you are watching water waves pass under the end of a pier. How can you figure out their frequency?

4. **Calculate** A wave has a speed of 3 m/s and a frequency of 6 (waves)/s. What is its wavelength?

CHALLENGE

5. **Apply** Imagine you are on a boat in the middle of the sea. You are in charge of recording the properties of passing ocean waves into the ship's logbook. What types of information could you record? How would this information be useful? Explain your answer.

CHAPTER INVESTIGATION

Wavelength

OVERVIEW AND PURPOSE The pendulum on a grandfather clock keeps time as it swings back and forth at a steady rate. The swings of a pendulum can be recorded as a wave with measurable properties. How do the properties of the pendulum affect the properties of the waves it produces? In this investigation you will use your understanding of wave properties to

- construct a pendulum and measure the waves it produces, and
- determine how the length of the pendulum affects the wavelength of the waves.

▶ Problem

How does changing the length of a pendulum affect the wavelength?

▶ Hypothesize

Write a hypothesis in "If . . . , then . . . , because . . ." form to answer the problem question.

▶ Procedure

MATERIALS
- 1/2 sheet white paper
- tape
- scissors
- string
- meter stick
- fine sand
- graduated cylinder
- 2 sheets colored construction paper

1. Make a data table like the one shown on the sample notebook page.

2. Make a cone with the half-sheet of paper by rolling it and taping it as shown. The hole in the bottom of the cone should be no larger than a pea.

3. Cut a hole in each side of the cone and tie the ends of the string to the cone to make a pendulum.

4. Hold the string on the pendulum so that the distance from your fingers holding the string to the bottom of the cone is 20 cm.

5. Cover the bottom of the cone with your fingertip. While you hold the cone, have your partner pour about 40 mL of sand into the cone.

6. Hold the pendulum about 5 cm above the construction paper as shown. Pull the pendulum from the bottom to one side of the construction paper. Be careful not to move the pendulum at the top, or to pull the pendulum over the edge of the paper.

7. Let the pendulum go while your partner gently pulls the paper forward so that the sand makes waves on the paper. Be sure to pull the paper at a steady rate. Let the remaining sand pile up on the end of the paper.

8. Measure the wavelength from crest to crest or trough to trough. Record the wavelength in your table.

9. Run two more trials, repeating steps 5–8. Be sure to pull the paper at the same speed for each trial. Calculate the average wavelength over all three trials, and record it in your table.

10. Repeat steps 4–8, changing the length of the pendulum to 30 cm and then to 40 cm.

▶ Observe and Analyze | Write It Up

1. **RECORD OBSERVATIONS** Draw the setup of your procedure. Be sure your data table is complete.

2. **IDENTIFY VARIABLES AND CONSTANTS** Identify the variables and constants that affected the wave produced by the moving pendulum. List them in your notebook.

3. **ANALYZE** What patterns can you find in your data? For example, do the numbers increase or decrease as you read down each column?

▶ Conclude | Write It Up

1. **INFER** Answer your problem question.

2. **INTERPRET** Compare your results with your hypothesis. Do your data support your hypothesis?

3. **IDENTIFY LIMITS** What possible limitations or sources of error could have affected your results?

4. **APPLY** Suppose you were examining the tracing made by a seismograph, a machine that records an earthquake wave. What would happen if you increased the speed at which the paper ran through the machine? What do you think the amplitude of the tracing represents?

▶ INVESTIGATE Further

CHALLENGE Revise your experiment to change one variable other than the length of the pendulum. Run a new trial, changing the variable you choose but keeping everything else constant. How did changing the variable affect the wave produced?

Wavelength

Problem How does changing the length of a pendulum affect the wavelength?

Hypothesize

Observe and Analyze

Table 1. Wavelengths Produced by Pendulums

Pendulum Length (cm)	Trial 1	Trial 2	Trial 3	Average Wavelength (cm)
20				
30				
40				

Conclude

Waves behave in predictable ways.

 BEFORE, you learned

- Waves transfer energy
- Amplitude, wavelength, and frequency can be measured

 NOW, you will learn

- How waves change as they encounter a barrier
- What happens when waves enter a new medium
- How waves interact with other waves

VOCABULARY

reflection p. 25
refraction p. 25
diffraction p. 26
interference p. 27

EXPLORE Reflection

How do ripples reflect?

PROCEDURE

1. Put a few drops of food coloring into the pan of water.

2. Dip the pencil in the water at one end of the pan to make ripples in the water.

3. Observe the ripples as they reflect off the side of the pan. Draw a sketch of the waves reflecting.

MATERIALS
- wide pan, half full of water
- food coloring
- pencil

WHAT DO YOU THINK?
- What happens when the waves reach the side of the pan?
- Why do you think the waves behave as they do?

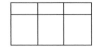
COMBINATION NOTES
Use combination notes in your notebook to describe how waves interact with materials.

Waves interact with materials.

You have read that mechanical waves travel through a medium like air, water, or the ground. In this section, you will read how the motion of waves changes when they encounter a new medium. For instance, when an ocean wave rolls into a ship or a sound wave strikes a solid wall, the wave encounters a new medium.

When waves interact with materials in these ways, they behave predictably. All waves, from water waves to sound waves and even light waves, show the behaviors that you will learn about next. Scientists call these behaviors reflection, refraction, and diffraction.

 CHECK YOUR READING What behaviors do all waves have in common?

Reflection

What happens to water waves at the end of a swimming pool? The waves cannot travel through the wall of the pool. Instead, the waves bounce off the pool wall. The bouncing back of a wave after it strikes a barrier is called **reflection.**

Remember what you have learned about forces. A water wave, like all waves, transfers energy. When the water wave meets the wall of the pool, it pushes against the wall. The wall applies an equal and opposite force on the water, sending the wave back in another direction. In the illustration on the right, you can see water waves reflecting off a barrier.

Sound and light waves reflect too. Sound waves reflecting off the walls of a canyon produce an echo. Light waves reflecting off smooth metal behind glass let you see an image of yourself in the mirror. The light waves bounce off the metal just as the water waves bounce off the pool wall. You will learn more about how sound and light waves reflect in the next chapters.

Reflection Water waves move in predictable ways. Here waves are shown from above as they reflect off a barrier.

 How would you define *reflection* in your own words?

Refraction

Sometimes, a wave does not bounce back when it encounters a new medium. Instead, the wave continues moving forward. When a wave enters a new medium at an angle, it bends, or refracts. **Refraction** is the bending of a wave as it enters a new medium at an angle other than 90 degrees. Refraction occurs because waves travel at different speeds in different mediums. Because the wave enters the new medium at an angle, one side of the wave enters the new medium before the rest of the wave. When one side of a wave speeds up or slows down before the other side, it causes the wave to bend.

You have probably noticed the refraction of light waves in water. Objects half-in and half-out of water look broken or split. Look at the photograph of the straw in the glass. What your eyes suggest—that the straw is split—is not real, is it? You are seeing the refraction of light waves caused by the change of medium from air to water. You will learn more about the refraction of light waves in Chapter 4.

Refraction Light waves refract as they pass from air to water, making this straw look split.

Diffraction

You have seen how waves reflect off a barrier. For example, water waves bounce off the side of a pool. But what if the side of the pool had an opening in it? Sometimes, waves interact with a partial barrier, such as a wall with an opening. As the waves pass through the opening, they spread out, or diffract. **Diffraction** is the spreading out of waves through an opening or around the edge of an obstacle. Diffraction occurs with all types of waves.

Look at the photograph on the right. It shows water waves diffracting as they pass through a small gap in a barrier. In the real world, ocean waves diffract through openings in cliffs or rock formations.

Similarly, sound waves diffract as they pass through an open doorway. Turn on a TV or stereo, and walk into another room. Listen to the sound with the door closed and then open. Then try moving around the room. You can hear the sound wherever you stand because the waves spread out, or diffract, through the doorway and reflect from the walls.

Diffraction through an opening

INVESTIGATE Diffraction

How can you make a wave diffract?

PROCEDURE

1. Put a few drops of food coloring into the container of water.

2. Experiment with quick motions of the ruler to set off waves in the container.

3. Place the block on its side in the center of the container. Set the bag of sand on the block to hold it down. Predict how the waves will interact with the barrier you have added.

4. Make another set of waves, and observe how they interact with the barrier.

WHAT DO YOU THINK?

- How did you make the waves diffract?
- How did your observations compare with your prediction?

CHALLENGE How could you change the experiment to make the effect of the diffraction more obvious?

SKILL FOCUS
Predicting

MATERIALS
- wide pan of water
- food coloring
- ruler
- wooden block
- bag of sand

TIME
20 minutes

Diffraction also occurs as waves pass the edge of an obstacle. The photograph at the right shows water waves diffracting as they pass an obstacle. Ocean waves also diffract in this way as they pass large rocks in the water.

Light waves diffract around the edge of an obstacle too. The edges of a shadow appear fuzzy because of diffraction. The light waves spread out, or diffract, around the object that is making the shadow.

Diffraction around an obstacle

 Describe what happens when waves diffract.

Waves interact with other waves.

Just as waves sometimes interact with new mediums, they can also interact with other waves. Two waves can add energy to or take away energy from each other in the place where they meet. **Interference** is the meeting and combining of waves.

Waves Adding Together

Suppose two identical waves coming from opposite directions come together at one point. The waves' crests and troughs are aligned briefly, which means they join up exactly. When the two waves merge into a temporary, larger wave, their amplitudes are added together. When the waves separate again, they have their original amplitudes and continue in their original directions.

The adding of two waves is called constructive interference. It builds up, or constructs, a larger wave out of two smaller ones. Look at the diagram at the right to see what happens in constructive interference.

Because the waves in the example joined together perfectly, the amplitude of the new wave equals the combined amplitudes of the 2 original waves. For example, if the crest of a water wave with an amplitude of 1 meter (3.3 ft) met up with the crest of another wave with an amplitude of 1 meter (3.3 ft), there would be a 2 meter (6.6 ft) crest in the spot where they met.

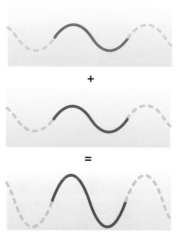
Constructive Interference

When two wave crests with amplitudes of 1 m each combine, a wave with an amplitude of 2 m is formed.

Waves Canceling Each Other Out

Imagine again that two very similar waves come together. This time, however, the crest of one wave joins briefly with the trough of the other. The energy of one wave is subtracted from the energy of the other. The new wave is therefore smaller than the original wave. This process is called destructive interference. Look at the diagram below to see what happens in destructive interference.

For example, if a 2-meter (6.6 ft) crest met up with a 1-meter (3.3 ft) trough, there would be a temporary crest of only 1 meter (3.3 ft) where they met. If the amplitudes of the two original waves are identical, the two waves can cancel each other out completely!

When identical waves meet, they are usually not aligned. Instead, the crests meet up with crests in some places and troughs in others. As a result, the waves add in some places and subtract in others. The photograph on the left shows a pattern resulting from waves both adding and subtracting on the surface of a pond. Have you ever listened to music on stereo speakers that were placed at a distance from each other? The music may have sounded loud in some places and soft in others, as the sound waves from the two speakers interfered with each other.

Wave interference produces this pattern on a pond as two sets of waves interact.

Destructive Interference

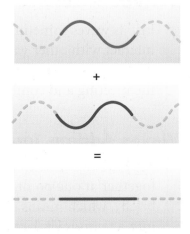

When a 1 m wave crest meets a 1 m wave trough, the amplitudes cancel each other out. A wave with an amplitude of 0 m is formed where they meet.

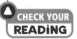 **CHECK YOUR READING** Summarize in your own words what happens during interference.

1.3 Review

KEY CONCEPTS

1. Explain what happens when waves encounter a medium that they cannot travel through.

2. Describe a situation in which waves would diffract.

3. Describe two ways that waves are affected by interference.

CRITICAL THINKING

4. **Synthesize** Explain how reflection and diffraction can happen at the same time in a wave.

5. **Compare** How is interference similar to net force? How do you think the two concepts might be related? **Hint:** Think about how forces are involved in wave motion.

● CHALLENGE

6. **Predict** Imagine that you make gelatin in a long, shallow pan. Then you scoop the gelatin out of one end of the pan and add icy cold water to the exact same depth as the gelatin. Now suppose you set off waves at the water end. What do you think will happen when the waves meet the gelatin?

Tsunamis!

Tsunamis (tsu-NAH-mees) are among the most powerful waves on Earth. They can travel fast enough to cross the Pacific Ocean in less than a day! When they reach shore, these powerful waves strike with enough force to destroy whole communities.

What Causes Tsunamis?

Tsunamis are caused by an undersea volcanic eruption, an earthquake, or even a landslide. This deep-sea event sends out a series of waves. Surprisingly, if you were out at sea, you would not even notice these powerful waves. The reason has to do with the physics of waves—their velocity, wavelength, and amplitude.

Diagram of a Wave

1 open ocean

2 near shore

Amplitude (A) = 1 m
Wavelength (λ) = 200 km
Speed (S) = 1000 km/h

Amplitude = 30 m
Wavelength = 1.5 km
Speed = 80 km/h

The Changing Wave

1 On the open ocean, the waves of a tsunami are barely visible. The amplitude of the waves is less than a few meters, but the energy of the waves extends to the sea floor. The tsunami's wavelength is extremely long—up to 200 kilometers (120 mi). These long, low waves can travel as fast as a jet—almost 1000 kilometers per hour (600 mi/h).

2 Near shore, the waves slow down as they approach shallow water. As their velocity drops, their wavelengths get shorter, but their amplitude gets bigger. All the energy that was spread out over a long wave in deep water is now compressed into a huge wave that can reach a height of more than 30 meters (100 ft).

Individual tsunami waves may arrive more than an hour apart. Many people have lost their lives returning home between waves, making the fatal mistake of thinking the danger was over.

EXPLORE

1. **VISUALIZE** Look at **2** on the diagram. How tall is 30 meters (100 ft)? Find a 100-foot building or structure near you to visualize the shore height of a tsunami.

2. **CHALLENGE** Use library or Internet resources to prepare a chart on the causes and effects of a major tsunami event.

A tsunami generated by a powerful earthquake struck Japan in 1983. The photograph above shows a scene before the tsunami struck. What changes do you see in the picture below showing the scene after the tsunami struck?

Chapter Review

the **BIG** idea

Waves transfer energy and interact in predictable ways.

KEY CONCEPTS SUMMARY

1.1 Waves transfer energy.

Transverse Wave

direction of disturbance

direction of wave

transfer of energy

Longitudinal Wave

direction of disturbance

direction of wave

transfer of energy

VOCABULARY
wave p. 9
medium p. 11
mechanical wave p. 11
transverse wave p. 13
longitudinal wave p. 14

1.2 Waves have measurable properties.

water level at rest

wavelength

crest

amplitude

fixed point

trough

Frequency is the number of waves passing a fixed point in a certain amount of time.

VOCABULARY
crest p. 17
trough p. 17
amplitude p. 17
wavelength p. 17
frequency p. 17

1.3 Waves behave in predictable ways.

Reflection

Refraction

Diffraction

VOCABULARY
reflection p. 25
refraction p. 25
diffraction p. 26
interference p. 27

Reviewing Vocabulary

Draw a word triangle for each of the terms below. On the bottom row, write the term and your own definition of it. Above that, write a sentence in which you use the term correctly. At the top, draw a small picture to show what the term looks like. A sample is completed for you.

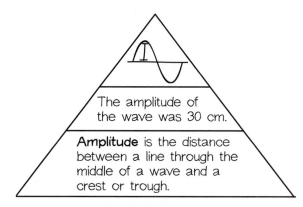

The amplitude of the wave was 30 cm.

Amplitude is the distance between a line through the middle of a wave and a crest or trough.

1. transverse wave
2. diffraction
3. frequency
4. medium
5. crest

6. interference
7. reflection
8. trough
9. refraction
10. wavelength

Reviewing Key Concepts

Multiple Choice *Choose the letter of the best answer.*

11. The direction in which a transverse wave travels is
    a. the same direction as the disturbance
    b. toward the disturbance
    c. from the disturbance downward
    d. at right angles to the disturbance

12. An example of a longitudinal wave is a
    a. water wave
    b. stadium wave
    c. sound wave
    d. rope wave

13. Which statement best defines a wave medium?
    a. the material through which a wave travels
    b. a point halfway between the crest and trough of a wave
    c. the distance from one wave crest to the next
    d. the speed at which waves travel in water

14. As you increase the amplitude of a wave, you also increase the
    a. frequency   **c.** speed
    b. wavelength   **d.** energy

15. To identify the amplitude in a longitudinal wave, you would measure areas of
    a. reflection   **c.** crests
    b. compression   **d.** refraction

16. Which statement describes the relationship between frequency and wavelength?
    a. When frequency increases, wavelength increases.
    b. When frequency increases, wavelength decreases.
    c. When frequency increases, wavelength remains constant.
    d. When frequency increases, wavelength varies unpredictably.

17. For wave refraction to take place, a wave must
    a. increase in velocity
    b. enter a new medium
    c. increase in frequency
    d. merge with another wave

18. Which setup in a wave tank would best enable you to demonstrate diffraction?
    a. water only
    b. water and sand
    c. water and food coloring
    d. water and a barrier with a small gap

19. Two waves come together and interact to form a new, smaller wave. This process is called
    a. destructive interference
    b. constructive interference
    c. reflective interference
    d. positive interference

Thinking Critically

Use the diagram below to answer the next two questions.

20. What two letters in the diagram measure the same thing? What do they both measure?

21. In the diagram above, what does the letter *c* measure?

Use the diagram below to answer the next three questions. The diagram shows waves passing a fixed point.

22. At 0 seconds, no waves have passed. How many waves have passed after 1 second?

23. What is being measured in the diagram?

24. How would you write the measurement taken in the diagram?

25. **EVALUATE** Do you think the following is an accurate definition of medium? Explain your answer.

A **medium** is any solid through which waves travel.

26. **APPLY** Picture a pendulum. The pendulum is swinging back and forth at a steady rate. How could you make it swing higher? How is swinging a pendulum like making a wave?

27. **PREDICT** What might happen to an ocean wave that encounters a gap or hole in a cliff along the shore?

28. **EVALUATE** Do you think *interference* is an appropriate name for the types of wave interaction you read about in Section 1.3? Explain your answer.

Using Math in Science

29. At what speed is the wave below traveling if it has a frequency of 2/s?

30. An ocean wave has a wavelength of 9 m and a frequency of 0.42/s. What is the wave's speed?

31. Suppose a sound wave has a frequency of 10,000/s. The wave's speed is 340 m/s. Calculate the wavelength of this sound wave.

32. A water wave is traveling at a speed of 2.5 m/s. The wave has a wavelength of 4 m. Calculate the frequency of this water wave.

the BIG idea

33. **INTERPRET** Look back at the photograph at the start of the chapter on pages 6–7. How does this photograph illustrate a transfer of energy?

34. **SYNTHESIZE** Describe three situations in which you can predict the behavior of waves.

35. **SUMMARIZE** Write a paragraph summarizing this chapter. Use the big idea from page 6 as the topic sentence. Then write an example from each of the key concepts listed under the big idea.

UNIT PROJECTS

If you are doing a unit project, make a folder for your project. Include in your folder a list of the resources you will need, the date on which the project is due, and a schedule to track your progress. Begin gathering data.

Interpreting Diagrams

Study the illustration below and then answer the questions.

The illustration below shows a wave channel, a way of making and studying water waves. The motor moves the rod, which moves the paddle back and forth. The movement of the paddle makes waves, which move down the length of the channel. The material behind the paddle absorbs the waves generated in that direction.

1. An experimenter can adjust the position of the rod on the arm of the motor. Placing it closer to the motor makes shallower waves. Placing it farther from the motor makes deeper waves.
   What property of waves does this affect?

   a. amplitude

   b. direction

   c. frequency

   d. wavelength

2. By changing motor speeds, an experimenter can make the paddle move faster or slower. What property of waves does this affect?

   a. amplitude

   b. direction

   c. trough depth

   d. wavelength

3. Sand is piled up in the channel at the end of the tank opposite the motor. When waves pass over this sand, their wavelengths shorten. Assuming that the speed of the waves stays the same, their frequency

   a. stays the same

   b. increases

   c. decreases

   d. cannot be predicted

4. Suppose there was no sand at the end of the tank opposite the paddle. In that case, the waves would hit the glass wall. What would they do then?

   a. stop

   b. reflect

   c. refract

   d. diffract

Extended Response

Answer the two questions below in detail.

5. Suppose temperatures in one 10-day period were as follows: 94°, 96°, 95°, 97°, 95°, 98°, 99°, 97°, 99°, and 98°. Make a simple line graph of the data.
   In what ways is the series of temperatures similar to a wave, and in what ways does it differ?

6. Lydia and Bill each drop a ball of the same size into the same tank of water but at two different spots. Both balls produce waves that spread across the surface of the water. As the two sets of waves cross each other, the water forms high crests in some places. What can you say about both waves? Explain your answer.

CHAPTER 2 Sound

the BIG idea

Sound waves transfer energy through vibrations.

Key Concepts

SECTION 2.1 Sound is a wave.
Learn how sound waves are produced and detected.

SECTION 2.2 Frequency determines pitch.
Learn about the relationship between the frequency of a sound wave and its pitch.

SECTION 2.3 Intensity determines loudness.
Learn how the energy of a sound wave relates to its loudness.

SECTION 2.4 Sound has many uses.
Learn how sound waves are used to detect objects and to make music.

Internet Preview

CLASSZONE.COM

Chapter 2 online resources: Content Review, two Visualizations, three Resource Centers, Math Tutorial, Test Practice

How is this guitar player producing sound?

What Gives a Sound Its Qualities?

Tap your finger lightly on a table. Then tap it hard. Try scratching the table with your finger. Now, place your head on the table so that your ear is flat against its surface. Tap the table again.

Observe and Think How did the sounds differ each time? What did you feel?

How Does Size Affect Sound?

Hang three large nails of different sizes from the edge of a table so that they are not touching. Tap each nail with a metal spoon to make it vibrate. Listen to the sounds that are made by tapping each nail.

Observe and Think Which nail produced the highest sound? the lowest? How does the size of a vibrating object affect its sound?

Internet Activity: Sound

Go to **ClassZone.com** to discover how particles move as sound waves move through the air.

Observe and Think How are the sound waves in the animation similar to the waves you have already learned about?

NSTA
scilinks.org
SCiLINKS

What Is Sound? **Code: MDL028**

Getting Ready to Learn

◀ CONCEPT REVIEW

- A wave is a disturbance that transfers energy from one place to another.
- Mechanical waves are waves that travel through matter.

◀ VOCABULARY REVIEW

medium p. 11

longitudinal wave p. 14

amplitude p. 17

wavelength p. 17

frequency p. 17

CONTENT REVIEW
CLASSZONE.COM
Review concepts and vocabulary.

▶ TAKING NOTES

OUTLINE

As you read, copy the headings on your paper in the form of an outline. Then add notes in your own words that summarize what you have read.

VOCABULARY STRATEGY

Place each vocabulary term at the center of a **description wheel** diagram. Write some words on the spokes describing it.

See the Note-Taking Handbook on pages R45–R51.

SCIENCE NOTEBOOK

I. Sound is a type of mechanical wave.
   A. How sound waves are produced
      1.
      2.
      3.
   B. How sound waves are detected
      1.
      2.
      3.

rapid back-and-forth motion

can produce a sound

VIBRATION

usually too small to see

can make with vocal cords

Sound is a wave.

◀ BEFORE, you learned	▶ NOW, you will learn
• Waves transfer energy • Waves have wavelength, amplitude, and frequency	• How sound waves are produced and detected • How sound waves transfer energy • What affects the speed of sound waves

VOCABULARY

sound p. 37
vibration p. 37
vacuum p. 41

EXPLORE Sound

What is sound?

PROCEDURE

MATERIALS
• piece of string
• large metal spoon

1. Tie the middle of the string to the spoon handle.

2. Wrap the string ends around your left and right index fingers. Put the tips of these fingers gently in your ears and hold them there.

3. Stand over your desk so that the spoon dangles without touching your body or the desk. Then move a little to make the spoon tap the desk lightly. Listen to the sound.

WHAT DO YOU THINK?
• What did you hear when the spoon tapped the desk?
• How did sound travel from the spoon to your ears?

Sound is a type of mechanical wave.

OUTLINE
Start an outline for this heading. Remember to leave room for details.

I. Main idea
  A. Supporting idea
    1. Detail
    2. Detail
  B. Supporting idea

In the last chapter, you read that a mechanical wave travels through a material medium. Such mediums include air, water, and solid materials. Sound is an example of a mechanical wave. **Sound** is a wave that is produced by a vibrating object and travels through matter.

The disturbances that travel in a sound wave are vibrations. A **vibration** is a rapid, back-and-forth motion. Because the medium vibrates back and forth in the same direction as the wave travels, sound is a longitudinal wave. Like all mechanical waves, sound waves transfer energy through a medium.

CHECK YOUR READING What do sound waves have in common with other mechanical waves? Your answer should include the word *energy*.

How Sound Waves Are Produced

READING TiP

When you see the word *push* or *pull*, think of force.

The disturbances in a sound wave are vibrations that are usually too small to see. Vibrations are also required to start sound waves. A vibrating object pushes and pulls on the medium around it and sends out waves in all directions.

You have a sound-making instrument within your own body. It is the set of vocal cords within the voice box, or larynx, in your throat. Put several of your fingers against the front of your throat. Now hum. Do you feel the vibrations of your vocal cords?

Your vocal cords relax when you breathe to allow air to pass in and out of your windpipe. Your vocal cords tense up and draw close together when you are about to speak or sing. The illustration below shows how sound waves are produced by the human vocal cords.

1. Your muscles push air up from your lungs and through the narrow opening between the vocal cords.

2. The force of the air causes the vocal cords to vibrate.

3. The vibrating vocal cords produce sound waves.

CHECK YOUR READING How do human vocal cords produce sound waves?

How Vocal Cords Produce Sound

Sound waves are produced by vibrations.

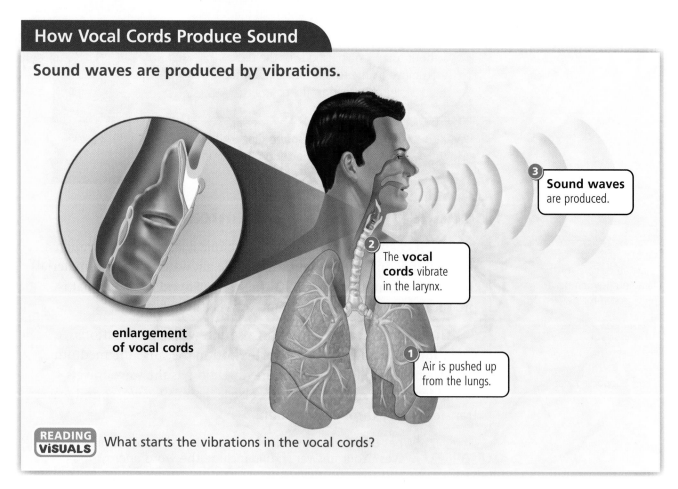

enlargement of vocal cords

3 **Sound waves** are produced.

2 The **vocal cords** vibrate in the larynx.

1 Air is pushed up from the lungs.

READING VISUALS What starts the vibrations in the vocal cords?

How Sound Waves Are Detected

The shape of a human ear helps it collect sound waves. Picture a satellite dish. It collects radio waves from satellites. Your ear works in much the same way. Actually, what we typically call the ear is only the outer section of the ear. The illustration below shows the main parts of the human ear.

1 Your outer ear collects sound waves and reflects them into a tiny tube called the ear canal. At the end of the ear canal is a thin, skin-like membrane stretched tightly over the opening, called the eardrum. When sound waves strike the eardrum, they make it vibrate.

2 The middle ear contains three tiny, connected bones called the hammer, anvil, and stirrup. These bones carry vibrations from the eardrum to the inner ear.

3 One of the main parts of the inner ear, the cochlea (KAWK-lee-uh), contains about 30,000 hair cells. Each of these cells has tiny hairs on its surface. The hairs bend as a result of the vibrations. This movement triggers changes that cause the cell to send electrical signals along nerves to your brain. Only when your brain receives and processes these signals do you actually hear a sound.

READING TiP

As you read each numbered description here, match it to the number on the illustration below.

How the Ear Detects Sound

Sound waves are detected in the human ear, beginning with vibrations of the eardrum.

The vibrations travel through the **hammer, anvil, and stirrup** to the inner ear.

inner ear

Cells in the **cochlea** detect the vibrations and send a message to the brain.

Sound waves cause the **eardrum** to vibrate.

outer ear

middle ear

Enlargement of hairs on a single cell in the cochlea (magnified 2185x)

READING VISUALS How do vibrations get from the eardrum to the cochlea?

Sound waves vibrate particles.

You can see the motion of waves in water. You can even ride them with a surfboard. But you cannot see air. How, then, can you picture sound waves moving through air? Sound waves transfer the motion of particles too small to see from one place to another.

For example, think about a drum that has been struck. What happens between the time the drum is struck and the sound is heard?

- The drum skin vibrates rapidly. It pushes out and then in, over and over again. Of course, this happens very, very fast. The vibrating drum skin pushes against nearby particles in the air. The particles in the air become bunched together, or compressed.

- When the drum skin pushes the opposite way, a space opens up between the drum's surface and the particles. The particles rush back in to fill the space.

- The back-and-forth movement, or vibration, of the particles is the disturbance that travels to the listener. Both the bunched up areas, or compressions, and the spaces between the compressions are parts of the wave.

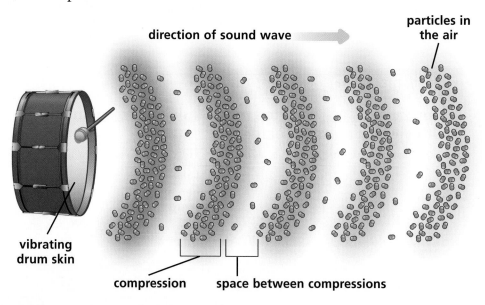

direction of sound wave

particles in the air

vibrating drum skin

compression   space between compressions

Notice that the waves consist of repeating patterns of compressions and spaces between the compressions. The compressions are areas of high air pressure. The spaces between the compressions are areas of low air pressure. The high- and low-pressure air pushes and pulls on the surrounding air, which then pushes and pulls on the air around that. Soon a sound wave has traveled through the air and has transferred kinetic energy from one place to another.

REMINDER
Kinetic energy is the energy of motion.

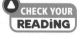
CHECK YOUR READING Summarize in your own words how sound travels through air.

In the middle 1600s, scientists began to do experiments to learn more about air. They used pumps to force the air out of enclosed spaces to produce a vacuum. A **vacuum** is empty space. It has no particles—or very, very few of them. Robert Boyle, a British scientist, designed an experiment to find out if sound moves through a vacuum.

Boyle put a ticking clock in a sealed jar. He pumped some air out of the jar and still heard the clock ticking. Then he pumped more air out. The ticking grew quieter. Finally, when Boyle had pumped out almost all the air, he could hear no ticking at all. Boyle's experiment demonstrated that sound does not travel through a vacuum.

The photograph at the right shows equipment that is set up to perform an experiment similar to Boyle's. A bell is placed in a sealed jar and powered through the electrical connections at the top. The sound of the loudly ringing bell becomes quieter as air is pumped out through the vacuum plate.

Sound is a mechanical wave. It can move only through a medium that is made up of matter. Sound waves can travel through air, solid materials, and liquids, such as water, because all of these mediums are made up of particles. Sound waves cannot travel through a vacuum.

connections

sealed jar

bell

vacuum plate

INFER As air is pumped out of the jar, the sound of the bell becomes quieter. Why do you think the bell is suspended?

 CHECK YOUR READING How did Boyle's experiment show that sound cannot travel through a vacuum?

INVESTIGATE Sound Energy

How does sound transfer energy?

PROCEDURE

1. Sprinkle a few grains of salt into the jar. Put the jar on a flat surface in a well-lit place.

2. Cut off the neck of the balloon with the scissors.

3. Stretch the balloon over the mouth of the jar and pull the sides down past the rim of the jar's mouth. Use a rubber band to make a tight fit.

4. Tap the balloon with the eraser end of the pencil. Observe what happens to the salt on the bottom of the jar.

WHAT DO YOU THINK?

• What happens to the salt?

• How can you explain what you observed?

CHALLENGE Suppose you could pump all the air out of the jar and could leave the salt grains in the jar and the tight rubber cover on top. If you repeated the experiment, do you think the results would be different? Explain your answer.

SKILL FOCUS
Observing

MATERIALS
• clean jar
• table salt
• balloon
• scissors
• rubber band
• pencil with good eraser end

TIME
10 minutes

salt

The speed of sound depends on its medium.

Suppose you are in the baseball stands during an exciting game. A pitch flies from the mound toward home plate, and you see the batter draw back, swing, and hit the ball high. A split second later you hear the crack of the bat meeting the ball. You notice that the sound of the hit comes later than the sight. Just how fast does sound travel?

Sound travels more slowly than light, and it does not always travel at the same speed. Two main factors affect the speed of sound: the material that makes up the medium—such as air or water—and the temperature. If we know the medium and the temperature, however, we can predict the speed of sound.

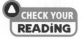 **CHECK YOUR READING** Which two factors affect the speed of sound?

The Effect of the Material

You have probably heard sounds in more than one medium. Think about the medium in which you most often hear sound—air. You listen to a radio or a compact disk player. You hear the siren of a fire truck. These sound waves travel through air, a mixture of gases.

Now think about going swimming. You dip below the water's surface briefly. Someone jumps into the water nearby and splashes water against the pool wall. You hear strange underwater sounds. These sound waves travel through water, a liquid.

Sound travels faster through liquids than it does through gases because liquids are denser than gases. That means that the particles are packed closer together. It takes less time for a water particle to push on the water particles around it because the particles are already closer together than are the particles in air. As a result, divers underwater would hear a sound sooner than people above water would.

Sound can also travel through solid materials that are elastic, which means they can vibrate back and forth. In solid materials, the particles are packed even closer together than they are in liquids or gases. Steel is an example of an elastic material that is very dense. Sound travels very rapidly through steel. Look at the chart on the left. Compare the speed of sound in air with the speed of sound in steel.

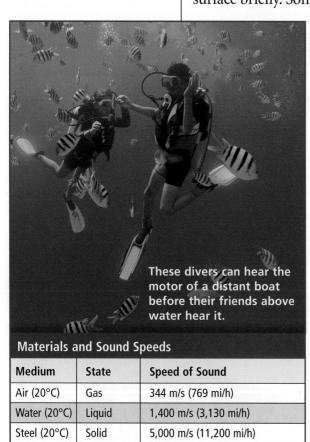

These divers can hear the motor of a distant boat before their friends above water hear it.

Materials and Sound Speeds

Medium	State	Speed of Sound
Air (20°C)	Gas	344 m/s (769 mi/h)
Water (20°C)	Liquid	1,400 m/s (3,130 mi/h)
Steel (20°C)	Solid	5,000 m/s (11,200 mi/h)

The Effect of Temperature

Sound also travels faster through a medium at higher temperatures than at lower ones. Consider the medium of air, a mixture of gases. Gas particles are not held tightly together as are particles in solids. Instead, the gas particles bounce all around. The higher the temperature, the more the gas particles wiggle and bounce. It takes less time for particles that are already moving quickly to push against the particles around them than it takes particles that are moving slowly. Sound, therefore, travels faster in hot air than in cold air.

Look at the picture of the snowboarders. The sound waves they make by yelling will travel more slowly through air than similar sounds made on a hot day. If you could bear to stand in air at a temperature of 100°C (212°F—the boiling point of water) and listen to the same person yelling, you might notice that the sound of the person's voice reaches you faster.

The chart on the right shows the speed of sound in air at two different temperatures. Compare the speed of sound at the temperature at which water freezes with the speed of sound at the temperature at which water boils. Sound travels about 17 percent faster in air at 100°C than in air at 0°C.

These snowboarders' shouts reach their friends more slowly in this cold air than they would in hot air.

Temperature and Sound Speeds

Medium	Temperature	Speed of Sound
Air	0°C (32°F)	331 m/s (741 mi/h)
Air	100°C (212°F)	386 m/s (864 mi/h)

CHECK YOUR READING What is the difference between the speed of sound in air at 0°C and at 100°C?

2.1 Review

KEY CONCEPTS

1. Describe how sound waves are produced.
2. Describe how particles move as energy is transferred through a sound wave.
3. Explain how temperature affects the speed of sound.

CRITICAL THINKING

4. **Predict** Would the sound from a distant train travel faster through air or through steel train tracks? Explain.
5. **Evaluate** Suppose an audience watching a science fiction movie hears a loud roar as a spaceship explodes in outer space. Why is this scene unrealistic?

CHALLENGE

6. **Evaluate** A famous riddle asks this question: If a tree falls in the forest and there is no one there to hear it, is there any sound? What do you think? Give reasons for your answer.

RESOURCE CENTER
CLASSZONE.COM

Find out more about supersonic aircraft.

This photograph may actually show the wake of a sonic boom. It was taken on a very humid day, and water vapor may have condensed in the low-pressure part of the sound wave.

Boom Notes

- The pilot of an airplane cannot hear the sonic boom because the sound waves are behind the plane.

- Lightning heats particles in the air so rapidly that they move faster than the speed of sound and cause a shock wave, which is what makes the boom of thunder. If a lightning strike is very close, you will hear a sharp crack.

- Large meteors enter the atmosphere fast enough to make a sonic boom.

Sonic Booms

Airplanes traveling faster than the speed of sound can produce an incredibly loud sound called a sonic boom. The sonic boom from a low-flying airplane can rattle and even break windows!

How It Works

Breaking the Barrier

The sound waves produced by this airplane begin to pile up and produce a pressure barrier.

This airplane has broken through the pressure barrier and has produced a loud boom.

When an airplane reaches extremely high speeds, it actually catches up to its own sound waves. The waves start to pile up and form a high-pressure area in front of the plane. If the airplane has enough acceleration, it breaks through the barrier, making a sonic boom. The airplane gets ahead of both the pressure barrier and the sound waves and is said to be traveling at supersonic speeds—speeds faster than the speed of sound.

Boom and It's Gone

If an airplane that produces a boom is flying very high, it may be out of sight by the time the sonic boom reaches a hearer on the ground. To make a sonic boom, a plane must be traveling faster than about 1240 kilometers per hour (769 mi/h)! The sound does not last very long—about one-tenth of a second for a small fighter plane to one-half second for a supersonic passenger plane.

EXPLORE

1. **PREDICT** Specially designed cars have traveled faster than the speed of sound. Would you expect them to produce a sonic boom?

2. **CHALLENGE** The space shuttles produce sonic booms when they are taking off and landing, but not while they are orbiting Earth, even though they are moving much faster than 1240 km/h. Can you explain why?

Frequency determines pitch.

 BEFORE, you learned

- Sound waves are produced by vibrations
- Frequency measures the number of waves passing a fixed point per second

 NOW, you will learn

- How the frequency of a wave affects the way it sounds
- How sound quality differs from pitch
- How the Doppler effect works

VOCABULARY

pitch p. 45
hertz p. 46
ultrasound p. 46
resonance p. 48
Doppler effect p. 50

EXPLORE Pitch

Why does the sound change?

PROCEDURE

MATERIALS
ruler

1. Hold the ruler flat on the edge of a desk so that it sticks out about 25 centimeters beyond the edge.

2. With your free hand, push the tip of the ruler down and then let it go. As the ruler vibrates, slide it back onto the desk. Listen to the sounds the ruler makes.

WHAT DO YOU THINK?
- What happened to the sound as you slid the ruler back onto the desk?
- Describe the motion of the ruler.

Pitch depends on the frequency of a sound wave.

VOCABULARY
Remember to add a description wheel in your notebook for each new term.

When you listen to music, you hear both high and low sounds. The characteristic of highness or lowness of a sound is called **pitch.** The frequency of a sound wave determines the pitch of the sound you hear. Remember that frequency is the number of waves passing a fixed point in a given period of time. A high-frequency wave with short wavelengths, such as that produced by a tiny flute, makes a high-pitched sound. A low-frequency wave with long wavelengths, such as the one produced by the deep croak of a tuba, makes a low-pitched sound. An object vibrating very fast produces a high-pitched sound, while an object vibrating slower produces a lower-pitched sound.

CHECK YOUR READING How is frequency related to pitch?

High and Low Frequencies

Frequency is a measure of how often a wave passes a fixed point. One complete wave can also be called a cycle. The unit for measuring frequency, and also pitch, is the hertz. A **hertz** (Hz) is one complete wave, or cycle, per second. For example, a wave with a frequency of 20 hertz has 20 cycles per second. In a wave with a frequency of 100 hertz, 100 waves pass a given point every second. The diagram below shows how frequency and pitch are related.

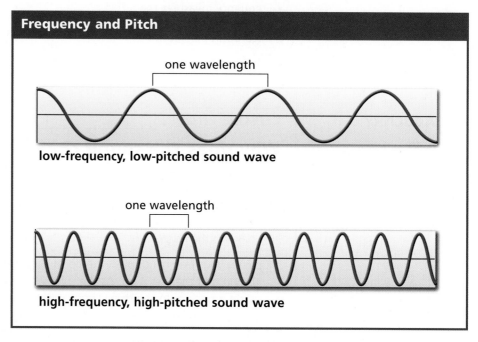

Frequency and Pitch

one wavelength

low-frequency, low-pitched sound wave

one wavelength

high-frequency, high-pitched sound wave

Human ears can hear a wide range of pitches. Most people with good hearing can hear sounds in the range of 20 hertz to 20,000 hertz. The note of middle C on a piano, for example, has a frequency of 262 hertz.

Sound waves with wavelengths below 20 hertz are called infrasound. People cannot hear sounds in this range. Infrasound waves have a very long wavelength and can travel great distances without losing much energy. Elephants may use infrasound to communicate over long distances. Some of the waves that elephants use travel through the ground instead of the air, and they may be detected by another elephant up to 32 kilometers (about 20 miles) away.

The highest frequency that humans can hear is 20,000 hertz. Sound waves in the range above 20,000 hertz are called **ultrasound.** Though people cannot hear ultrasound, it is very useful. Later in this chapter, you will learn about some of the uses of ultrasound. Many animals can hear sound waves in the ultrasound range. The chart on page 47 shows the hearing ranges of some animals.

READING TiP

The prefix *infra* means "below," and the prefix *ultra* means "beyond."

CHECK YOUR READING What is the range of frequencies that humans can hear?

Sound Frequencies Heard by Animals

Frequencies
in Hz

0   50,000   100,000

mosquito 200–400 Hz

tree frog 50–4,000 Hz

elephant 16–12,000 Hz

human 20–20,000 Hz

chimpanzee 100–33,000 Hz

dog 40–50,000 Hz

bat 2,000–110,000 Hz

porpoise 75–150,000 Hz

Although people can hear a wide range of frequencies, there are many sounds that people cannot hear.

Some animals can hear frequencies that are higher than those that people can hear. Dog whistles produce ultrasound.

READING VISUALS Which animals on this chart can hear frequencies above those that humans can hear?

INVESTIGATE Sound Frequency

How is frequency related to pitch?

SKILL FOCUS
Inferring

PROCEDURE

(1) Stretch the rubber bands around the open box.

(2) Pull one of the rubber bands tightly across the open part of the box so that it vibrates with a higher frequency than the looser rubber band. Tape the rubber band in place.

(3) Pluck each rubber band and listen to the sound it makes.

WHAT DO YOU THINK?

• Which rubber band produces a sound wave with a higher pitch?

• How is frequency related to pitch?

CHALLENGE Suppose you are tuning a guitar and want to make one of the strings sound higher in pitch. Do you tighten or loosen the string? Explain your answer.

MATERIALS
• 2 rubber bands of different sizes
• small open box
• tape

TIME
20 minutes

Natural Frequencies

You have read that sound waves are produced by vibrating objects. Sound waves also cause particles in the air to vibrate as they travel through the air. These vibrations have a frequency, or a number of cycles per second. All objects have a frequency at which they vibrate called a natural frequency.

You may have seen a piano tuner tap a tuning fork against another object. The tuner does this to make the fork vibrate at its natural frequency. He or she then listens to the pitch produced by the tuning fork's vibrations and tunes the piano string to match it. Different tuning forks have different frequencies and can be used to tune instruments to different pitches.

When a sound wave with a particular frequency encounters an object that has the same natural frequency, constructive interference takes place. The amplitude of the sound from the vibrating object adds together with the amplitude of the initial sound wave. The strengthening of a sound wave in this way is called **resonance.** When a tuning fork is struck, a nearby tuning fork with the same natural frequency will also begin to vibrate because of resonance.

How is natural frequency related to resonance?

Sound Quality

Have you ever noticed that two singers can sing exactly the same note, or pitch, and yet sound very different? The singers produce sound waves with their vocal cords. They stretch their vocal cords in just the right way to produce sound waves with a certain frequency. That frequency produces the pitch that the note of music calls for. Why, then, don't the singers sound exactly the same?

Each musical instrument and each human voice has its own particular sound, which is sometimes called the sound quality. Another word for sound quality is timbre (TAM-buhr). Timbre can be explained by the fact that most sounds are not single waves but are actually combinations of waves. The pitch that you hear is called the fundamental tone. Other, higher-frequency pitches are called overtones. The combination of pitches is the main factor affecting the quality of a sound.

Another factor in sound quality is the way in which a sound starts and stops. Think about a musician who is crashing cymbals. The cymbals' sound blasts out suddenly. A sound produced by the human voice, on the other hand, starts much more gently.

CHECK YOUR READING What are two factors that affect sound quality? Which sentences above tell you?

The illustration below shows oscilloscope (uh-SIHL-uh-SKOHP) screens. An oscilloscope is a scientific instrument that tracks an electrical signal. The energy of a sound wave is converted into a signal and displayed on an oscilloscope screen. The screens below show sound wave diagrams made by musicians playing a piano and a clarinet. Both of these musical instruments are producing the same note, or pitch. Notice that the diagrams look slightly different from each other. Each has a different combination of overtones, producing a unique sound quality.

Both oscilloscope images at left show diagrams of sound waves of the same pitch produced on two different instruments. The waves, however, have different sound qualities.

piano

clarinet

The motion of the source of a sound affects its pitch.

Sometimes in traffic, a screeching siren announces that an ambulance must pass through traffic. Drivers slow down and pull over to the side, leaving room for the ambulance to speed by. Suppose you are a passenger in one of these cars. What do you hear?

When the ambulance whizzes past you, the pitch suddenly seems to drop. The siren on the ambulance blasts the same pitches again and again. What has made the difference in what you hear is the rapid motion of the vehicle toward you and then away from you. The motion of the source of a sound affects its pitch.

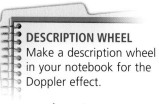

DESCRIPTION WHEEL
Make a description wheel in your notebook for the Doppler effect.

The Doppler Effect

In the 1800s an Austrian scientist named Christian Doppler hypothesized about sound waves. He published a scientific paper about his work. In it, he described how pitch changes when a sound source moves rapidly toward and then away from a listener. Doppler described the scientific principle we notice when a siren speeds by. The **Doppler effect** is the change in perceived pitch that occurs when the source or the receiver of a sound is moving.

Before long, a Dutch scientist learned of Doppler's work. In 1845 he staged an experiment to test the hypothesis that Doppler described. In the experiment, a group of trumpet players were put on a train car. Other musicians were seated beside the railroad track. Those musicians had perfect pitch—that is, the ability to identify a pitch just by listening to it. The train passed by the musicians while the trumpeters on the train played their instruments. The musicians recorded the pitches they heard from one moment to the next. At the end of the demonstration, the musicians reported that they had heard the pitch of the trumpets fall as the train passed. Their experiment showed that the Doppler effect exists.

CHECK YOUR READING How does the motion of a sound's source affect its pitch?

To listeners outside a train, the sound made by the train seems higher in pitch while it approaches them than while it speeds away.

The Doppler Effect

The perceived pitch of a sound changes as the source of the sound moves toward or away from the hearer.

Sound waves arrive at these people farther apart, so the frequency is lower.

Sounds waves arrive at these people closer together, so the frequency is higher.

READING VISUALS Which people hear a higher pitch?

Frequency and Pitch

Again imagine sitting in a car as an ambulance approaches. The siren on the ambulance continually sends out sound waves. As the ambulance pulls closer to you, it catches up with the sound waves it is sending out. As a result, the sound waves that reach your ears are spaced closer together. The frequency, and therefore the pitch, is higher when it reaches you. As the ambulance continues, it gets farther and farther away from you, while the sound waves still move toward you. Now the waves arrive farther and farther apart. As the frequency decreases, you hear a lower pitch.

VISUALIZATION
CLASSZONE.COM

Explore the Doppler effect.

2.2 Review

KEY CONCEPTS

1. Describe what is different about the sound waves produced by a low note and a high note on a musical instrument.

2. Explain why two people singing the same pitch do not sound exactly the same.

3. How does perceived pitch change as a sound source passes a listener?

CRITICAL THINKING

4. **Apply** How could you produce vibrations in a tuning fork without touching it? Explain your answer.

5. **Predict** Suppose you could view the waves produced by a high-pitched and a low-pitched voice. Which wave would display the greater number of compressions in 1 s? Why?

◐ CHALLENGE

6. **Infer** Offer a possible explanation for why no one noticed the Doppler effect before the 1800s.

KEY CONCEPT
2.3 Intensity determines loudness.

◀ **BEFORE,** you learned

- Sound waves are produced by vibrations
- Frequency determines the pitch of a sound
- Amplitude is a measure of the height of a wave crest

▶ **NOW,** you will learn

- How the intensity of a wave affects its loudness
- How sound intensity can be controlled
- How loudness can affect hearing

VOCABULARY

intensity p. 52
decibel p. 52
amplification p. 55
acoustics p. 55

THINK ABOUT

What makes a sound louder?

A drum player has to play softly at some times and loudly at others. Think about what the drummer must do to produce each type of sound. If you could watch the drummer in the photograph in action, what would you see? How would the drummer change the way he moves the drumsticks to make a loud, crashing sound? What might he do to make a very soft sound?

Intensity depends on the amplitude of a sound wave.

OUTLINE
Make an outline for this heading. Remember to include main ideas and details.

I. Main idea
  A. Supporting idea
    1. Detail
    2. Detail
  B. Supporting idea

Earlier you read that all waves carry energy. The more energy a sound wave carries, the more intense it is and the louder it will sound to listeners. The **intensity** of a sound is the amount of energy its sound wave has. A unit called the **decibel** (dB) is used to measure sound intensity. The faint rustling of tree leaves on a quiet summer day can hardly be heard. Some of the softest sounds measure less than 10 decibels. On the other hand, the noise from a jet taking off or the volume of a TV set turned all the way up can hurt your ears. Very loud sounds measure more than 100 decibels. Remember that amplitude is related to wave energy. The greater the amplitude, the more intensity a sound wave has and the louder the sound will be.

○ **CHECK YOUR READING** How is energy related to loudness?

INVESTIGATE Loudness

How is amplitude related to loudness?

PROCEDURE

① Cut a notch in the middle of both ends of the cardboard. Stretch the rubber band around the cardboard so that it fits into the notches as shown.

② Mark lines on the cardboard at one and four centimeters away from the rubber band.

③ Slide the pencils under the rubber band at each end.

④ Pull the rubber band to the one-centimeter line and let it go so that it vibrates with a low amplitude. Notice the sound it makes. Pull the rubber band to the four-centimeter line and let it go again. This time the amplitude is higher. Notice the sound it makes this time.

WHAT DO YOU THINK?

- How did the loudness of the sounds compare?
- How is amplitude related to loudness?

CHALLENGE Using what you learned from experimenting with the rubber band, explain why swinging a drumstick harder on a drum would make a louder sound than swinging a drumstick lightly.

SKILL FOCUS
Observing

MATERIALS
- piece of cardboard
- scissors
- large rubber band
- 2 pencils
- ruler

TIME
15 minutes

The drummer varies the loudness of a sound by varying the energy with which he hits the drum. Loudness is also affected by the distance between the source and the listener.

Have you ever wondered why sound gradually dies out over distance? Think about someone walking away from you with a radio. When the radio is close, the radio seems loud. As the person walks away, the sound grows fainter and fainter. Sound waves travel in all directions from their source. As the waves travel farther from the radio, their energy is spread out over a greater area. This means that their intensity is decreased. The sound waves with lower intensities are heard as quieter sounds.

Other forces can take energy away from sound waves, too. Forces can act within the medium of a sound wave to decrease the intensity of the waves. This effect on sound is probably a good thing. Imagine what the world would be like if every sound wave continued forever!

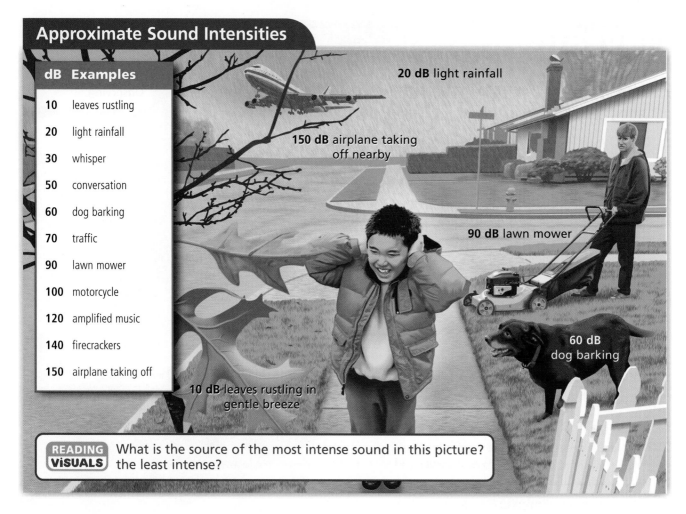

Approximate Sound Intensities

dB	Examples
10	leaves rustling
20	light rainfall
30	whisper
50	conversation
60	dog barking
70	traffic
90	lawn mower
100	motorcycle
120	amplified music
140	firecrackers
150	airplane taking off

20 dB light rainfall

150 dB airplane taking off nearby

90 dB lawn mower

60 dB dog barking

10 dB leaves rustling in gentle breeze

READING VISUALS What is the source of the most intense sound in this picture? the least intense?

The intensity of sound can be controlled.

REMINDER

Remember, amplitude is related to wave energy.

Over time and distance, a sound wave gets weaker and weaker until the sound becomes undetectable. The pitch, however, does not typically change as the sound grows weaker. In other words, even as the amplitude decreases, the frequency stays the same.

Sometimes it is desirable to change sound intensity without changing the pitch and quality of a sound. We can do this by adding energy to or taking energy away from a sound wave. As you have already seen, intensity is the amount of energy in a sound wave. Changing the intensity of a sound wave changes its amplitude.

Sound intensity can be controlled in many ways. Mufflers on cars and trucks reduce engine noise. Have you ever heard a car with a broken muffler? You were probably surprised at how loud it was. Burning fuel in an engine produces hot gases that expand and make a very loud noise. A muffler is designed to absorb some of the energy of the sound waves and so decrease their amplitude. As a result, the intensity of the sound you hear is much lower than it would be without the muffler.

CHECK YOUR READING How could you change the intensity of a sound without changing the pitch?

Amplification

In addition to being reduced, as they are in a muffler, sound waves can be amplified. The word *amplify* may remind you of *amplitude,* the measure of the height of a wave's crest. These words are related. To amplify something means to make it bigger. **Amplification** is the increasing of the strength of an electrical signal. It is often used to increase the intensity of a sound wave.

When you listen to a stereo, you experience the effects of amplification. Sound input to the stereo is in the form of weak electrical signals from a microphone. Transistors in an electronic circuit amplify the signals. The electrical signals are converted into vibrations in a coil in your stereo's speaker. The coil is attached to a cone, which also vibrates and sends out sound waves. You can control the intensity of the sound waves by adjusting your stereo's volume.

sound waves in

Amplifier

coil

cone

sound waves out

Acoustics

The scientific study of sound is called **acoustics** (uh-KOO-stihks). Acoustics involves both how sound is produced and how it is received and heard by humans and animals.

Acoustics also refers to the way sound waves behave inside a space. Experts called acoustical engineers help design buildings to reduce unwanted echoes. An echo is simply a reflected sound wave. To control sound intensity, engineers design walls and ceilings with acoustical tiles. The shapes and surfaces of acoustical tiles are designed to absorb or redirect some of the energy of sound waves.

The pointed tiles in this sound-testing room are designed to absorb sound waves and prevent any echoes.

The shapes and surfaces in this concert hall direct sound waves to the audience.

READING VISUALS COMPARE AND CONTRAST Imagine sound waves reflecting off the surfaces in the two photographs above. How do the reflections differ?

Intense sound can damage hearing.

healthy hair cells

damaged hair cells

When a train screeches to a stop in a subway station, the sound of the squealing brakes echoes off the tunnel walls. Without thinking about it, you cover your ears with your hands. This response helps protect your ears from possible damage.

In the first section of this chapter, you read about the main parts of the human ear. The part of the inner ear called the cochlea is lined with special cells called hair cells. As you have seen, these cells are necessary for hearing.

The hair cells are extremely sensitive. This sensitivity makes hearing possible, but it also makes the cells easy to damage. Continual exposure to sounds of 90 dB or louder can damage or destroy the cells. This is one reason why being exposed to very loud noises, especially for more than a short time, is harmful to hearing.

CHECK YOUR READING How do high-intensity sounds damage hearing?

RESOURCE CENTER
CLASSZONE.COM
Find out more about sound and protecting your hearing.

Using earplugs can prevent damage from too much exposure to high-intensity sounds such as amplified music. The intensity at a rock concert is between 85 and 120 dB. Ear protection can also protect the hearing of employees in factories and other noisy work sites. In the United States, there are laws that require employers to reduce sounds at work sites to below 90 dB or to provide workers with ear protection.

Even a brief, one-time exposure to an extremely loud noise can destroy hair cells. Noises above 130 dB are especially dangerous. Noises above 140 dB are even painful. It is best to avoid such noises altogether. If you find yourself exposed suddenly to such a noise, covering your ears with your hands may be the best protection.

2.3 Review

KEY CONCEPTS

1. Explain how the terms *intensity, decibel,* and *amplitude* are related.

2. Describe one way in which sound intensity can be controlled.

3. How do loud sounds cause damage to hearing?

CRITICAL THINKING

4. **Synthesize** A wind chime produces both soft and loud sounds. If you could see the waves, how would they differ?

5. **Design an Experiment** How could you demonstrate that sound dies away over distance? Suppose you could use three volunteers, a radio, and a tape recorder.

⬥ CHALLENGE

6. **Apply** Which of these acoustical designs would be best for a concert hall? Why?
a. bare room with hard walls, floor, and ceiling
b. room padded with sound-absorbing materials such as acoustical tile
c. room with some hard surfaces and some sound padding

MATH TUTORIAL
CLASSZONE.COM

Click on Math Tutorial for more help with interpreting line graphs.

This air traffic ground controller wears ear protection to prevent hearing loss.

Measuring Hearing Loss

An audiogram is a graph that can be used to determine if a patient has hearing loss. The vertical axis shows the lowest intensity, in decibels, that the patient can hear for each frequency tested. Notice that intensity is numbered from top to bottom on an audiogram.

To determine the lowest intensity heard at a given frequency, find the frequency on the horizontal axis. Follow the line straight up until you see the data points, shown as ✖ for the right ear and ● for the left ear. Look to the left to find the intensity. For example, the lowest intensity heard in both ears at 250 Hz is 10 dB.

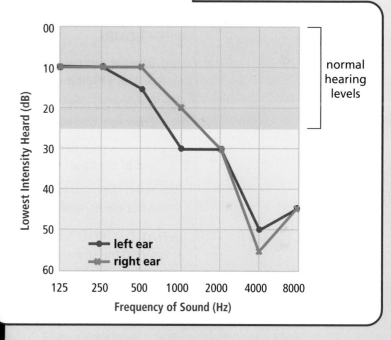

Audiogram for Patient A

normal hearing levels

Lowest Intensity Heard (dB)

—●— left ear
—✖— right ear

Frequency of Sound (Hz)

Use the graph to answer the following questions.

1. What is the lowest intensity heard in the patient's left ear at 1000 Hz? the right ear at the same frequency?

2. At which frequencies are the data points for both ears within normal hearing levels?

3. Data points outside the normal hearing levels indicate hearing loss. At which frequencies are the data points for both ears outside the normal levels?

CHALLENGE A dip in the graph at 3000 to 4000 Hz is a sign that the hearing loss was caused by exposure to loud noises. The patient is referred to a specialist for further testing. Should Patient A get further testing? Why or why not?

Sound has many uses.

 BEFORE, you learned

- Sound waves are produced by vibrations
- Sound waves have amplitude, frequency, and wavelength

 NOW, you will learn

- How ultrasound is used
- How musical instruments work
- How sound can be recorded and reproduced

VOCABULARY

echolocation p. 59
sonar p. 59

EXPLORE Echoes

How can you use sound to detect an object?

PROCEDURE

1. Tape the two cardboard tubes onto your desk at a right angle as shown.

2. Put your ear up to the end of one of the tubes. Cover your other ear with your hand.

3. Listen as your partner whispers into the outside end of the other tube.

4. Stand the book upright where the tubes meet. Repeat steps 2 and 3.

WHAT DO YOU THINK?

- How did the sound change when you added the book?
- How can an echo be used to detect an object?

MATERIALS

- 2 cardboard tubes
- tape
- book

Ultrasound waves are used to detect objects.

A ringing telephone, a honking horn, and the sound of a friend's voice are all reminders of how important sound is. But sound has uses that go beyond communication. For example, some animals and people use reflected ultrasound waves to detect objects. Some animals, such as bats, use the echoes of ultrasound waves to find food. People use ultrasound echoes to detect objects underwater or even to produce images of the inside of the body.

 CHECK YOUR READING   Other than communication, what are three uses of sound?

Echolocation

Sending out ultrasound waves and interpreting the returning sound echoes is called **echolocation** (*echo* + *location*). Bats flying at night find their meals of flying insects by using echolocation. They send out as many as 200 ultrasound squeaks per second. By receiving the returning echoes, they can tell where prey is and how it is moving. They can also veer away from walls, trees, and other big objects.

sound waves emitted by bat

sound waves reflected off prey

A number of animals that live in water use echolocation, too. Dolphins, toothed whales, and porpoises produce ultrasound squeaks or clicks. They listen to the returning echo patterns to find fish and other food in the water.

Sonar

People use the principles of echolocation to locate objects underwater. During World War I (1914–1918), scientists developed instruments that used sound waves to locate enemy submarines. Instruments that use echolocation to locate objects are known as **sonar.** Sonar stands for "sound navigation and ranging." The sonar machines could detect sounds coming from submarine propellers. Sonar devices could also send out ultrasound waves and then use the echoes to locate underwater objects. The information from the echoes could then be used to form an image on a screen.

Later, people found many other uses for sonar. Fishing boats use sonar to find schools of fish. Oceanographers—scientists who study the ocean—use it to map the sea floor. People have even used sonar to find ancient sunken ships in deep water.

This woman is using sonar to monitor for submarines.

Sonar is used to locate sunken ships. The image of the sunken ship above was produced on the basis of information from sonar.

Medical Uses of Ultrasound

Ultrasound has many uses in medicine. Because ultrasound waves are not heard by humans, ultrasound can be used at very high intensities. For example, high-intensity vibrations from ultrasound waves are used to safely break up kidney stones in patients. The energy transferred by ultrasound waves is also used to clean medical equipment.

One of the most important medical uses of ultrasound is the ultrasound scanner. This device relies on the same scientific principle as sonar. It sends sound waves into a human body and then records the waves that are reflected from inside the body. Information from these echoes forms a picture on a screen. The ultrasound scanner is used to examine internal organs such as the heart, pancreas, bladder, ovaries, and brain. Doppler ultrasound is a technology that can detect the movement of fluids through the body and is used to examine blood flow.

The image of these triplets was produced by reflected ultrasound waves.

CHECK YOUR READING How is an ultrasound scanner similar to sonar?

One of the most well-known uses of ultrasound is to check on the health of a fetus during pregnancy. Problems that are discovered may possibly be treated early. The scan can also reveal the age and gender of the fetus and let the expecting parents know if they will be having twins or triplets. Ultrasound is safer than other imaging methods, such as the x-ray, which might harm the development of the fetus.

Sound waves can produce music.

Why are some sounds considered noise and other sounds considered music? Music is sound with clear pitches or rhythms. Noise is random sound; that means it has no intended pattern.

RESOURCE CENTER
CLASSZONE.COM

Explore musical instruments from around the world.

Musical instruments produce pitches and rhythms when made to vibrate at their natural frequencies. Some musical instruments have parts that vibrate at different frequencies to make different pitches. All of the pitches, together with the resonance of the instrument itself, produce its characteristic sound. The three main types of musical instruments are stringed, wind, and percussion. Some describe electronic instruments as a fourth type of musical instrument. Look at the illustration on the next page to learn more about how each type of musical instrument works.

How Musical Instruments Work

The way a musical instrument vibrates when it is played determines the sound it produces.

Stringed Instruments

Stringed instruments, such as the guitar, are played by plucking the strings. The plucking starts the vibrations that produce sound waves.

soundboard

1 The vibrations begin when a player plucks one of the **strings**.

5 To play a different pitch, the player presses on a string to shorten it. A shorter string produces a higher pitch.

bridge

sound hole

4 The sound waves exit the guitar through the **sound hole**.

2 The vibrations travel through the **bridge** to the **soundboard**, which makes the entire soundboard vibrate.

body

3 As the **soundboard** vibrates, the air inside the **body** also vibrates, which amplifies the sound waves.

Wind Instruments

Musicians play the trombone by blowing into a mouthpiece. Sound waves are produced by a column of vibrating air. Like the length of a musical string, the length of the air column determines the pitch.

Percussion Instruments

Musicians play a drum by striking a tightly stretched skin. The vibrations of the tight skin send out sound waves. The size and tightness of the drum skin determine the pitch.

Sound can be recorded and reproduced.

For most of human history, people had no way to send their voices farther than they could shout. Nor could people before the 1800s record and play back sound. The voices of famous people were lost when they died. Imagine having a tape or a compact disk recording of George Washington giving a speech!

Then in the late 1800s, two inventions changed the world of sound. In 1876, the telephone was invented. And in 1877, Thomas Edison played the first recorded sound on a phonograph, or sound-recording machine.

READING TiP

The prefix *phono* means "sound," and the suffix *graph* means "writing."

The Telephone

The telephone has made long-distance voice communication possible. Many people today use cell phones. But whether phone signals travel over wires or by microwaves, as in cell phones, the basic principles are similar. You will learn more about the signal that is used in cell phones when you read about microwaves in Chapter 3. In general, a telephone must do two things. It must translate the sound that is spoken into it into a signal, and it must reproduce the sound that arrives as a signal from somewhere else.

earpiece

sound waves out

diaphragm

mouthpiece

sound waves in

microphone

Suppose you are phoning your best friend to share some news. You speak into the mouthpiece. Sound waves from your voice cause a thin disk inside the mouthpiece to vibrate. A microphone turns these vibrations into electrical signals. Your handset sends these signals over wire to a switching station. Computers in the switching station connect phone callers and keep them connected until they finish their conversation.

Your friend receives the news by listening to the earpiece on his handset. There the process is more or less reversed. The electrical signals that arrive in the earpiece are turned into vibrations that shake another thin disk called a diaphragm. The vibrating diaphragm produces sound waves. The sound your friend hears is a copy of your voice, though it sounds like the real you.

CHECK YOUR READING What part of a telephone detects sound waves?

Recorded Sound

Sound occurs in real time, which means it is here for a moment and then gone. That is why Thomas Edison's invention of the phonograph—a way to preserve sound—was so important.

Edison's phonograph had a needle connected to a diaphragm that could pick up sound waves. The vibrations transferred by the sound waves were sent to a needle that cut into a piece of foil. The sound waves were translated into bumps along the grooves cut into the foil. These grooves contained all the information that was needed to reproduce the sound waves. Look at the image on top at the right to view an enlargement of record grooves. To play back the sound, Edison used another needle to track along the grooves etched in the foil. Later, phonographs were developed that changed sound waves into electrical signals that could be amplified.

Most people today listen to music on audio tapes or CDs. Tape consists of thin strips of plastic coated with a material that can be magnetized. Sounds that have been turned into electrical signals are stored on the tape as magnetic information. A CD is a hard plastic disc that has millions of microscopic pits arranged in a spiral. The bottom photograph at the right shows an enlargement of pits on the surface of a CD. These pits contain the information that a CD player can change into electrical signals, which are then turned into sound waves.

needle

record grooves

CD pits

The images above were taken by a scanning electron micrograph (SEM). Both the record grooves (top) and CD pits (bottom) store all of the information needed to reproduce sound.

 CHECK YOUR READING Describe three devices on which sound is recorded.

2.4 Review

KEY CONCEPTS

1. Describe one medical use of ultrasound.

2. How are vibrations produced by each of the three main types of musical instruments?

3. How does a telephone record and reproduce sound?

CRITICAL THINKING

4. **Model** Draw a simple diagram to show how telephone communication works. Begin your diagram with the mouthpiece and end with the earpiece.

5. **Classify** The pitch of a musical instrument is changed by shortening the length of a vibrating column of air. What type of instrument is it?

⬥ CHALLENGE

6. **Synthesize** How is the earpiece of a telephone similar to the amplifier you read about in Section 3? Look again at the diagram of the amplifier on page 55 to help you find similarities.

CHAPTER INVESTIGATION

Build a Stringed Instrument

OVERVIEW AND PURPOSE

People make music by plucking strings, blowing through tubes, and striking things. Part of each musical instrument vibrates to produce sounds that form the building blocks of music. In this lab, you will use what you have learned about sound to

- make a simple stringed instrument and see how the vibrating string produces sounds and
- change the design so that your stringed instrument produces more than one pitch.

▶ Problem

How does the length of a string affect the pitch of the sound it produces when plucked?

▶ Hypothesize

Write a hypothesis to explain how changing the length of the string affects the pitch of sound that is produced. Your hypothesis should take the form of an "If . . . , then . . . , because . . ." statement. Complete steps 1–3 before writing your hypothesis.

MATERIALS
- book
- 3–5 rubber bands
- 2 pencils
- ruler
- shoebox
- scissors

▶ Procedure

1. Make a data table like the one shown. Try out the following idea for a simple stringed instrument. Stretch a rubber band around a textbook. Put two pencils under the rubber band to serve as bridges.

2. Put the bridges far apart at either end of the book. Find the string length by measuring the distance between the two bridges. Record this measurement in your **Science Notebook.** Pluck the rubber band to make it vibrate. Watch it vibrate and listen to the sound it makes.

3. Move the bridges closer together. What effect does this have on the length of the string? Measure and record the new length. How does this affect the tone that is produced? Record your observations.

4. Make a musical instrument based on the principles you just identified. Begin by stretching rubber bands of the same weight or thickness over the box.

5. If necessary, reinforce the box with an extra layer of cardboard or braces so that it can withstand the tension of the rubber bands without collapsing.

6. Place pencils under the rubber bands at each end of the box. Arrange one pencil at an angle so that each string is a different length. Record the length of each string and your observations of the sounds produced. Experiment with the placement of the bridges.

7. You might also try putting one bridge at the center of the box and plucking on either side of it. How does this affect the range of pitches your instrument produces?

8. Experiment with the working model to see how you can vary the sounds. Try this variation: cut a hole in the center of the box lid. Put the lid back on the box. Replace the rubber bands and bridges. How does the hole change the sound quality?

Observe and Analyze
Write It Up

1. **RECORD OBSERVATIONS** Draw a picture of your completed instrument design. Be sure your data table is complete.

2. **ANALYZE** Explain what effect moving the bridges farther apart or closer together has on the vibrating string.

3. **SYNTHESIZE** Using what you have learned from this chapter, write a paragraph that explains how your instrument works. Be sure to describe how sound waves of different frequencies and different intensities can be produced on your instrument.

Conclude
Write It Up

1. **INTERPRET** Answer the question posed in the problem.

2. **ANALYZE** Compare your results with your hypothesis. Did your results support your hypothesis?

3. **EVALUATE** Describe any difficulties with or limitations of the materials that you encountered as you made your instrument.

4. **APPLY** Based on your experiences, how would you explain the difference between music and noise?

INVESTIGATE Further

CHALLENGE Stringed instruments vary the pitch of musical sounds in several other ways. In addition to the length of the string, pitch depends on the tension, weight, and thickness of the string. Design an experiment to test one of these variables. How does it alter the range of sounds produced by your stringed instrument?

Build a Stringed Instrument
Problem How does the length of a string affect the pitch of the sound it produces when plucked?
Hypothesize

Observe and Analyze

Simple instrument: initial string length _____
Simple instrument: new string length _____
Table 1. Stringed Instrument Sound Observations

Stringed Instrument Designs	Length of Strings (cm)	Observations About Pitch and Sound Quality
Bridges at each end		
Bridge in middle		
After adding sound hole		

Conclude

the BIG idea

Sound waves transfer energy through vibrations.

CONTENT REVIEW
CLASSZONE.COM

◀ KEY CONCEPTS SUMMARY

2.1 Sound is a wave.

disturbance →

wave

Sound is a longitudinal wave that travels through a material medium, such as air.

VOCABULARY
sound p. 37
vibration p. 37
vacuum p. 41

2.2 Frequency determines pitch.

A sound wave with a lower frequency and longer wavelength is perceived to have a lower pitch.

A sound wave with a higher frequency and shorter wavelength is perceived to have a higher pitch.

VOCABULARY
pitch p. 45
hertz p. 46
ultrasound p. 46
resonance p. 48
Doppler effect p. 50

2.3 Intensity determines loudness.

A sound wave with a lower amplitude and energy is perceived as a softer sound.

A sound wave with a higher amplitude and energy is perceived as a louder sound.

VOCABULARY
intensity p. 52
decibel p. 52
amplification p. 55
acoustics p. 55

2.4 Sound has many uses.

Human uses of sound:
sonar
ultrasound
music
telephone
recording

Bats use sound to locate objects.

VOCABULARY
echolocation p. 59
sonar p. 59

Reviewing Vocabulary

Copy and complete the chart below by using vocabulary terms from this chapter.

Property of Wave	Unit of Measurement	Characteristic of Sound
Frequency	1.	2.
3.	4.	loudness

Make a frame for each of the vocabulary words listed below. Write the word in the center. Decide what information to frame it with. Use definitions, examples, descriptions, parts, or pictures. An example is shown.

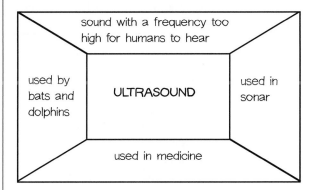

sound with a frequency too high for humans to hear

used by bats and dolphins

ULTRASOUND

used in sonar

used in medicine

5. resonance

6. Doppler effect

7. amplification

8. acoustics

9. echolocation

10. sonar

Reviewing Key Concepts

Multiple Choice *Choose the letter of the best answer.*

11. Sound is a mechanical wave, so it always
   a. travels through a vacuum
   b. has the same amplitude
   c. is made by a machine
   d. travels through matter

12. Which unit is a measure of sound frequency?
   a. hertz
   b. decibel
   c. amp
   d. meter

13. In which of the following materials would sound waves move fastest?
   a. water
   b. cool air
   c. hot air
   d. steel

14. Which of the following effects is caused by amplification?
   a. wavelength increases
   b. amplitude increases
   c. frequency decreases
   d. decibel measure decreases

15. The frequency of a sound wave determines its
   a. pitch
   b. loudness
   c. amplitude
   d. intensity

16. As sound waves travel away from their source, their
   a. intensity increases
   b. energy increases
   c. intensity decreases
   d. frequency decreases

17. A telephone mouthpiece changes sound waves into
   a. electric signals
   b. vibrations
   c. CD pits
   d. grooves on a cylinder

Short Answer *Look at the diagrams of waves below. For the next two items, choose the wave diagram that best fits the description, and explain your choice.*

a.   b.   c.

18. the sound of a basketball coach blowing a whistle during practice

19. the sound of a cow mooing in a pasture

Thinking Critically

Look at the photograph of an instrument above. Write a short answer to the next two questions.

20. HYPOTHESIZE How might sound waves be produced using the instrument in the photograph?

21. APPLY How might a person playing the instrument in the photograph vary the intensity?

22. COMMUNICATE Two people are singing at the same pitch, yet they sound different. Explain why.

23. SEQUENCE Copy the following sequence chart on your paper. Write the events in the correct sequence on the chart.

Events

a. Sound waves race out from the wind chime.

b. Forces in air gradually weaken the chime sound.

c. A breeze makes a wind chime vibrate.

d. A person nearby hears the wind chime.

24. COMPARE AND CONTRAST Write a description of the similarities and differences between each of the following pairs of terms: frequency—amplitude; intensity—amplitude; pitch—quality; fundamental tone—overtones.

Using Math in Science

Read the line graph below showing freeway noise levels at a toll collector's booth. Use the data in the graph to answer the next four questions.

25. Which is the noisiest quarter-hour?

26. Estimate the loudest level of sound that the toll collector is exposed to.

27. If ear protection should be worn for a sound level above 90 dB, should the toll collector wear hearing protection? If so, during which times?

28. Describe how you could turn the line graph into a bar graph. Would the bar graph be as informative? Explain your answer.

the BIG idea

29. ANALYZE Look back at the picture at the start of the chapter on pages 34–35. How are sound waves being produced?

30. SUMMARIZE Write a paragraph summarizing this chapter. Use the Big Idea on page 34 as your topic sentence. Write examples of each key concept listed on page 34.

UNIT PROJECTS

Check your schedule for your unit project. How are you doing? Be sure that you've placed data or notes from your research in your project folder.

Analyzing Experiments

Read the following description of the way scientists study animals' hearing. Then answer the questions below.

Scientists test the hearing ranges of a human by making a sound and asking the person to say whether it was heard. This cannot be done with animals. Scientists use different methods to find animals' hearing ranges. In some experiments, they train animals—by rewarding them with food or water—to make specific behaviors when they hear a sound. Another method is to study an animal's nervous system for electrical reactions to sounds.

Researchers have found that dogs and cats can hear a wide range of sounds. Both dogs and cats can hear much higher frequencies than humans can. Lizards and frogs can only hear sounds in a much narrower range than humans can. Elephants can hear a wider range than lizards and frogs but not as wide a range as dogs and cats. Elephants can hear the lowest frequency sounds of all these animals.

1. What type of behavior would be best for scientists to train animals to make as a signal that they hear a sound?
   a. a typical motion that the animal makes frequently
   b. a motion that is difficult for the animal to make
   c. a motion the animal makes rarely but does make naturally
   d. a complicated motion of several steps

2. According to the passage, which animals can hear sounds with the highest frequencies?
   a. cats
   b. elephants
   c. frogs
   d. lizards

3. The high-pitched sounds of car brakes are sometimes more bothersome to pet dogs than they are to their owners. Based on the experimental findings, what is the best explanation for that observation?
   a. The dogs have not been trained to respond to the high-frequency sounds.
   b. The dogs have not been trained to respond to the low-frequency sounds.
   c. The dogs hear low-frequency sounds that their owners cannot hear.
   d. The dogs hear high-frequency sounds that their owners cannot hear.

4. Which animal hears sounds with the longest wavelengths?
   a. cat
   b. dog
   c. elephant
   d. frog

Extended Response

Answer the two questions below in detail. Include some of the terms from the word box in your answer. Underline each term you use in your answer.

| amplitude | distance | Doppler effect |
| frequency | pitch | wavelength |

5. Suppose you are riding in a car down the street and pass a building where a fire alarm is sounding. Will the sound you hear change as you move up to, alongside, and past the building? Why or why not?

6. Marvin had six glass bottles that held different amounts of water. He blew air into each bottle, producing a sound. How would the sounds produced by each of the six bottles compare to the others? Why?

Electromagnetic Waves

the BIG idea

Electromagnetic waves transfer energy through radiation.

How does this phone stay connected?

Key Concepts

SECTION
3.1 **Electromagnetic waves have unique traits.**
Learn how electromagnetic waves differ from mechanical waves.

SECTION
3.2 **Electromagnetic waves have many uses.**
Learn about the behaviors and uses of different types of electromagnetic waves.

SECTION
3.3 **The Sun is the source of most visible light.**
Learn about the natural and artificial production of light.

SECTION
3.4 **Light waves interact with materials.**
Learn how light waves behave in a material medium.

Internet Preview

CLASSZONE.COM

Chapter 3 online resources: Content Review, Simulation, Visualization, two Resource Centers, Math Tutorial, Test Practice.

EXPLORE (the BIG idea)

What Melts the Ice Cubes?

Put an ice cube in each of two sandwich bags, and place the bags in sunlight. Cover one with a sheet of white paper, and cover the other with a sheet of black paper. Lift the sheets of paper every five minutes and observe the cubes. Continue until they are melted.

Observe and Think
What did you notice about the way the ice cubes melted? How can you explain what you observed?

What Is White Light Made Of?

Use the shiny side of a compact disk (CD) to reflect light from the Sun onto a sheet of white paper. If bright sunlight is not available, use a flashlight. Try holding the CD at different angles and at different distances from the paper.

Observe and Think
What did you see on the paper? Where do you think that what you observed came from?

Internet Activity: Electromagnetic Waves

Go to **ClassZone.com** to explore images of the Sun based on different wavelengths.

Observe and Think
Why can we see only some of the waves coming from the Sun?

NSTA
scilinks.org

Light and Color **Code: MDL029**

Getting Ready to Learn

◀ CONCEPT REVIEW

- A wave is a disturbance that transfers energy.
- Mechanical waves have a medium.
- Waves can be measured.
- Waves react to a change in medium.

◀ VOCABULARY REVIEW

mechanical wave p. 11

wavelength p. 17

frequency p. 17

reflection p. 25

field *See Glossary.*

CONTENT REVIEW
CLASSZONE.COM
Review concepts and vocabulary.

▶ TAKING NOTES

SUPPORTING MAIN IDEAS

Make a chart to show main ideas and the information that supports them. Copy each blue heading. Below each heading, add supporting information, such as reasons, explanations, and examples.

VOCABULARY STRATEGY

Write each new vocabulary term in the center of a **frame game** diagram. Decide what information to frame it with. Use examples, descriptions, parts, sentences that use the term in context, or pictures. You can change the frame to fit each term.

See the Note-Taking Handbook on pages R45–R51.

MAIN IDEA
Electromagnetic waves have unique properties.

→ EM waves are disturbances in a field rather than in a medium.

→ EM waves can travel through a vacuum.

→ EM waves travel at the speed of light.

passes through a vacuum

RADIATION

travels at the speed of light

interacts with a medium

3.1 Electromagnetic waves have unique traits.

◀ BEFORE, you learned

- Waves transfer energy
- Mechanical waves need a medium to travel

▶ NOW, you will learn

- How electromagnetic waves differ from mechanical waves
- Where electromagnetic waves come from
- How electromagnetic waves transfer energy

VOCABULARY

electromagnetic wave p. 73
radiation p. 75

EXPLORE Electromagnetic Waves

How does the signal from a remote control travel?

PROCEDURE

① Turn the TV on and off using the remote control.

② Work with a partner to try to turn on the TV by aiming the remote control at the mirror.

WHAT DO YOU THINK?
How did you have to position the remote control and the mirror in order to operate the TV? Why do you think this worked?

MATERIALS
- TV with remote control unit
- mirror with stand

An electromagnetic wave is a disturbance in a field.

Did you know that you are surrounded by thousands of waves at this very moment? Waves fill every cubic centimeter of the space around you. They collide with or pass through your body all the time.

Most of these waves are invisible, but you can perceive many of them. Light is made up of these waves, and heat can result from them. Whenever you use your eyes to see, or feel the warmth of the Sun on your skin, you are detecting their presence. These waves also allow radios, TVs, and cell phones to send or receive information over long distances. These waves have the properties shared by all waves, yet they are different from mechanical waves in important ways. This second type of wave is called an electromagnetic wave. An **electromagnetic wave** (ih-LEHK-troh-mag-NEHT-ihk) is a disturbance that transfers energy through a field. Electromagnetic waves are also called EM (EE-EHM) waves.

VOCABULARY
Create a frame game diagram for the term *electromagnetic wave.*

A field is an area around an object where the object can apply a force—a push or a pull—to another object without touching it. You have seen force applied through a field if you have ever seen a magnet holding a card on the door of a refrigerator. The magnet exerts a pull on the door, even though it does not touch the door. The magnet exerts a force through the magnetic field that surrounds the magnet. When a disturbance occurs in an electric or magnetic field rather than in a medium, the wave that results is an electromagnetic wave.

How EM Waves Form

VISUALIZATION
CLASSZONE.COM

Learn more about the nature of EM waves.

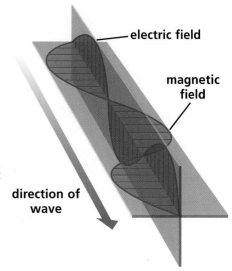

electric field

magnetic field

direction of wave

EM waves occur when electrically charged atomic particles move. Charged particles exert an electric force on each other, so they have electric fields. A moving charged particle creates a magnetic force, so a moving charge also has a magnetic field around it.

When electrically charged particles move quickly, they can start a disturbance of electric and magnetic fields. The fields vibrate at right angles to each other, as shown in the diagram above. The EM wave travels in the form of these vibrating fields. As you read in Chapter 1, waves have the properties of wavelength and frequency. In an EM wave, both the electric and the magnetic fields have these properties.

 What are the two types of fields that make up an EM wave?

Sources of EM Waves

Many of the EM waves present in Earth's environment come from the Sun. The Sun's high temperature allows it to give off countless EM waves. Other stars give off as many EM waves as the Sun, but because these bodies are so far away, fewer of their EM waves reach Earth. In addition to the Sun, technology is a source of EM waves that humans use for a wide variety of purposes.

EM waves from the Sun provide most of the energy for the environment on Earth. Some of the energy goes into Earth's surface, which then gives off EM waves of different wavelengths.

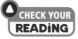 What are two sources of EM waves on Earth?

Electromagnetic waves can travel in a vacuum.

Energy that moves in the form of EM waves is called **radiation** (RAY-dee-AY-shuhn). Radiation is different from the transfer of energy through a medium by a mechanical wave. A mechanical wave must vibrate the medium as it moves, and this uses some of the wave's energy. Eventually, every mechanical wave will give up all of its energy to the medium and disappear. An EM wave can travel without a material medium—that is, in a vacuum or space empty of matter—and does not lose energy as it moves. In theory, an EM wave can travel forever.

READING TiP

EM waves are also called rays. The words *radiation* and *radiate* come from the Latin word *radius,* which means "ray" or "spoke of a wheel."

How EM Waves Travel in a Vacuum

Because they do not need a medium, EM waves can pass through outer space, which is a near vacuum. Also, because they do not give up energy in traveling, EM waves can cross the great distances that separate stars and galaxies. For example, rays from the Sun travel about 150 million kilometers (93 million mi) to reach Earth. Rays from the most distant galaxies travel for billions of years before reaching Earth.

Usually, EM waves spread outward in all directions from the source of the disturbance. The waves then travel until something interferes with them. The farther the waves move from their source, the more they spread out. As they spread out, there are fewer waves in a given area and less energy is transferred. Only a very small part of the energy radiated from the Sun is transferred to Earth. But that energy is still a great amount—enough to sustain life on the planet.

The Speed of EM Waves in a Vacuum

In a vacuum, EM waves travel at a constant speed, and they travel very fast—about 300,000 kilometers (186,000 mi) per second. In 1 second, an EM wave can travel a distance greater than 7 times the distance around Earth. Even at this speed, rays from the Sun take about 8 minutes to reach Earth. This constant speed is called the speed of light. The vast distances of space are often measured in units of time traveled at this speed. For example, the Sun is about 8 light-minutes away from Earth. The galaxy shown in the photograph is 60 million light-years from Earth.

The light and other EM waves from this galaxy took approximately 60 million years to reach Earth.

CHECK YOUR READING How are EM waves used to measure distances in space?

Electromagnetic waves can interact with a material medium.

When EM waves encounter a material medium, they can interact with it in much the same way that mechanical waves do. They can transfer energy to the medium itself. Also, EM waves can respond to a change of medium by reflecting, refracting, or diffracting, just as mechanical waves do. When an EM wave responds in one of these ways, its direction changes. When the direction of the wave changes, the direction in which the energy is transferred also changes.

Transferring Energy

REMINDER

Potential energy comes from position or form; kinetic energy comes from motion.

A mechanical wave transfers energy in two ways. As it travels, the wave moves potential energy from one place to another. It also converts potential energy into kinetic energy by moving the medium back and forth.

In a vacuum, EM waves transfer energy only by moving potential energy from one place to another. But when EM waves encounter matter, their energy can be converted into many different forms.

CHECK YOUR READING In what form do EM waves transfer energy in a vacuum?

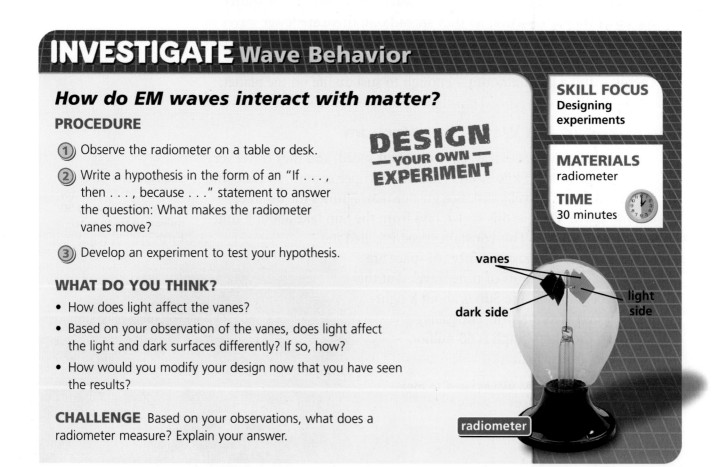

INVESTIGATE Wave Behavior

How do EM waves interact with matter?

PROCEDURE

DESIGN
— YOUR OWN —
EXPERIMENT

1. Observe the radiometer on a table or desk.

2. Write a hypothesis in the form of an "If . . . , then . . . , because . . ." statement to answer the question: What makes the radiometer vanes move?

3. Develop an experiment to test your hypothesis.

WHAT DO YOU THINK?

• How does light affect the vanes?

• Based on your observation of the vanes, does light affect the light and dark surfaces differently? If so, how?

• How would you modify your design now that you have seen the results?

CHALLENGE Based on your observations, what does a radiometer measure? Explain your answer.

SKILL FOCUS
Designing experiments

MATERIALS
radiometer

TIME
30 minutes

vanes

light side

dark side

radiometer

Converting Energy from One Form to Another

How EM waves interact with a medium depends on the type of the wave and the nature of the material. For example, a microwave oven uses a type of EM wave called microwaves. Microwaves pass through air with very little interaction. However, they reflect off the oven's fan and sides. But when microwaves encounter water, such as that inside a potato, their energy is converted into thermal energy. As a result, the potato gets cooked, but the oven remains cool.

reflecting fan

microwave source

1 A device on the oven produces microwaves and sends them toward the reflecting fan.

2 Microwaves are reflected in many directions by the blades of the fan and then again by the sides of the oven.

microwaves

3 Microwaves move through the air without transferring energy to the air.

4 Microwaves transfer energy to the water molecules inside the potato in the form of heat, cooking the potato.

EM waves usually become noticeable and useful when they transfer energy to a medium. You do not observe the microwaves in a microwave oven. All you observe is the potato cooking. In the rest of this chapter, you will learn about different types of EM waves, including microwaves, and about how people use them.

CHECK YOUR READING How does microwave cooking depend on reflection?

3.1 Review

KEY CONCEPTS

1. How are EM waves different from mechanical waves?

2. What are two sources of EM waves in Earth's environment?

3. How can EM waves transfer energy differently in a material medium as compared to a vacuum?

CRITICAL THINKING

4. **Predict** What would happen to an EM wave that never came into contact with matter?

5. **Infer** What might be one cause of uneven heating in a microwave oven?

⬤ CHALLENGE

6. **Synthesize** EM waves can interact with a medium. How might this fact be used to make a device for detecting a particular type of EM radiation?

MATH in SCIENCE

MATH TUTORIAL
CLASSZONE.COM

Click on Math Tutorial for more help with positive and negative exponents.

The top photograph shows an image of the Crab Nebula made using three frequencies of visible light. The bottom photograph shows the same nebula as it appears at higher—x-ray—frequencies.

SKILL: USING EXPONENTS

EM Frequencies

The Chandra X-Ray Observatory in the photograph is a space telescope that detects high-frequency EM waves called x-rays. An x-ray might have a frequency of 10 billion billion cycles per second, or hertz. In standard form—using zeros—10 billion billion Hz looks like this:

10,000,000,000,000,000,000 Hz

Because this number is hard to read, scientists use an exponent to write it. Ten billion billion is written using an exponent as **10^{19}**.

Exponents can also represent very small numbers. For example, an x-ray with a frequency of 10^{19} Hz is about one hundredth of one billionth of a meter long. That wavelength can be written in standard form as **0.00000000001 m.** Using exponents, the wavelength can be written more simply as **10^{-11} m.**

Examples

Large Numbers

To write a multiple of 10 in exponential form, count the number of zeros. Then use the total as the exponent.

(1) 10,000 has 4 zeros.

(2) 4 is the exponent.

ANSWER 10^4 is the way to write 10,000 using exponents.

Decimals

To convert a decimal into exponential form, count the number of places to the right of the decimal point, including the first nonzero place. Then, use the total with a negative sign as the exponent.

(1) 0.000001 has 6 places to the right of the decimal point.

(2) Add a negative sign to make the exponent –6.

ANSWER 10^{-6} is the way to write 0.000001 using exponents.

Answer the following questions.

Write each wavelength or frequency using an exponent.

1. 10,000,000 Hz (radio)
2. 0.00001 m (IR)
3. 100,000 m (radio)
4. 0.0001 m (IR)
5. 10,000,000,000 Hz (microwave)

Write the number in standard form.

6. 10^8 Hz (radio)
7. 10^{-8} m (UV)
8. 10^{17} Hz (UV)
9. 10^{-15} m (gamma)

CHALLENGE Using exponents, multiply 10^2 m by 10^3 Hz. Explain how you got your result.

KEY CONCEPT

3.2 Electromagnetic waves have many uses.

 BEFORE, you learned

- EM waves transfer energy through fields
- EM waves have measurable properties
- EM waves interact with matter

 NOW, you will learn

- How EM waves differ from one another
- How different types of EM waves are used

VOCABULARY

electromagnetic spectrum p. 80
radio waves p. 82
microwaves p. 83
visible light p. 84
infrared light p. 84
ultraviolet light p. 85
x-rays p. 86
gamma rays p. 86

EXPLORE Radio Waves

How can you make radio waves?

PROCEDURE

① Tape one end of one length of wire to one end of the battery. Tape one end of the second wire to the other end of the battery.

② Wrap the loose end of one of the wires tightly around the handle of the fork.

③ Turn on the radio to the AM band and move the selector past all stations until you reach static.

④ Hold the fork close to the radio. Gently pull the free end of wire across the fork's prongs.

WHAT DO YOU THINK?

- What happens when you stroke the prongs with the wire?
- How does changing the position of the dial affect the results?

MATERIALS

- two 25 cm lengths of copper wire
- C or D battery
- electrical tape
- metal fork
- portable radio

EM waves have different frequencies.

It might seem hard to believe that the same form of energy browns your toast, brings you broadcast television, and makes the page you are now reading visible. Yet EM waves make each of these events possible. The various types of EM waves differ from each other in their wavelengths and frequencies.

The frequency of an EM wave also determines its characteristics and uses. Higher-frequency EM waves, with more electromagnetic vibrations per second, have more energy. Lower-frequency EM waves, with longer wavelengths, have less energy.

REMINDER

Remember that frequency is the number of waves that pass a given point per second. The shorter the wavelength, the higher the frequency.

The Electromagnetic Spectrum

RESOURCE CENTER
CLASSZONE.COM

Learn more about
the electromagnetic
spectrum.

The range of all EM frequencies is known as the **electromagnetic spectrum** (SPEHK-truhm), or EM spectrum. The spectrum can be represented by a diagram like the one below. On the left are the waves with the longest wavelengths and the lowest frequencies and energies. Toward the right, the wavelengths become shorter, and the frequencies and energies become higher. The diagram also shows different parts of the spectrum: radio waves, microwaves, infrared light, visible light, ultraviolet light, x-rays, and gamma rays.

The EM spectrum is a smooth, gradual progression from the lowest frequencies to the highest. Divisions between the different parts of the spectrum are useful, but not exact. As you can see from the diagram below, some of the sections overlap.

The Electromagnetic Spectrum

Frequency in Hertz (1 hertz = 1 wavelength/second)

10^4 10^5 10^6 10^7 10^8 10^9 10^{10} 10^{11} 10^{12} 10^{13}

Radio Waves   Infrared Light

Microwaves

This woman is speaking on the radio. **Radio waves** are used for radio and television broadcasts. They are also used for cordless phones, garage door openers, alarm systems, and baby monitors.

Not all astronomy involves visible light. Telescopes like the one above pick up **microwaves** from space. Microwaves are also used for radar, cell phones, ovens, and satellite communications.

The amount of **infrared light** an object gives off depends on its temperature. Above, different colors indicate different amounts of infrared light.

Measuring EM Waves

Because all EM waves move at the same speed in a vacuum, the frequency of an EM wave can be determined from its wavelength. EM wavelengths run from about 30 kilometers for the lowest-frequency radio waves to trillionths of a centimeter for gamma rays. EM waves travel so quickly that even those with the largest wavelengths have very high frequencies. For example, a low-energy radio wave with a wavelength of 30 kilometers has a frequency of 10,000 cycles per second.

EM wave frequency is measured in hertz (Hz). One hertz equals one cycle per second. The frequency of the 30-kilometer radio wave mentioned above would be 10,000 Hz. Gamma ray frequencies reach trillions of trillions of hertz.

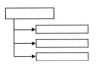

SUPPORTING MAIN IDEAS
Write details that support the main idea that EM waves form a spectrum based on frequency.

CHECK YOUR READING Why is wavelength all you need to know to calculate EM wave frequency in a vacuum?

10^{14} 10^{15} 10^{16} 10^{17} 10^{18} 10^{19} 10^{20} 10^{21} 10^{22} 10^{23} 10^{24}

Ultraviolet Light

Gamma Rays

Visible Light

X-Rays

Gamma rays can be used to treat illnesses and to create images like this one of a person's thyroid gland.

Visible light is the part of the EM spectrum that can be seen with the human eye. This bird's colors come from different wavelengths.

X-rays are useful for showing hard tissues inside the body, such as bones. To make images like the one above, x-ray images have to be displayed using visible light.

The researcher in this photograph is using **ultraviolet light** in the process of DNA analysis. A chemical in the samples gives off visible pink light when ultraviolet rays are present.

Radio waves and microwaves have long wavelengths and low frequencies.

Radio waves are EM waves that have the longest wavelengths, the lowest frequencies, and the lowest energies. Radio waves travel easily through the atmosphere and many materials. People have developed numerous technologies to take advantage of the properties of radio waves.

Radio Waves

Radio was the first technology to use EM waves for telecommunication, which is communication over long distances. A radio transmitter converts sound waves into radio waves and broadcasts them in different directions. Radio receivers in many locations pick up the radio waves and convert them back into sound waves.

1. Sound waves enter the microphone, which produces electrical impulses.

2. The electrical impulses are used by the transmitter to produce radio waves.

3. The radio waves reach a radio receiver which produces sound waves.

AM Signal

Information is encoded in the signal by varying the radio wave's amplitude.

FM Signal

Information is encoded in the signal by varying the radio wave's frequency.

Different radio stations broadcast radio waves at different frequencies. To pick up a particular station, you have to tune your radio to the frequency for that station. The numbers you see on the radio—such as 670 or 99.5—are frequencies.

Simply transmitting EM waves at a certain frequency is not enough to send music, words, or other meaningful sounds. To do that, the radio transmitter must attach information about the sounds to the radio signal. The transmitter attaches the information by modulating—that is, changing—the waves slightly. Two common ways of modulating radio waves are varying the amplitude of the waves and varying the frequency of the waves. Amplitude modulation is used for AM radio, and frequency modulation is used for FM radio.

You might be surprised to learn that broadcast television also uses radio waves. The picture part of a TV signal is transmitted using an AM signal. The sound part is transmitted using an FM signal.

CHECK YOUR READING What two properties of EM waves are used to attach information to radio signals?

Microwaves

A type of EM waves called microwaves comes next on the EM spectrum. **Microwaves** are EM waves with shorter wavelengths, higher frequencies, and higher energy than other radio waves. Microwaves get their name from the fact that their wavelengths are generally shorter than those of radio waves. Two important technologies that use microwaves are radar and cell phones.

Radar The term *radar* stands for "radio detection and ranging." Radar came into wide use during World War II (1939–1945) as a way of detecting aircraft and ships from a distance and estimating their locations. Radar works by transmitting microwaves, receiving reflections of the waves from objects the waves strike, and converting these patterns into visual images on a screen. Today, radar technology is used to control air traffic at airports, analyze weather conditions, and measure the speed of a moving vehicle.

Radar led to the invention of the microwave oven. The discovery that microwaves could be used to cook food was made by accident when microwaves melted a candy bar inside a researcher's pocket.

Cell Phones A cell phone is actually a radio transmitter and receiver that uses microwaves. Cell phones depend on an overlapping network of cells, or areas of land several kilometers in diameter. Each cell has at its center a tower that sends and receives microwave signals. The tower connects cell phones inside the cell to each other or to the regular wire-based telephone system. These two connecting paths are shown below.

READING **TiP**

As you read about the different categories of EM waves, refer to the diagram on pages 80 and 81.

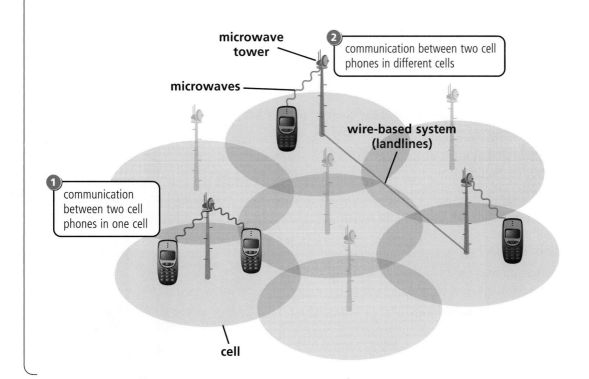

microwave tower

② communication between two cell phones in different cells

microwaves

wire-based system (landlines)

① communication between two cell phones in one cell

cell

Infrared, visible, and ultraviolet light have mid-range wavelengths and frequencies.

READING TIP

Infrared means "below red." *Ultraviolet* means "beyond violet."

Visible light is the part of the EM spectrum that human eyes can see. It lies between 10^{14} Hz and 10^{15} Hz. We perceive the longest wavelengths of visible light as red and the shortest as violet. This narrow band is very small compared with the rest of the spectrum. In fact, visible light is only about 1/100,000 of the complete EM spectrum. The area below visible light and above microwaves is the infrared part of the EM spectrum. Above visible light is the ultraviolet part of the spectrum. You will read more about visible light in the next section.

Infrared Light

The **infrared light** part of the spectrum consists of EM frequencies between microwaves and visible light. Infrared radiation is the type of EM wave most often associated with heat. Waves in this range are sometimes called heat rays. Although you cannot see infrared radiation, you can feel it as warmth coming from the Sun, a fire, or a radiator. Infrared lamps are used to provide warmth in bathrooms and to keep food warm after it is cooked. Infrared rays also help to cook food—for example, in a toaster or over charcoal.

INVESTIGATE The Electromagnetic Spectrum

How can you detect invisible light?

PROCEDURE

1. Find a place that has both bright sunlight and shade, such as a windowsill. Place the white paper in the shade.

2. Using the marker, color the bulbs of the thermometers black. Place one thermometer on the paper. After three minutes, record the temperature.

3. Position the prism so that it shines a bright color spectrum on the white paper. Place the thermometers so that one bulb is in the blue area, one in the red, and one just outside the red, as shown.

4. After five minutes, record the three temperatures.

WHAT DO YOU THINK?

- How did the temperature in the shade compare to the temperature in the light and just outside of it?

- How might you explain the difference?

CHALLENGE How could you modify the experiment to find the hottest location in the infrared range?

SKILL FOCUS
Drawing conclusions

MATERIALS
- white paper
- black marker
- 3 thermometers
- prism

TIME
30 minutes

Some animals, such as pit viper snakes, can actually see infrared light. Normally, human beings cannot see infrared light. However, infrared scopes and cameras convert infrared radiation into visible wavelengths. They do this by representing different levels of infrared radiation with different colors of visible light. This technology can create useful images of objects based on the objects' temperatures.

 How do human beings perceive infrared radiation?

In this infrared image, warmer areas appear red and orange, while cooler ones appear blue, green, and purple.

Ultraviolet Light

The **ultraviolet light** part of the EM spectrum consists of frequencies above those of visible light and partially below those of x-rays. Because ultraviolet (UV) light has higher frequencies than visible light, it also carries more energy. The waves in this range can damage your skin and eyes. Sunblock and UV-protection sunglasses are designed to filter out these frequencies.

Ultraviolet light has beneficial effects as well. Because it can damage cells, UV light can be used to sterilize medical instruments and food by killing harmful bacteria. In addition, UV light causes skin cells to produce vitamin D, which is essential to good health. Ultraviolet light can also be used to treat skin problems and other medical conditions.

Like infrared light, ultraviolet light is visible to some animals. Bees and other insects can see higher frequencies than people can. They see nectar guides—marks that show where nectar is located—that people cannot see with visible light. The photographs below show how one flower might look to a person and to a bee.

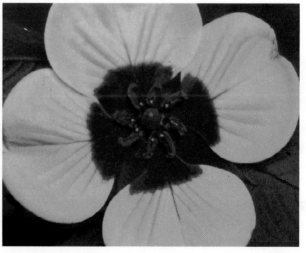

This photograph shows the flower as it appears in visible light.

This photograph shows how different areas appear bright in ultraviolet light.

X-rays and gamma rays have short wavelengths and high frequencies.

At the opposite end of the EM spectrum from radio waves are x-rays and gamma rays. Both have very high frequencies and energies. **X-rays** have frequencies from about 10^{16} Hz to 10^{21} Hz. **Gamma rays** have frequencies from about 10^{19} Hz to more than 10^{24} Hz. Like other EM waves, x-rays and gamma rays are produced by the Sun and by other stars. People have also developed technologies that use these EM frequencies.

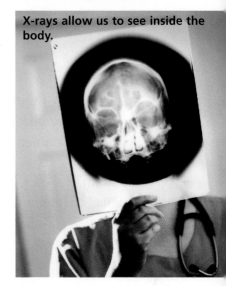
X-rays allow us to see inside the body.

X-rays pass easily through the soft tissues of the body, but many are absorbed by denser matter such as bone. If photographic film is placed behind the body and x-rays are aimed at the film, only the x-rays that pass through the body will expose the film. This makes x-ray images useful for diagnosing bone fractures and finding dense tumors. But too much exposure to x-rays can damage tissue. Even in small doses, repeated exposure to x-rays can cause cancer over time. When you have your teeth x-rayed, you usually wear a vest made out of lead for protection. Lead blocks high-frequency radiation.

Gamma rays have the highest frequencies and energies of any EM waves. Gamma rays are produced by some radioactive substances as well as by the Sun and other stars. Gamma rays can penetrate the soft and the hard tissues of the body, killing normal cells and causing cancer cells to develop. If carefully controlled, this destructive power can be beneficial. Doctors can also use gamma rays to kill cancer cells and fight tumors.

3.2 Review

KEY CONCEPTS

1. What two properties of EM waves change from one end of the EM spectrum to the other?

2. Describe two uses for microwave radiation.

3. How are EM waves used in dentistry and medicine?

CRITICAL THINKING

4. **Infer** Why do you think remote controls for TVs, VCRs, and stereos use infrared light rather than ultraviolet light?

5. **Apply** For a camera to make images of where heat is escaping from a building in winter, what type of EM wave would it need to record?

◐ CHALLENGE

6. **Synthesize** When a person in a car is talking on a cell phone, and the car moves from one cell to another, the conversation continues without interruption. How might this be possible?

Talking on a cell phone while driving may increase the risk of accidents.

Are Cell Phones Harmful?

In 1993, a man appearing on a popular television talk show claimed that cell phone radiation had caused his wife's brain cancer. Since that time, concerned scientists have conducted more than a dozen studies. None of them have shown clear evidence of a connection between cell phones and cancer. However, researchers have made a number of experimental observations.

▶ Experimental Observations

Here are some results from scientists' investigations.

1. Substances that cause cancer work by breaking chemical bonds in DNA.
2. Only EM radiation at ultraviolet frequencies and above can break chemical bonds.
3. Microwave radiation may make it easier for molecules called free radicals to damage DNA bonds.
4. Other factors such as psychological stress may cause breaks in DNA bonds.
5. Performing multiple tasks like driving and talking on the phone reduces the brain's ability to perform either task.
6. Exposing the brain to microwave radiation may slow reaction times.

▶ Hypotheses

Here are some hypotheses that could be used for further research.

A. Microwaves from cell phones can break DNA bonds.
B. Cell phones may contribute to cancer.
C. Holding and talking into a cell phone while driving increases a person's risk of having an accident.
D. Worrying about cell phones may be a health risk.

▶ Determining Relevance

On Your Own On a piece of paper, write down each hypothesis. Next to the hypothesis write each observation that you think is relevant. Include your reasons.

As a Group Discuss how each observation on your list is or is not relevant to a particular hypothesis.

CHALLENGE Based on the observations listed above, write a question that you think would be a good basis for a further experiment. Then explain how the answer to this question would be helpful.

The Sun is the source of most visible light.

 BEFORE, you learned

- Visible light is part of the EM spectrum
- EM waves are produced both in nature and by technology

▶ **NOW, you will learn**

- How visible light is produced by materials at high temperatures
- How some living organisms produce light
- How humans produce light artificially

VOCABULARY

incandescence p. 89
luminescence p. 89
bioluminescence p. 89
fluorescence p. 91

THINK ABOUT

Why is light important?

This railroad worm has eleven pairs of green lights on its sides and a red light on its head. The animal probably uses these lights for illumination and to frighten away predators. Almost every living organism, including humans, depends on visible light. Think of as many different ways as you can that plants, animals, and people use light. Then, think of all the sources of visible light that you know of, both natural and artificial. Why is light important to living organisms?

Light comes from the Sun and other natural sources.

RESOURCE CENTER
CLASSZONE.COM

Learn more about visible light.

It is hard to imagine life without light. Human beings depend on vision in countless ways, and they depend on light for vision. Light is the only form of EM radiation for which human bodies have specialized sensory organs. The human eye is extremely sensitive to light and color and the many kinds of information they convey.

Most animals depend on visible light to find food and to do other things necessary for their survival. Green plants need light to make their own food. Plants, in turn, supply food directly or indirectly for nearly all other living creatures. With very few exceptions, living creatures depend on light for their existence.

CHECK YOUR READING How is plants' use of light important to animals?

Most of the visible light waves in the environment come from the Sun. The Sun's high temperature produces light of every wavelength. The production of light by materials at high temperatures is called **incandescence** (IHN-kuhn-DEHS-uhns). When a material gets hot enough, it gives off light by glowing or by bursting into flames.

Other than the Sun, few natural sources of incandescent light strongly affect life on Earth. Most other stars give off as much light as the Sun, or even more, but little light from stars reaches Earth because they are so far away. Lightning produces bright, short-lived bursts of light. Fire, which can occur naturally, is a lower-level, longer-lasting source of visible light. The ability to make and use fire was one of the first light technologies, making it possible for human beings to see on a dark night or inside a cave.

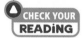 **CHECK YOUR READING** Why does little light reach Earth from stars other than the Sun?

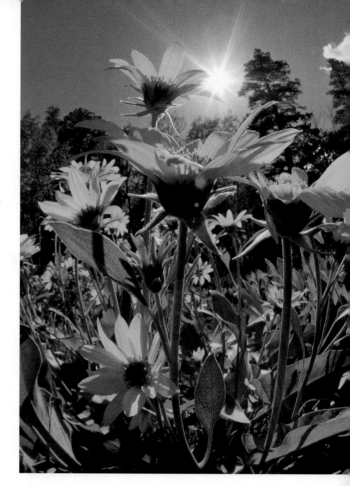

Some living things produce visible light.

Many organisms produce their own visible light, which they use in a variety of ways. They produce this light through luminescence. **Luminescence** is the production of light without the high temperatures needed for incandescence. The production of light by living organisms is called **bioluminescence.** Bioluminescent organisms produce light from chemical reactions rather than from intense heat. Bioluminescence enables organisms to produce light inside their tissues without being harmed.

Bioluminescent organisms include insects, worms, fish, squid, jellyfish, bacteria, and fungi. Some of these creatures have light-producing organs that are highly complex. These organs might include light-producing cells but also reflectors, lenses, and even color filters.

The firefly, a type of beetle, uses bioluminescence to attract mates. A chemical reaction in its abdomen allows the firefly to glow at specific intervals. The pattern of glowing helps fireflies of the same species identify each other at night. Most often, the male flashes a signal while flying, and the female responds with a flash. After they have identified each other, the fireflies may continue to exchange flashes until the male has located the female.

VOCABULARY
Don't forget to make word frames for the terms *luminescence* and *bioluminescence.*

The process of bioluminescence is very efficient. Almost all of the energy released by the chemical reactions of bioluminescence is converted into light. Very little heat is produced. Researchers in lighting technology wanted for years to imitate this efficiency, and that became possible with the development of light-emitting diodes (LEDs). LEDs produce little heat, converting almost all of the incoming electrical energy into light.

CHECK YOUR READING How is bioluminescence different from incandescence?

A female firefly responds to a male's signal.

Human technologies produce visible light.

Human beings invented the first artificial lighting when they learned to make and control fire. For most of human history, people have made light with devices that use fire in some form, such as oil lamps, candles, and natural gas lamps. After the discovery of electricity, people began to make light through a means other than fire. However, the technique of using a very hot material as a light source stayed the same until the invention of fluorescent lighting. In recent years, "cool" lighting has become much more common.

INVESTIGATE Artificial Lighting

Is all artificial light the same?

Many types of artificial light sources are available. These sources differ in the amount of light they produce, the way the light beams are directed, and the characteristics of the light itself.

DESIGN — YOUR OWN — EXPERIMENT

PROCEDURE

1. Design a procedure to discover and record differences among several different types of artificial lighting. Your procedure should test how different colored materials appear in different types of lighting. You should compare the results with how these materials appear in direct sunlight.

2. Write up your experiment and carry it out.

WHAT DO YOU THINK?
- What differences did you discover among bulbs of different types and sizes?
- How would you improve your design if you were to repeat your experiment?

SKILL FOCUS
Designing experiments

MATERIALS
Artificial lighting with a variety of bulb types and sizes

TIME
30 minutes

Incandescent and Fluorescent Lighting

The development of the electric light bulb in the late 1800s made light available at a touch. An ordinary light bulb is a sealed glass tube with a thin tungsten wire running through it. This wire is called a filament. When electrical current passes through the filament, the tungsten gets hotter and begins to glow. Because these light bulbs use high temperatures to produce light, they are called incandescent bulbs.

Tungsten can become very hot—about 3500 degrees Celsius (6300°F)—without melting. At such high temperatures, tungsten gives off a bright light. However, the tungsten filament also produces much infrared radiation. In fact, the filament produces more infrared light than visible light. As a result, incandescent bulbs waste a lot of energy that ends up as heat. At such high temperatures, tungsten also slowly evaporates and collects on the inside of the bulb. Eventually, the filament weakens and breaks, and the bulb burns out.

SUPPORTING MAIN IDEAS
List the characteristics of incandescent lighting and the different types that are available.

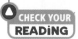 **CHECK YOUR READING** What causes ordinary light bulbs to burn out?

Since the 1980s, halogen (HAL-uh-juhn) bulbs have come into wide use. Halogen bulbs have several advantages over ordinary incandescent bulbs. They contain a gas from the halogen group. This gas combines with evaporating tungsten atoms and deposits the tungsten back onto the filament. As a result, the filament lasts longer. The filament can also be raised to a higher temperature without damage, so it produces more light. Halogen bulbs, which are made of quartz, resist heat better than glass.

Incandescent Light Bulb

tungsten filament

glass bulb

Halogen Light Bulb

tungsten filament

halogen gas mixture

quartz bulb

Fluorescent Light Bulb

mercury vapor and other gases

phosphor coating

electric current

electrode

Many electric lights in use today are fluorescent. **Fluorescence** (flu-REHS-uhns) occurs when a material absorbs EM radiation of one wavelength and gives off EM radiation of another. Fluorescent bulbs are filled with a mixture of mercury vapor and other gases that give off ultraviolet light when an electric current passes through them.

The insides of the bulbs are coated with a powder called phosphor that fluoresces. Phosphor absorbs ultraviolet light and gives off visible light. Because fluorescent lighting is cool and does not waste much energy as heat, it is more efficient and more economical than incandescent lighting.

CHECK YOUR READING Why are fluorescent lights more efficient than incandescent lights?

Other Types of Artificial Lighting

LEDs are being used more and more in place of incandescent bulbs.

Like fluorescent lights, many other artificial light sources use a gas in place of a filament. For example, neon lights use gas-filled tubes to produce light. However, instead of ultraviolet light, the gas gives off visible light directly. The colors of neon lights come from the particular mixtures of gases and filters used. Vapor lights, which are commonly used for street lights, work in a similar way. In a vapor light, a material such as sodium is heated until it becomes a gas, or vapor. The vapor responds to an electric current by glowing brightly.

One of fastest-growing types of artificial lighting is the light emitting diode, or LED. LEDs do not involve bulbs, filaments, or gases. Instead, they produce light electronically. A diode is a type of semiconductor—a device that regulates electric current. An LED is a semiconductor that converts electric energy directly into visible light.

LEDs have many advantages over traditional forms of lighting. They produce a very bright light, do not break easily, use little energy, produce little heat, and can last for decades. Some technologists believe that LEDs will eventually replace most traditional forms of artificial lighting.

3.3 Review

KEY CONCEPTS

1. Describe natural, nonliving sources of incandescent light.
2. What advantages does bioluminescence have over incandescence as a way for living organisms to produce light?
3. What are some advantages and disadvantages of artificial incandescent lighting?

CRITICAL THINKING

4. **Classify** Make a chart summarizing the different types of artificial lighting discussed in this section.
5. **Infer** Why do you think moonlight does not warm you, even though the Moon reflects light from the hot Sun?

CHALLENGE

6. **Compare and Contrast** What does LED lighting have in common with bioluminescence? How are the two different?

Light waves interact with materials.

◀ BEFORE, you learned	▶ NOW, you will learn
• Mechanical waves respond to a change in medium • Visible light is made up of EM waves • EM waves interact with a new medium in the same ways that mechanical waves do	• How the wave behavior of light affects what we see • How light waves interact with materials • Why objects have color • How different colors are produced

VOCABULARY

transmission p. 93
absorption p. 93
scattering p. 95
polarization p. 96
prism p. 97
primary colors p. 98
primary pigments p. 99

EXPLORE Light and Matter

How can a change in medium affect light?

PROCEDURE

① Fill the container with water.

② Add 10 mL (2 tsp) of milk to the water. Put on the lid, and gently shake the container until the milk and water are mixed.

③ In a dark room, shine the light at one side of the container from about 5 cm (2 in.) away. Observe what happens to the beam of light.

WHAT DO YOU THINK?
• What happened to the beam of light from the flashlight?
• Why did the light behave in this way?

MATERIALS
• clear plastic container with lid
• water
• measuring spoons
• milk
• flashlight

Light can be reflected, transmitted, or absorbed.

You have read that EM waves can interact with a material medium in the same ways that mechanical waves do. Three forms of interaction play an especially important role in how people see light. One form is reflection. Most things are visible because they reflect light. The two other forms of interaction are transmission and absorption.

Transmission (trans-MIHSH-uhn) is the passage of an EM wave through a medium. If the light reflected from objects did not pass through the air, windows, or most of the eye, we could not see the objects. **Absorption** (uhb-SAWRP-shun) is the disappearance of an EM wave into the medium. Absorption affects how things look, because it limits the light available to be reflected or transmitted.

VOCABULARY
Don't forget to make word frames for *transmission* and *absorption*.

How Materials Transmit Light

Materials can be classified according to the amount and type of light they transmit.

1 Transparent (trans-PAIR-uhnt) materials allow most of the light that strikes them to pass straight through. It is possible to see objects through a transparent material. Air, water, and clear glass are transparent. Transparent materials are used for items such as windows, light bulbs, thermometers, sandwich bags, and clock faces.

2 Translucent (trans-LOO-suhnt) materials transmit some light, but they also cause it to spread out in all directions. You can see light through translucent materials, but you cannot see objects clearly through them. Some examples are lampshades, frosted light bulbs, frosted windows, sheer fabrics, and notepaper.

3 Opaque (oh-PAYK) materials do not allow any light to pass through them, because they reflect light, absorb light, or both. Heavy fabrics, construction paper, and ceramic mugs are opaque. Shiny materials may be opaque mainly because they reflect light. Other materials, such as wood and rock, are opaque mainly because they absorb light.

CHECK YOUR READING What is the difference between translucent and opaque materials?

This stained-glass window contains transparent, translucent, and opaque materials.

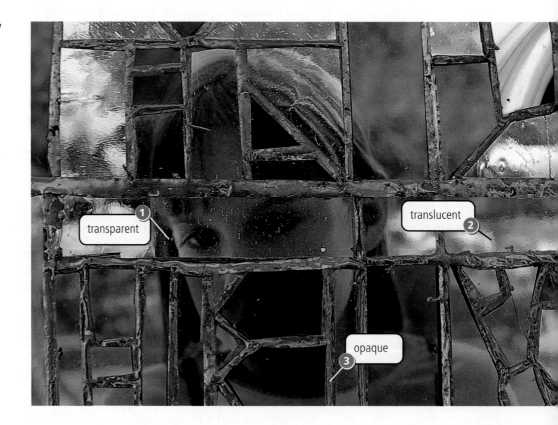

A light filter is a material that is transparent to some kinds of light and opaque to others. For example, clear red glass transmits red light but absorbs other wavelengths. Examples of light filters are the colored covers on taillights and traffic lights, infrared lamp bulbs, and UV-protected sunglasses. Filters that transmit only certain colors are called color filters.

Scattering

Sometimes fine particles in a material interact with light passing through the material to cause scattering. **Scattering** is the spreading out of light rays in all directions, because particles reflect and absorb the light. Fog or dust in the air, mud in water, and scratches or smudges on glass can all cause scattering. Scattering creates glare and makes it hard to see through even a transparent material. Making the light brighter causes more scattering, as you might have noticed if you have ever tried to use a flashlight to see through fog.

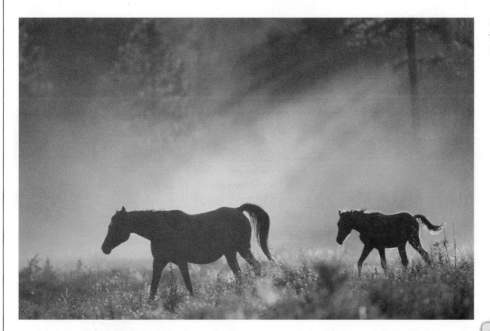

Fine particles, such as those in fog, scatter light and reduce visibility.

Scattering is what makes the sky blue. Molecules in Earth's atmosphere scatter the blue part of visible light more than they scatter the other wavelengths. This process makes the sky light and blue. It is too bright to see the faint stars beyond Earth's atmosphere. At dawn and dusk, light from the Sun must travel farther through the atmosphere before it reaches your eyes. By the time you see it, the greens and blues are scattered away and the light appears reddish. At night, because there is so little sunlight, the sky is dark and you can see the stars.

SUPPORTING MAIN IDEAS
Be sure to add to your chart the different ways light interacts with materials.

⏶ CHECK YOUR READING   How does scattering make the sky blue?

Polarization

Polarizing filters reduce glare and make it easier to see objects. **Polarization** (POH-luhr-ih-ZAY-shuhn) is a quality of light in which all of its waves vibrate in the same direction. Remember that EM waves are made of electric and magnetic fields vibrating at right angles to each other. Polarization describes the electric fields of a light wave. When all of the electric fields of a group of light waves vibrate in the same direction, the light is polarized.

Light can be polarized by a particular type of light filter called a polarizing filter. A polarizing filter acts on a light wave's electric field like the bars of a cage. The filter allows through only waves whose electric fields vibrate in one particular direction. Light that passes through the filter is polarized. In the illustration below, these waves are shown in darker yellow.

Light reflecting off the surface of this pond causes glare.

A polarizing filter reduces glare, making it possible to see objects under the water.

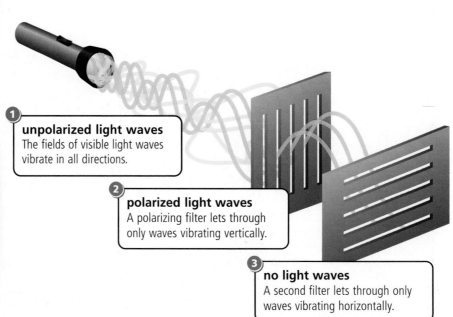

1 unpolarized light waves
The fields of visible light waves vibrate in all directions.

2 polarized light waves
A polarizing filter lets through only waves vibrating vertically.

3 no light waves
A second filter lets through only waves vibrating horizontally.

What do you think happens when polarized light passes into a second polarizing filter? If the direction of the second filter is the same as the first, then all of the light will pass through the second filter. The light will still be polarized. If the second filter is at a right angle to the first, as in the illustration above, then no light at all will pass through the second filter.

Wavelengths determine color.

The section of the EM spectrum called visible light is made up of many different wavelengths. When all of these wavelengths are present together, as in light from the Sun or a light bulb, the light appears white.

Seen individually, different wavelengths appear as different colors of light. This fact can be demonstrated by using a prism. A **prism** is a tool that uses refraction to spread out the different wavelengths that make up white light. The prism bends some of the wavelengths more than others. The lightwaves, bent at slightly different angles, form a color spectrum. The color spectrum could be divided into countless individual wavelengths, each with its own color. However, the color spectrum is usually divided into seven named color bands. In order of decreasing wavelength, the bands are red, orange, yellow, green, blue, indigo, and violet. You see a color spectrum whenever you see a rainbow.

Prisms split light into colors by refracting wavelengths in different amounts.

Color Reflection and Absorption

The color of an object or material is determined by the wavelengths it absorbs and those it reflects. An object has the color of the wavelengths it reflects. A material that reflects all wavelengths of visible light appears white. A material that absorbs all wavelengths of visible light appears black. A green lime absorbs most wavelengths but reflects green, so the lime looks green, as shown below.

SUPPORTING MAIN IDEAS
Describe the roles of reflection and absorption in color.

1. In this simplified diagram, light of all colors strikes the lime.

2. The lime absorbs all wavelengths except green.

3. The lime reflects mostly green, so it appears green.

The color that an object appears to the eye depends on another factor besides the wavelengths the object absorbs and reflects. An object can reflect only wavelengths that are in the light that shines on it. In white light, a white object reflects all the wavelengths of visible light and appears white. If you shine only red light on a white piece of paper, however, the paper will appear red, not white, because only red light is available to be reflected.

In summary, two factors determine the color of an object: first, the wavelengths that the object itself reflects or absorbs, and second, the wavelengths present in the light that shines on the object.

 CHECK YOUR READING What color band or bands does a red apple absorb? a white flower?

Primary Colors of Light

The human eye can detect only three color bands: red, green, and blue. Your brain perceives these three colors and various mixtures of them as all the colors. These three colors of light, which can be mixed to produce all possible colors, are called **primary colors.** When all three colors are mixed together equally, they appear white. Whenever colored light is added to a mixture, specific wavelengths are added. Mixing colors by adding wavelengths is called additive color mixing.

An example of the practical use of primary colors is a color television or computer monitor. The screen is divided into thousands of tiny bundles of red, green, and blue dots, or pixels. A television broadcast or DVD sends signals that tell the monitor which pixels to light up and when to do so. By causing only some pixels to give off light, the monitor can mix the three colors to create an amazing variety of colorful images.

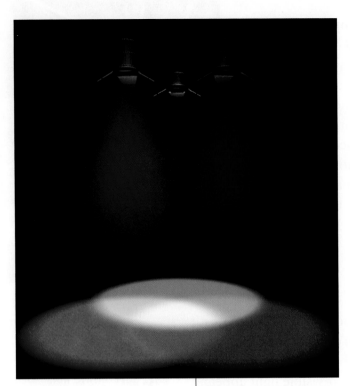

Primary colors of light combine to make the secondary colors yellow, cyan (light blue), and magenta (dark pink).

CHECK YOUR READING What does an equal mix of all three primary colors produce?

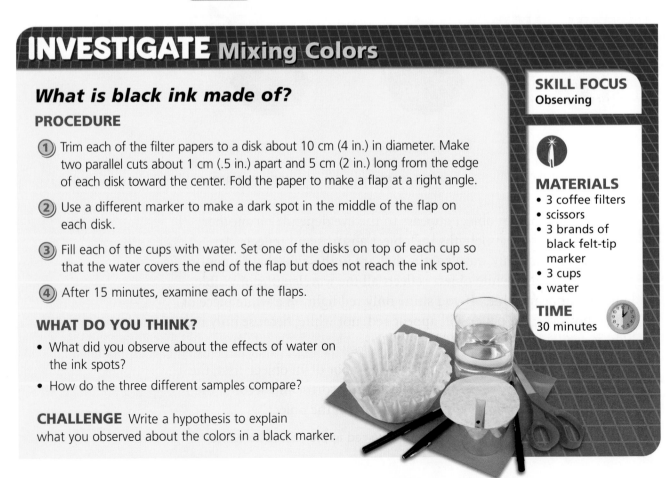

INVESTIGATE Mixing Colors

What is black ink made of?

PROCEDURE

1. Trim each of the filter papers to a disk about 10 cm (4 in.) in diameter. Make two parallel cuts about 1 cm (.5 in.) apart and 5 cm (2 in.) long from the edge of each disk toward the center. Fold the paper to make a flap at a right angle.

2. Use a different marker to make a dark spot in the middle of the flap on each disk.

3. Fill each of the cups with water. Set one of the disks on top of each cup so that the water covers the end of the flap but does not reach the ink spot.

4. After 15 minutes, examine each of the flaps.

WHAT DO YOU THINK?

- What did you observe about the effects of water on the ink spots?
- How do the three different samples compare?

CHALLENGE Write a hypothesis to explain what you observed about the colors in a black marker.

SKILL FOCUS
Observing

MATERIALS
- 3 coffee filters
- scissors
- 3 brands of black felt-tip marker
- 3 cups
- water

TIME
30 minutes

Primary Pigments

Remember that two factors affect an object's color. One is the wavelengths present in the light that shines on the object. The other is the wavelengths that the object's material reflects or absorbs. Materials can be mixed to produce colors just as light can. Materials that are used to produce colors are called pigments. The **primary pigments** are cyan, yellow, and magenta. You can mix primary pigments just as you can mix primary colors to produce all the colors.

The primary pigment colors are the same as the secondary colors of light. The secondary pigment colors are red, blue, and green—the same as the primary colors of light.

The effect of mixing pigments is different from the effect of mixing light. Remember that a colored material absorbs all wavelengths except those of the color it reflects. Yellow paint absorbs all wavelengths except yellow. Because pigments absorb wavelengths, whenever you mix pigments, you are subtracting wavelengths rather than adding them. Mixing colors by subtracting wavelengths is called subtractive color mixing. When all three primary pigments are mixed together in equal amounts, all wavelengths are subtracted. The result is black—the absence of reflected light.

The inks used to make the circles on this page are primary pigments. They combine to make the secondary pigments red, blue, and green.

 CHECK YOUR READING How is mixing pigments different from mixing light?

3.4 Review

KEY CONCEPTS

1. What are some ways in which materials affect how light is transmitted?

2. How does a polarizing filter reduce glare?

3. In order for an object to appear white, which wavelengths must the light contain and the object reflect?

CRITICAL THINKING

4. **Apply** Imagine that you are a firefighter searching a smoke-filled apartment. Would using a stronger light help you see better? Explain your answer.

5. **Predict** Higher-energy EM waves penetrate farthest into a dense medium. What colors are more likely to penetrate to the bottom of a lake?

CHALLENGE

6. **Synthesize** If you focus a red light, a green light, and a blue light on the same part of a black curtain, what color will the curtain appear to be? Why?

CHAPTER INVESTIGATION

Wavelength and Color

OVERVIEW AND PURPOSE Lighting directors use color filters to change the look of a scene. The color an object appears depends on both the wavelengths of light shining on it and the wavelengths of light it reflects. In this exercise, you will investigate the factors that affect these wavelengths and so affect the color of an object. You will

- make a light box
- study the effect of different colors of light on objects of different colors

▶ Problem

How does the appearance of objects of different colors change in different colors of light?

▶ Hypothesize

Read the procedure below and look at the sample notebook page. Predict what color each object will appear in each color of light. Give a reason for each prediction.

▶ Procedure

MATERIALS
- 3 sheets of acetate (red, blue, and green)
- ruler
- scissors
- shoe box
- masking tape
- light source
- 4 solid-colored objects (white, black, red, and yellow)

1 Draw a data table like the one in the sample **Science Notebook.**

2 Make 3 color filters by cutting a 10 cm (4 in.) square from each color of acetate.

3 Make a 3 cm (1 in.) wide hole in the middle of the top of the box. This will be the viewing hole.

4 Make an 8 cm (3 in.) hole in one end of the box. This will be the light hole.

5 You will observe each of the four colored objects four times—with no filter and with the red, blue, and green filters. Use masking tape to position the filters in the light hole, as shown.

step 5

6 Place the light box on a flat surface near a strong white light source, such as sunlight or a bright lamp. Position the box with the uncovered light hole facing the light source. Place the white object inside the box, look through the eyehole, and observe the object's color. Record your observations.

step 7

7 Use the light box to test each of the combinations of object color and filter shown in the table on the sample notebook page. Record your results.

▶ Observe and Analyze
Write It Up

1. **RECORD OBSERVATIONS** Be sure your data table is complete.

2. **COMPARE** What color did the red object appear to be when viewed with a blue filter? a red filter?

▶ Conclude
Write It Up

1. **INTERPRET** Answer your problem question.

2. **ANALYZE** Compare your results to your predictions. How do the results support your hypothesis?

3. **IDENTIFY VARIABLES** What different variables affected the outcome of your experiment?

4. **INFER** Why do colors of objects appear to change in different types of light?

5. **IDENTIFY LIMITS** What possible limitations or sources of error could have affected your results?

6. **APPLY** If you were going to perform on a stage that was illuminated using several different color filters, what color clothing should you wear in order to look as bright and colorful as possible?

▶ INVESTIGATE Further

CHALLENGE Perform this experiment using different kinds of artificial light. Try it with a low-wattage incandescent bulb, a high-wattage incandescent bulb, a fluorescent bulb, or a full-spectrum bulb. How do different kinds of artificial light affect the colors that objects appear to be?

Wavelength and Color

Problem

How does the appearance of objects of different colors change in different colors of light?

Hypothesize

Observe and Analyze

Table 1. Predicted and Observed Colors of Objects with Different Colored Filters

Predicted	no filter	red filter	blue filter	green filter
white object				
black object				
red object				
yellow object				
Observed	no filter	red filter	blue filter	green filter
white object				

the BIG idea

Electromagnetic waves transfer energy through radiation.

CONTENT REVIEW
CLASSZONE.COM

◀ **KEY CONCEPTS SUMMARY**

3.1 Electromagnetic waves have unique traits.

- Electromagnetic (EM) waves are made of vibrating electric and magnetic fields.
- EM waves travel at the speed of light through a vacuum.
- EM waves transfer energy and can interact with matter.

VOCABULARY
electromagnetic wave p. 73
radiation p. 75

3.2 Electromagnetic waves have many uses.

- EM waves are grouped by frequency on the EM spectrum.
- The EM spectrum is divided into radio waves, microwaves, infrared light, visible light, ultraviolet light, x-rays, and gamma rays.

VOCABULARY
EM spectrum p. 80
radio waves p. 82
microwaves p. 83
visible light p. 84
infrared light p. 84
ultraviolet light p. 85
x-rays p. 86
gamma rays p. 86

3.3 The Sun is the source of most visible light.

- Most visible light in the environment comes from the Sun.
- Many living organisms produce visible light for their own use.
- Humans produce visible light artificially.

VOCABULARY
incandescence p. 89
luminescence p. 89
bioluminescence p. 89
fluorescence p. 91

3.4 Light waves interact with materials.

- Reflection, transmission, and absorption affect what light we see.
- Light can be scattered and polarized.
- Visible light is made up of many wavelengths.
- The primary colors are red, blue, and green.
- The primary pigments are yellow, cyan, and magenta.

VOCABULARY
transmission p. 93
absorption p. 93
scattering p. 95
polarization p. 96
prism p. 97
primary colors p. 98
primary pigments p. 99

Reviewing Vocabulary

Make a four-square diagram for each of the listed terms. Write the term in the center. Define the term in one square. Write characteristics, examples, and nonexamples in other squares. A sample is shown below.

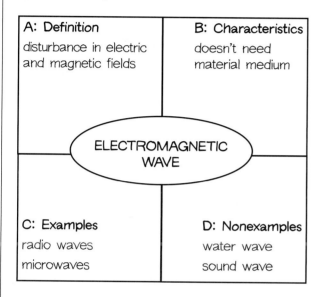

A: Definition	B: Characteristics
disturbance in electric and magnetic fields	doesn't need material medium

ELECTROMAGNETIC WAVE

C: Examples	D: Nonexamples
radio waves microwaves	water wave sound wave

1. gamma rays
2. infrared light
3. transmission
4. absorption
5. pigment

6. radiation
7. bioluminescence
8. EM spectrum
9. incandescence
10. polarization

Reviewing Key Concepts

Multiple Choice *Choose the letter of the best answer.*

11. An electromagnetic wave is a disturbance that transfers energy through a field. In this sense, a disturbance is the same as a
    a. confusion   c. vibration
    b. magnification   d. conflict

12. Unlike mechanical waves, EM waves can travel through
    a. a vacuum   c. the ground
    b. water   d. air

13. A light year is a measure of
    a. time   c. speed
    b. distance   d. wavelength

14. The Sun and a light bulb both produce light through
    a. bioluminescence   c. luminescence
    b. incandescence   d. polarization

15. Which of the following types of light bulb converts ultraviolet waves into visible light waves?
    a. incandescent   c. halogen
    b. fluorescent   d. tungsten

16. An object seen through translucent material appears less clear than one seen through transparent material because the translucent material
    a. transmits none of the light coming from the object
    b. reflects all the light coming from the object
    c. transmits all the light coming from the object
    d. diffuses some light coming from the object

17. An object appears red because it
    a. reflects light waves of all colors
    b. reflects light waves of red
    c. absorbs light waves of red
    d. transmits light waves of all colors

18. Primary colors of light can combine to make
    a. black light   c. primary pigments
    b. white light   d. ultraviolet light

Short Answer *Write a short answer to each question.*

19. What vibrates in an EM wave?

20. How can EM waves be used to measure distance?

21. Describe how microwaves are used in communications.

22. What two properties of an EM wave change as you move from one part of the EM spectrum to another?

23. How does visible light differ from other EM waves? How is it similar?

24. Explain briefly how an incandescent light bulb works.

Thinking Critically

The diagram below shows how far different wavelengths of visible light penetrate into ocean water. Use information from this diagram to answer the next three questions.

25. OBSERVE An EM wave can interact with a material in different ways. Which type of interaction keeps some light waves from reaching the ocean floor?

26. PREDICT How would violet light behave in the same water? Think of where violet is on the color spectrum.

27. SYNTHESIZE How is the apparent color of objects near the ocean floor affected by the interactions shown in the diagram?

28. ANALYZE Under what circumstances can an EM wave begin to convert some of its electromagnetic energy into other forms of energy?

29. ANALYZE What two things must be true about the light source and the material of an object for you to see an object as red?

30. PREDICT If you shine a blue light on a white object, what color will the object appear to be? What color light would you need to add to make the white object appear white?

31. APPLY Why might incandescent lighting become less common in the future? Explain your reasoning.

32. IDENTIFY CAUSE AND EFFECT Liquid crystal displays like the ones used in some calculators work by polarizing light. Describe how two polarizing filters could cause the numbers on the display panel to appear black.

33. COMPARE AND CONTRAST In what way would a sieve be a good model for a polarizing light filter? In what ways would it not be?

34. CONTRAST In what ways is a fluorescent bulb more efficient than incandescent and halogen bulbs?

35. PREDICT What color will a white object appear to be if you look at it through a blue filter?

the BIG idea

36. ANALYZE Return to the question on page 70. Answer the question again, using what you have learned in the chapter.

37. SUMMARIZE Write a summary of this chapter. Use the Big Idea statement from page 70 as the title for your summary. Use the Key Concepts listed on page 70 as the topic sentences for each paragraph. Provide an example for each key concept.

38. ANALYZE Describe all of the EM wave behaviors and interactions that occur when a radiator warms a kitten.

UNIT PROJECTS

Check your schedule for your unit project. How are you doing? Be sure that you've placed data or notes from your research in your project folder.

Standardized Test Practice

For practice on your
state test, go to . . .
TEST PRACTICE
CLASSZONE.COM

Interpreting Diagrams

The diagram below shows part of the electromagnetic (EM) spectrum. The lower band shows frequency in hertz. The upper band shows part of the spectrum used by different technologies.

Use the diagram to answer the following questions.

1. Which of the technologies listed below uses the highest frequencies?

   a. AM radio
   b. CB radio
   c. FM radio
   d. TV channels 2–6

2. If you were receiving a signal at a frequency of nearly 10^9 Hz, what would you be using?

   a. a CB radio
   b. an AM radio
   c. an FM radio
   d. a cell phone

3. All of the technologies in the diagram use radio waves. High-frequency radio waves, starting about halfway between 10^8 Hz and 10^9 Hz, are also called microwaves. Which of these technologies uses microwaves?

   a. cell phone
   b. AM radio
   c. FM radio
   d. television

4. Signals with similar frequencies sometimes interfere with each other. For this reason, you might expect interference in which of the following?

   a. lower television channels from cell phones
   b. upper television channels from FM radio
   c. lower television channels from FM radio
   d. upper television channels from cell phones

Extended Response

Answer the two questions below in detail. Include some of the terms from the word box. Underline each term you use in your answer.

| frequency | energy | interaction |
| field | medium | vacuum |

5. What are the similarities and differences between mechanical waves and electromagnetic waves?

6. What are some advantages and disadvantages of different types of artificial lighting?

TIMELINES in Science

THE STORY OF LIGHT

Light has fascinated people since ancient times. The earliest ideas about light were closely associated with beliefs and observations about vision. Over the centuries, philosophers and scientists developed an increasingly better understanding of light as a physical reality that obeyed the laws of physics.

With increased understanding of the nature and behavior of light has come the ability to use light as a tool. Many applications of light technology have led to improvements in human visual abilities. People can now make images of a wide range of objects that were invisible to earlier generations. The study of light has also led to technologies that do not involve sight at all.

This timeline shows just a few of the many steps on the road to understanding light. The boxes below the timeline show how these discoveries have been applied and developed into new technologies.

400 B.C.
Light Travels in a Straight Line
Observing the behavior of shadows, Chinese philosopher Mo-Ti finds that light travels in a straight line. His discovery helps explain why light passing through a small opening forms an upside-down image.

300 B.C.
Reflection Obeys Law
Greek mathematician Euclid discovers that light striking mirrors obeys the law of reflection. The angle at which light reflects off a mirror is equal to the angle at which it strikes the mirror.

EVENTS

450 B.C.	425 B.C.	400 B.C.	375 B.C.	350 B.C.	325 B.C.	300 B.C.

APPLICATIONS AND TECHNOLOGY

APPLICATION

Camera Obscura
The principle described by Mo-Ti in 400 B.C. led to the development of the camera obscura. When light from an object shines through a small hole into a dark room, an image of the object appears on the far wall. The darkened room is called, in Latin, *camera obscura*. Because light travels in a straight line, the highest points on the object appear at the lowest points on the image; thus, the image appears upside down. Room-sized versions of the camera obscura like the one shown here were a popular attraction in the late 1800s.

1666
White Light Is Made of Colors

British scientist Isaac Newton makes a remarkable discovery. After studying the effects of a prism on white light, Newton realizes that white light is actually made up of different colors. This contradicts the long-held belief that white light is pure light, and that colored light gets its color from the impurities of different materials.

A.D. 1000
Eyes Do Not Shoot Rays

Egyptian mathematician and astronomer Ali Alhazen publishes his *Book of Optics*. A diagram of the eye, from this book, is shown below. Alhazen proves that light travels from objects to the eyes, not the other way around. The previously accepted theory, put forth by Greek philosopher Plato centuries ago, claimed that light travels from the eyes to objects.

1676
Light Speeds Into Distance

Looking through a telescope, Danish astronomer Olaus Roemer observes one of Jupiter's moons "setting" earlier and earlier as Earth approaches the planet—and later and later as Earth moves farther away. Roemer infers that distance affects the time it takes light to travel from Jupiter to Earth. He estimates the speed of light as 230,000 kilometers per second.

| A.D. 1000 | 1025 | | 1625 | 1650 | 1675 |

TECHNOLOGY
Reflecting Telescopes

Early astronomers such as Galileo used refracting telescopes. These telescopes, which used a lens to gather light, were difficult to focus because of the uneven refraction of different wavelengths. Isaac Newton built the first reflecting telescope, which overcame this difficulty by using a mirror to gather light and focus an image. All major astronomical telescopes, including the Hubble Space Telescope, now use mirrors.

1821
Light Waves Move Like Ripples in a Pond
French physicist Augustin-Jean Fresnel confirms the theory that light waves are transverse waves. Like water waves, light waves vibrate at right angles to the direction of their travel. This theory helps to explain many observed behaviors of light, including diffraction fringes like those surrounding this mountain climber.

1801
Light Makes Waves
British scientist Thomas Young finds that beams of light can interact to produce an interference pattern. He aims light through two slits and observes alternating light and dark bands on a screen. Young concludes that light acts as if it were made up of waves, which contradicts the theory put forth by Newton and others that light is made up of particles.

1887
No Medium Needed
U.S. scientists Albert Michelson and Edward Morley disprove the theory that light, like other waves, must have a medium. The men devise an experiment to detect the effect of ether—material that light supposedly uses to move through space—on a light beam. The experiment shows that no ether exists and therefore that light waves need no medium.

| 1750 | 1775 | 1800 | 1825 | 1850 | 1875 | 1900 |

APPLICATION
Holograms
Holograms are used today to create images for art, communications, and research. A hologram is an interference pattern created by a collision between the two halves of a split laser beam. One half shines on film, and the other half shines on the object. The object reflects this second beam onto the film, where it creates an interference pattern with the first beam. This interference pattern captures a three-dimensional image of the object, as in this hologram of a shark.

TECHNOLOGY
Gravitational Lenses
As part of his theory of relativity, Albert Einstein predicted that light would bend in a gravitational field. His theory was confirmed in 1919. During a solar eclipse, scientists witnessed the bending of light from more distant stars as that light passed near the Sun. Astronomers take advantage of this effect to get a better look at objects deep in space. Sometimes light from a distant object passes through a closer object's gravitational field on its way to Earth. By analyzing images of the object, scientists can learn more about it.

1960

Light Beams Line Up

U.S. inventor Theodore Harold Maiman builds a working laser by stimulating emission of light in a cylinder of ruby crystal. Laser light waves all have the same wavelength, and their peaks occur together.

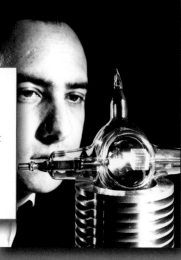

2001

Light Is Completely Stopped

After slowing light to the speed of a bicycle, Danish physicist Lene Vestergaard Hau brings it to a complete halt in a super-cold medium. Controlling the speed of light could revolutionize computers, communications, and other electronic technology.

RESOURCE CENTER
CLASSZONE.COM

Learn more about current research involving light.

1925	1950	1975	2000

APPLICATION

Lasers in Eye Surgery

For centuries, people have used corrective lenses to help their eyes focus images more clearly. Today, with the help of lasers, doctors can correct the eye itself. Using an ultraviolet laser, doctors remove microscopic amounts of a patient's cornea to change the way it refracts light. As a result, the eye focuses images exactly on the retina. For many nearsighted people, the surgery results in 20/20 vision or better.

SPOTLIGHT on
PERCY JULIAN

The chemist Percy Julian (1899–1975) synthesized the drug used to treat glaucoma, a disease in which fluid builds up slowly in the eye. This fluid can damage the optic nerve, leading to partial or total blindness. The drug, physostigmine, lowers pressure inside the eye. It also helps improve memory in Alzheimer's patients and can be used as an antidote to nerve gas.

Julian was interested in medicinal plants and believed in using natural products whenever possible. For example, he synthesized physostigmine from the Calabar bean. He used a soy protein to develop AeroFoam, a substance for putting out gasoline and oil fires. Julian also made an inexpensive substitute for cortisone, used for treating arthritis. He was awarded over 100 patents for his inventions and honored on a stamp issued by the U.S. Postal Service.

ACTIVITIES

Make a Camera Obscura

Take a small box and paint the interior black. On one side, make a pinhole. On a side next to that one, make a hole about 5 cm in diameter.

On a bright, sunny day, hold the box so that sunlight enters the box through the pinhole. Fit your eye snugly against the larger hole and look inside.

Writing About Science

Lasers are currently used in entertainment, medicine, communication, supermarkets, and so on. Write a prediction about a specific use of lasers in the future. You might describe a new invention.

CHAPTER

Light and Optics

the **BIG** idea

Optical tools depend on the wave behavior of light.

How can this device help a person to see better?

Key Concepts

SECTION
(4.1) **Mirrors form images by reflecting light.**
Learn how mirrors use reflection to create images.

SECTION
(4.2) **Lenses form images by refracting light.**
Learn how lenses use refraction to create images.

SECTION
(4.3) **The eye is a natural optical tool.**
Learn about how eyes work as optical tools.

SECTION
(4.4) **Optical technology makes use of light waves.**
Learn about complex optical tools.

Internet Preview

CLASSZONE.COM

Chapter 4 online resources: Content Review, Simulation, Visualization, three Resource Centers, Math Tutorial, Test Practice.

How Does a Spoon Reflect Your Face?

Look at the reflection of your face in the bowl of a shiny metal spoon. How does your face look? Is it different from what you would expect? Now turn the spoon over and look at your face in the round side. How does your face look this time?

Observe and Think Why do the two sides of the spoon affect the appearance of your face in these ways?

Why Do Things Look Different Through Water?

Fill a clear, round jar with straight, smooth sides with water. Look through the jar at different objects in the room. Experiment with different distances between the objects and the jar and between yourself and the jar.

Observe and Think How does the jar change the way things look? What do you think causes these changes?

Internet Activity: Optics

Go to **ClassZone.com** to learn more about optics.

Observe and Think How does research in optics benefit other areas of scientific investigation?

NSTA
scilinks.org
SCILINKS

Lenses Code: MDL030

Getting Ready to Learn

◄ CONCEPT REVIEW

- Light tends to travel in a straight line.
- The speed of light is affected by a material medium.
- Reflection and refraction are two ways light interacts with materials.

◄ VOCABULARY REVIEW

reflection p. 25
refraction p. 25
visible light p. 84

CONTENT REVIEW
CLASSZONE.COM
Review concepts and vocabulary.

▶ TAKING NOTES

COMBINATION NOTES

To take notes about a new concept, first make an informal outline of the information. Then make a sketch of the concept and label it so you can study it later.

CHOOSE YOUR OWN STRATEGY

Take notes about new vocabulary terms, using one or more of the strategies from earlier chapters—**four square, description wheel,** or **frame game.** Feel free to mix and match the strategies, or to use an entirely different vocabulary strategy.

See the Note-Taking Handbook on pages R45–R51.

SCIENCE NOTEBOOK

NOTES
The angle of incidence (x) equals the angle of reflection (y).

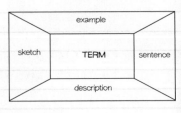

FOUR SQUARE

Definition	Characteristics
TERM	
Examples	Nonexamples

DESCRIPTION WHEEL

feature feature feature feature TERM feature feature

FRAME GAME

example
sketch TERM sentence
description

Mirrors form images by reflecting light.

▶ **BEFORE, you learned**

- EM waves interact with materials
- Light can be reflected

▶ **NOW, you will learn**

- About the science of optics
- How light is reflected
- How mirrors form images

VOCABULARY

optics p. 113
law of reflection p. 114
regular reflection p. 114
diffuse reflection p. 114
image p. 115
convex p. 116
concave p. 116
focal point p. 117

EXPLORE Reflection

How does surface affect reflection?

PROCEDURE

MATERIALS
aluminum foil

1. Tear off a square sheet of aluminum foil. Look at your reflection in the shiny side of the foil.

2. Turn the foil over and look at your reflection in the dull side.

3. Crumple up the piece of foil, then smooth it out again, shiny side up. Again, look at your reflection in the foil.

WHAT DO YOU THINK?

- How did the three reflections differ from one another?
- What might explain these differences?

Optics is the science of light and vision.

COMBINATION NOTES
Don't forget to include sketches of important concepts in your notebook.

Optics (AHP-tihks) is the study of visible light and the ways in which visible light interacts with the eye to produce vision. Optics is also the application of knowledge about visible light to develop tools—such as eyeglasses, mirrors, magnifying lenses, cameras, and lasers—that extend vision or that use light in other ways.

Mirrors, lenses, and other optical inventions are called optical tools. By combining optical tools, inventors have developed powerful instruments to extend human vision. For example, the microscope uses a combination of mirrors and lenses to make very small structures visible. Telescopes combine optical tools to extend vision far into space. As you will see, some of the latest optical technology—lasers—use visible light in ways that do not involve human vision at all.

Mirrors use regular reflection.

You have read that when light waves strike an object, they either pass through it or they bounce off its surface. Objects are made visible by light waves, or rays, bouncing off their surfaces. In section 3 you will see how the light waves create images inside the human eye.

Light rays bounce off objects in a very predictable way. For example, look at the diagram on the left below. Light rays from a flashlight strike a mirror at an angle of 60° as measured from the normal, an imaginary line perpendicular to the surface of the mirror. This angle is called the angle of incidence. The angle at which the rays reflect off the mirror, called the angle of reflection, is also 60° as measured from the normal. The example illustrates the **law of reflection,** which states that the angle of reflection equals the angle of incidence. As you can see in the second diagram, holding the flashlight at a different angle changes both the angle of incidence and the angle of reflection. However, the two angles remain equal.

normal

angle of incidence | angle of reflection

60° | 60°

40° | 40°

The angle of reflection equals the angle of incidence.

The light rays striking the mirror bounce back by regular reflection. Rays striking everything else bounce back by diffuse reflection.

If the surface of an object is very smooth, like a mirror, light rays that come from the same direction will bounce off in the same new direction. The reflection of parallel light rays all in the same direction is called **regular reflection.**

If the surface is not very smooth—even if it feels smooth to the touch, like a piece of paper—light rays striking it from the same direction bounce off in many new directions. Each light ray follows the law of reflection, but rays coming from the same direction bounce off different bumps and hollows of the irregular surface. The reflection of parallel light rays in many different directions is called **diffuse reflection.**

How can you use mirrors to see around a corner?

PROCEDURE

(1) To make a periscope, cut two flaps on opposite sides of the carton, one from the top and one from the bottom, as shown in the illustration.

(2) Fold each flap inward until it is at a 45-degree angle to the side cuts and tape it into place.

(3) Attach a mirror to the outside surface of each of the flaps.

(4) Holding the periscope straight up, look through one of the openings. Observe what you can see through the other opening.

WHAT DO YOU THINK?

• Where are the objects you see when you look through the periscope?

• How does the angle of the mirrors affect the path of light through the periscope?

CHALLENGE How would it affect what you see through the periscope if you changed the angle of the mirrors from 45 degrees to 30 degrees? Try it.

SKILL FOCUS
Analyzing

MATERIALS
• paper milk or juice carton
• scissors
• tape
• 2 mirrors slightly smaller than the bottom of the carton
• protractor

TIME
30 minutes

mirror

tape

flap 1
flap 2
45°
fold
cut
step 1

Shape determines how mirrors form images.

When you look in a mirror, you see an image of yourself. An **image** is a picture of an object formed by waves of light. The image of yourself is formed by light waves reflecting off you, onto the mirror, and back toward your eyes. Mirrors of different shapes can produce images that are distorted in certain ways.

VISUALIZATION
CLASSZONE.COM
See reflection in action.

Flat Mirrors

Your image in a flat mirror looks exactly like you. It appears to be the same size as you, and it's wearing the same clothes. However, if you raise your right hand, the image of yourself in the mirror will appear to raise its left hand. That is because you see the image as a person standing facing you. In fact, your right hand is reflected on the right side of the image, and your left on the left side.

CHECK YOUR READING If you wink your left eye while looking in the mirror, which eye in the image of you will wink?

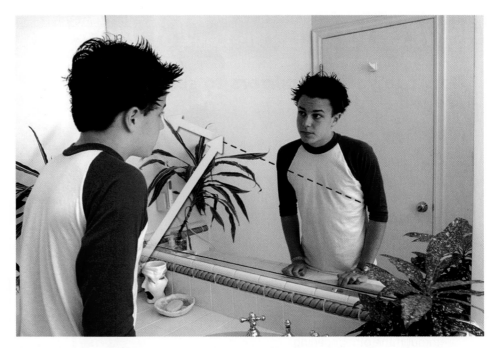

The solid line shows the actual path of light. The broken line shows where the light appears to be coming from.

If you look closely at your image in a mirror, you will notice that it actually appears to be on the far side of the mirror, exactly as far from the mirror as you are. This is a trick of light. The solid yellow arrows in the photograph above show the path of the light rays from the boy's elbow to the mirror and back to his eyes. The light rays reflect off the mirror. The broken line shows the apparent path of the light rays. They appear to his eyes to be coming through the mirror from a spot behind it.

Concave and Convex Mirrors

VOCABULARY
Try making sketches to help you remember the new terms on this page.

Unlike light rays hitting a flat mirror, parallel light rays reflecting off a curved mirror do not move in the same direction. A **convex** mirror is curved outward, like the bottom of a spoon. In a convex mirror, parallel light rays move away from each other, as you can see in the diagram below on the left. A **concave** mirror is curved inward toward the center, like the inside of a spoon. Parallel light rays reflecting off a concave mirror move toward each other, as shown on the right.

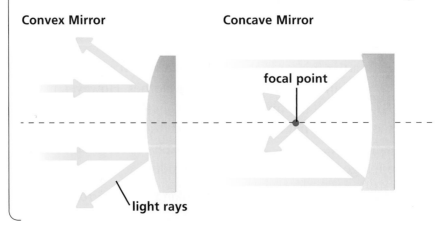

Convex Mirror

Concave Mirror

focal point

light rays

The rays striking a concave mirror cross and then move apart again. The point at which the rays meet is called the **focal point** of the mirror. The distance between the mirror and its focal point depends on the shape of the curve.

The images formed in these mirrors depend on the curve of the mirror's surface and the distance of the object from the mirror. Your image in a curved mirror may appear larger or smaller than you are, and it may even be upside down.

Convex Mirror

Your image in a convex mirror appears smaller than you.

Concave Mirror, Far Away

If you are standing far away, your image in a concave mirror appears upside down and smaller than you.

Concave Mirror, Up Close

If you are standing inside the focal point, your image in a concave mirror appears right-side up and larger.

All rays parallel to a line through the center of the mirror are reflected off the mirror and pass through the mirror's focal point. Rays from the top of the object are reflected downward and those from the bottom are reflected upward.

  How does your distance from the mirror affect the way your image appears in a concave mirror?

4.1 Review

KEY CONCEPTS

1. Explain the term *optics* in your own words.

2. How is diffuse reflection similar to regular reflection? How is it different?

3. Describe the path that light rays take when they form an image of your smile when you look into a flat mirror.

CRITICAL THINKING

4. **Infer** Imagine seeing your reflection in a polished table top. The image is blurry and hard to recognize. What can you tell about the surface of the table from your observations?

5. **Analyze** Why do images formed by concave mirrors sometimes appear upside down?

△ CHALLENGE

6. **Synthesize** Draw the letter *R* below as it would appear if you held the book up to (a) a flat mirror and (b) a convex mirror.

R

Send Help!

Survival kits often contain a small mirror that can be used to signal for help. If you were lost in the desert and saw a search plane overhead, you could use the mirror to reflect sunlight toward the plane and catch the pilot's attention. To aim your signal, you would use the law of reflection. The angle at which a ray of light bounces off a mirror—the angle of reflection—is always equal to the angle at which the ray strikes the mirror—the angle of incidence.

MATH TUTORIAL
CLASSZONE.COM

Click on Math Tutorial for more help with measuring angles.

Example

Measure the angle of incidence using a protractor as follows:

(1) Place the center mark of the protractor over the vertex of the angle formed by the incident ray and the normal.

(2) Place the left 0° mark of the protractor on the incident ray.

(3) Read the number where the normal crosses the scale (35°).

(4) The angle of incidence is 35°.

ANSWER Therefore, the angle of reflection will be 35°.

Copy each of the following angles of incidence, extend its sides, and use a protractor to measure it.

1.   2.   3.   4.

CHALLENGE Copy the drawing below. Use a protractor to find the angle of reflection necessary to signal the plane from point A.

• A

A mirror can be used to signal for help.

KEY CONCEPT

Lenses form images by refracting light.

 BEFORE, you learned

- Waves can refract when they move from one medium to another
- Refraction changes the direction of a wave

 NOW, you will learn

- How a material medium can refract light
- How lenses control refraction
- How lenses produce images

VOCABULARY

lens p. 121
focal length p. 123

EXPLORE Refraction

How does material bend light?

PROCEDURE

1. Place the pencil in the cup, as shown in the photograph. Look at the cup from the side so that you see part of the pencil through the cup.

2. Fill the cup one-third full with water and repeat your observations.

3. Gently add oil until the cup is two-thirds full. After the oil settles into a separate layer, observe.

WHAT DO YOU THINK?

- How did the appearance of the pencil change when you added the water? the oil?
- What might explain these changes?

MATERIALS
- clear plastic cup
- pencil
- water
- mineral oil

A medium can refract light.

When sunlight strikes a window, some of the light rays reflect off the surface of the glass. Other rays continue through the glass, but their direction is slightly changed. This slight change in direction is called refraction. Refraction occurs when a wave strikes a new medium—such as the window—at an angle other than 90° and keeps going forward in a slightly different direction.

Refraction occurs because one side of the wave reaches the new medium slightly before the other side does. That side changes speed, while the other continues at its previous speed, causing the wave to turn.

 How does the motion of a light wave change when it refracts?

Refraction of Light

COMBINATION NOTES
Sketch the ways light is refracted when it moves into a denser medium and into a thinner medium.

Recall that waves travel at different speeds in different mediums. The direction in which a light wave turns depends on whether the new medium slows the wave down or allows it to travel faster. Like reflection, refraction is described in terms of an imaginary line—called the normal—that is perpendicular to the new surface. If the medium slows the wave, the wave will turn toward the normal. If the new medium lets the wave speed up, the wave will turn away from the normal. The wave in the diagram below turns toward the normal as it slows down in the new medium.

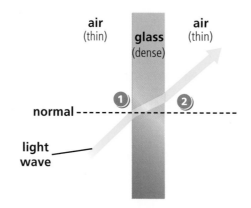

① Waves moving at an angle into a denser medium turn toward the normal.

② Waves moving at an angle into a thinner medium turn away from the normal.

READING TiP

A dense medium has more mass in a given volume than a thin medium.

Light from the Sun travels toward Earth through the near vacuum of outer space. Sunlight refracts when it reaches the new medium of Earth's upper atmosphere. Earth's upper atmosphere is relatively thin and refracts light only slightly. Denser materials, such as water and glass, refract light more.

By measuring the speed of light in different materials and comparing this speed to the speed of light in a vacuum, scientists have been able to determine exactly how different materials refract light. This knowledge has led to the ability to predict and control refraction, which is the basis of much optical technology.

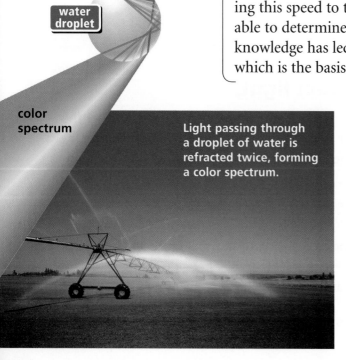

Light passing through a droplet of water is refracted twice, forming a color spectrum.

Refraction and Rainbows

You've seen rainbows in the sky after a rainstorm or hovering in the spray of a sprinkler. Rainbows are caused by refraction and reflection of light through spherical water drops, which act as prisms. Just as a prism separates the colors of white light, producing the color spectrum, each water drop separates the wavelengths of sunlight to produce a spectrum. Only one color reaches your eye from each drop. Red appears at the top of a rainbow because it is coming from higher drops, while violet comes from lower drops.

Shape determines how lenses form images.

When you look at yourself in a flat mirror, you see your image clearly, without distortions. Similarly, when you look through a plain glass window, you can see what is on the other side clearly. Just as curved mirrors distort images, certain transparent mediums called lenses alter what you see through them. A **lens** is a clear optical tool that refracts light. Different lenses refract light in different ways and form images useful for a variety of purposes.

Convex and Concave Lenses

Like mirrors, lenses can be convex or concave. A convex lens is curved outward; a concave lens is curved inward. A lens typically has two sides that are curved, as shown in the illustration below.

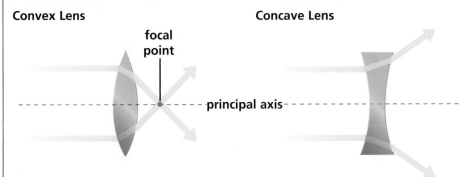

Convex Lens

focal point

principal axis

A convex lens causes parallel light rays to meet at a focal point.

Concave Lens

A concave lens causes parallel light rays to spread out.

Convex Parallel light rays passing through a convex lens are refracted inward. They meet at a focal point on the other side of the lens. The rays are actually refracted twice—once upon entering the lens and once upon leaving it. This is because both times they are entering a new medium at an angle other than 90 degrees. Rays closest to the edges of the lens are refracted most. Rays passing through the center of the lens—along the principal axis, which connects the centers of the two curved surfaces—are not refracted at all. They pass through to the same focal point as all rays parallel to them.

Concave Parallel light rays that pass through a concave lens are refracted outward. As with a convex lens, the rays are refracted twice. Rays closest to the edges of the lens are refracted most; rays at the very center of the lens pass straight through without being deflected. Because they are refracted away from each other, parallel light rays passing through a concave lens do not meet.

CHECK YOUR READING Compare what happens to parallel light rays striking a concave mirror with those striking a concave lens.

How a Convex Lens Forms an Image

A convex lens forms an image by refracting light rays. Light rays reflected from an object are refracted when they enter the lens and again when they leave the lens. They meet to form the image.

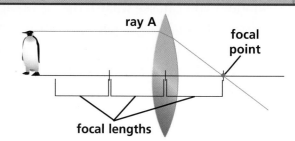

1 Light rays reflect off the penguin in all directions, and many enter the lens. Here a single ray (A) from the top of the penguin enters the lens and is refracted downward.

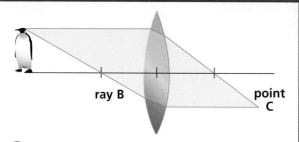

2 Another light ray (B) from the top of the penguin passes through the lens at the bottom and meets the first ray at point C. All of the rays from the top of the penguin passing through the lens meet at this point.

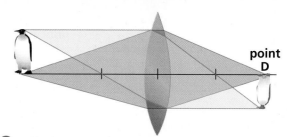

3 All of the light rays from the bottom of the penguin meet at a different point (D). Light rays from all parts of the penguin meet at corresponding points on the image.

READING VISUALS Where do light rays reflected from the middle of the penguin meet?

Images Formed by Lenses

SIMULATION
CLASSZONE.COM

Work with convex and concave lenses to form images.

When light rays from an object pass through a lens, an image of the object is formed. The type of image depends on the lens and, for convex lenses, on the distance between the lens and the object.

Notice the distance between the penguin and the lens in the illustration on page 122. The distance is measured in terms of a **focal length,** which is the distance from the center of the lens to the lens's focal point. The penguin is more than two focal lengths from the camera lens, which means the image formed is upside down and smaller.

If the penguin were between one and two focal lengths away from a convex lens, the image formed would be upside down and larger. Overhead projectors form this type of image, which is then turned right side up by a mirror and projected onto a screen for viewing.

Finally, if an object is less than one focal length from a convex lens, it will appear right side up and larger. In order to enlarge an object so that you can see details, you hold a magnifying lens close to the object. In the photograph, you see a face enlarged by a magnifying lens. The boy's face is less than one focal length from the lens.

If you look at an object through a concave lens, you'll see an image of the object that is right side up and smaller than the object normally appears. In the case of concave lenses, the distance between the object and the lens does not make a difference in the type of image that is formed. In the next section you'll see how the characteristics of the images formed by different lenses play a role in complex optical tools.

CHECK YOUR READING When will an image formed by a convex lens be upside down?

4.2 Review

KEY CONCEPTS

1. What quality of a material affects how much it refracts light?

2. How does the curve in a lens cause it to refract light differently from a flat piece of glass?

3. How does a camera lens form an image?

CRITICAL THINKING

4. **Infer** You look through a lens and see an image of a building upside down. What type of lens are you looking through?

5. **Make a Model** Draw the path of a light ray moving at an angle from air into water. Write a caption to explain the process.

CHALLENGE

6. Study the diagram on the opposite page. Describe the light rays that would pass through the labeled focal point. Where are they coming from, and how are they related to each other?

CHAPTER INVESTIGATION

Looking at Lenses

OVERVIEW AND PURPOSE Optical tools such as microscopes, telescopes, and eyeglasses use lenses to create images of objects. In this lab, you will use what you have learned about light and lenses to

- experiment with a convex lens to focus images of objects
- determine what makes it possible to focus images of objects.

▶ Procedure

PART A

1. Make a data table like the one shown on the sample notebook page.

2. Draw a stick figure on one index card. Assemble the cards, clay, and lens as shown in the photograph.

3. Position the convex lens so that you can see an enlarged, right-side up image of the stick figure. Measure the distances between the lens and the card, and between the lens and your eye. Record the distances in your data table.

4. Position the lens so that you can see an enlarged, upside down image of the stick figure. Measure the distances between the lens and the object, and between the lens and your eye. Record the distances in your data table.

5. Position the lens so that you can see a reduced, upside down image of the stick figure. Measure the distances between the lens and the object, and between the lens and your eye. Record the distances in your data table.

MATERIALS
- index cards
- marker
- modeling clay
- convex lens
- books
- meter stick
- flashlight
- masking tape
- white poster board

PART B

6 Put an arrow made of tape on the lens of the flashlight as shown.

7 Assemble poster board and clay to make a screen. Arrange the flashlight, lens, and screen as shown below right.

8 Shine the beam from the flashlight through the lens to form an enlarged, upside down image on the screen. Measure the distances between the lens and the flashlight and between the lens and the screen.

9 Position the light and screen to produce a reduced, upside down image. Measure the distances between the lens and the flashlight and between the lens and the screen.

10 Position the light and screen to produce an enlarged right-side up image.

step 6

▶ Observe and Analyze [Write It Up]

1. **RECORD OBSERVATIONS** Draw pictures of each setup in steps 3–9 to show what happened. Be sure your data table is complete.

2. **ANALYZE** What was the distance from the lens to the object in step 3? Answer this question for each of the other steps. How do the distances compare?

3. **ANALYZE** What happened when you tried to form the three types of images on the screen? How can you explain these results?

▶ Conclude [Write It Up]

1. **ANALYZE** What conclusions can you draw about the relationship between the distances you measured and the type of image that was produced?

2. **IDENTIFY LIMITS** Describe possible sources of error in your procedure or any places where errors might have occurred.

3. **APPLY** What kind of lenses are magnifying glasses? When a magnifying glass produces a sharp clear image, where is the object located in relation to the lens?

step 7

▶ INVESTIGATE Further

CHALLENGE If you were to repeat steps 8 and 9 with a concave lens, you would not be able to focus an image on the screen. Why not?

Looking at Lenses
Observe and Analyze
Table 1. Distances from Lens

Image	Object	Eye
Object enlarged and right-side up		
Object enlarged and upside down		
Object reduced and upside down		
	Flashlight	Screen
Object enlarged and right-side up		
Object enlarged and upside down		
Object reduced and upside down		

Conclude

4.3 The eye is a natural optical tool.

◀ **BEFORE**, you learned

- Mirrors and lenses focus light to form images
- Mirrors and lenses can alter images in useful ways

▶ **NOW**, you will learn

- How the eye depends on natural lenses
- How artificial lenses can be used to correct vision problems

VOCABULARY

cornea p. 127
pupil p. 127
retina p. 127

EXPLORE Focusing Vision

How does the eye focus an image?

PROCEDURE

① Position yourself so you can see an object about 6 meters (20 feet) away.

② Close one eye, hold up your index finger, and bring it as close to your open eye as you can while keeping the finger clearly in focus.

③ Keeping your finger in place, look just to the side at the more distant object and focus your eye on it.

④ Without looking away from the more distant object, observe your finger.

WHAT DO YOU THINK?

- How does the nearby object look when you are focusing on something distant?
- What might be happening in your eye to cause this change in the nearby object?

The eye gathers and focuses light.

The eyes of human beings and many other animals are natural optical tools that process visible light. Eyes transmit light, refract light, and respond to different wavelengths of light. Eyes contain natural lenses that focus images of objects. Eyes convert the energy of light waves into signals that can be sent to the brain. The brain interprets these signals as shape, brightness, and color. Altogether, these processes make vision possible.

In this section, you will learn how the eye works. You will also learn how artificial lenses can be used to improve vision.

How Light Travels Through the Human Eye

1 Light enters the eye through the **cornea** (KAWR-nee-uh), a transparent membrane that covers the eye. The cornea acts as a convex lens and does most of the refracting in the eye.

2 The light then continues through the **pupil,** a circular opening that controls how much light enters the eye. The pupil is surrounded by the iris, which opens and closes to change the size of the pupil.

3 Next the light passes through the part of the eye called the lens. The lens is convex on both sides. It refracts light to make fine adjustments for near and far objects. Unlike the cornea, the lens is attached to tiny muscles that contract and relax to control the amount of refraction that occurs and to move the focal point.

READING TiP

The word *lens* can refer both to an artificial optical tool and to a specific part of the eye.

4 The light passes through the clear center of the eye and strikes the **retina** (REHT-uhn-uh). The retina contains specialized cells that respond to light. Some of these cells send signals through the optic nerve to the brain. The brain interprets these signals as images.

How the Human Eye Forms an Image

The cornea and lens together focus a reduced, inverted image on the retina.

1 Light from an object is refracted by the **cornea.**

iris

2 The light passes through the iris and the **pupil.**

3 The **lens** refracts the light more.

4 An image is focused on the **retina.**

optic nerve

READING VISUALS What part of the illustration explains why the image is focused upside down? Explain your answer.

How the Eye Forms Images

COMBINATION NOTES
Make a chart showing how light interacts with different parts of the eye.

For you to see an object clearly, your eye must focus an image of the object on your retina. The light reflected from each particular spot on the object must converge on a matching point on your retina. Many such points make up an image of an entire object. Because the light rays pass through the lens's focal point, the image is upside down. The brain interprets this upside down image as an object that is right-side up.

For a complete image to be formed in the eye and communicated to the brain, more than the lens and the cornea are needed. The retina also plays an important role. The retina contains specialized cells that detect brightness and color and other qualities of light.

Rod Cells Rod cells distinguish between white and black and shades of gray. Rods respond to faint light, so they help with night vision.

Cone Cells Cone cells respond to different wavelengths of light, so they detect color. There are three types of cones, one for each of the colors red, blue, and green. Cones respond to other colors with combinations of these three, as the screen of a color monitor does. The brain interprets these combinations as the entire color spectrum.

CHECK YOUR READING Which type of cell in the retina detects color?

INVESTIGATE Vision

How does distance affect vision?

PROCEDURE

1. Arrange the materials as shown so that the lamp shines through the lens onto the plate. The lens should be about $\frac{2}{3}$ a meter from the lamp.

2. Adjust the distance between the plate and the lens until you see a focused image of the bulb on the plate. Measure this distance.

3. Move the lens until it is about a meter and a half from the lamp. Adjust the plate once again to get a focused image, then measure the distance between the plate and the lens.

WHAT DO YOU THINK?

- How does the distance needed between the plate and the lens change when the lamp is farther from the lens?
- How is what happens in the eye different from what you did to refocus the image?

CHALLENGE How could you change the model to make it more like what happens in the eye?

SKILL FOCUS
Observing

MATERIALS
- convex lens
- index card
- modeling clay
- white paper plate
- lamp

TIME
10 minutes

Corrective lenses can improve vision.

What happens when the image formed by the lens of the eye does not fall exactly on the retina? The result is that the image appears blurry. This can occur either because of the shape of the eye or because of how the lens works. Artificial lenses can be used to correct this problem.

Corrective Lenses

A person who is nearsighted cannot see objects clearly unless they are near. Nearsightedness occurs when the lens of the eye focuses the image in front of the retina. The farther away the object is, the farther in front of the retina the image forms. This problem can be corrected with glasses made with concave lenses. The concave lenses spread out the rays of light before they enter the eye. The point at which the rays meet then falls on the retina.

nearsighted eye   **concave lens**

① image in front of retina   ② image at retina

Objects are clearer to a farsighted person when the objects are farther away. Farsightedness occurs when the lens of the eye focuses an object's image behind the retina. This condition can result from aging, which may make the lens less flexible. The closer the object is, the farther behind the retina the image forms. Farsightedness can be corrected with glasses made from convex lenses. The convex lenses bend the light rays inward before they enter the eye. The point at which the rays meet then falls on the retina.

READING TiP

Nearsighted people can see objects near to them best. *Farsighted* people can see objects better when the objects are farther away.

farsighted eye   **convex lens**

① image behind retina   ② image at retina

CHECK YOUR READING   What kind of lens is used for correcting nearsightedness?

Surgery and Contact Lenses

Wearing glasses is an effective way to correct vision. It is also possible to change the shape of the cornea to make the eye refract properly. The cornea is responsible for two-thirds of the refraction that takes place inside the eye. As you know, the eye's lens changes shape to focus an image, but the shape of the cornea does not ordinarily change.

Contact lenses fit directly onto the cornea, changing the way light is refracted as it enters a person's eye.

However, using advanced surgical technology, doctors can change the shape of the cornea. By doing this, they change the way light rays focus in the eye so that the image lines up with the retina. To correct for nearsightedness, surgeons remove tissue from the center of the cornea. This flattens the cornea and makes it less convex so that it will refract less. To correct for farsightedness, surgeons remove tissue from around the edges of the cornea. This increases the cornea's curvature to make it refract more. Surgery changes the shape of the cornea permanently and can eliminate the need for eyeglasses.

Contact lenses also correct vision by changing the way the cornea refracts light. Contact lenses are corrective lenses that fit directly onto the cornea. The lenses actually float on a thin layer of tears. The moisture, the contact lens, and the cornea all function together. The lens of the eye then focuses the light further. Because the change is temporary, contacts, like eyeglasses, can be adapted to new changes in the eye.

CHECK YOUR READING What are two ways of changing the way the cornea refracts light to correct vision?

4.3 Review

KEY CONCEPTS

1. Where are images focused in an eye with perfect vision?

2. What causes people with nearsightedness to see blurry images of objects at a distance?

3. What kind of lens is used for correcting farsightedness? Why?

CRITICAL THINKING

4. **Make a Model** Draw a diagram to answer the following question: How does a convex lens affect the way a nearsighted eye focuses an image?

5. **Analyze** What distance would an eye doctor need to measure to correct a problem with nearsightedness or farsightedness?

CHALLENGE

6. **Apply** A person alternates between wearing glasses and wearing contact lenses to correct farsightedness. Are the contact lenses more or less convex than the lenses of the glasses? Explain the reasoning behind your response.

Optical technology makes use of light waves.

◀ BEFORE, you learned	▶ NOW, you will learn
• Mirrors are optical tools that use reflection	• How mirrors and lenses can be combined to make complex optical tools
• Lenses are optical tools that use refraction	• How optical tools are used to extend natural vision
• The eye is a natural optical tool	• How laser light is made and used in optical technology
• Lenses can correct vision	

VOCABULARY

laser p. 135
fiber optics p. 137

EXPLORE Combining Lenses

How can lenses be combined?

PROCEDURE

1. Assemble the lenses, clay, and index cards as shown in the photograph.

2. Line the lenses up so that you have a straight line of sight through them.

3. Experiment with different distances between
   • the lenses
   • the far lens and an object
   • the near lens and your eye
   Find an arrangement that allows you to see a clear image of an object through both lenses.

MATERIALS

• 2 convex lenses
• modeling clay
• 2 index cards

WHAT DO YOU THINK?

• What kind of image could you see? What arrangement or arrangements work best to produce an image?
• How do you think the lenses are working together to focus the image?

Mirrors and lenses can be combined to make more powerful optical tools.

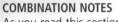

COMBINATION NOTES
As you read this section, make a list of optical tools. Add sketches to help you remember important concepts.

If you know about submarines, then you know how much they depend on their periscopes to see above the water. Periscopes are made by combining mirrors. Lenses can also be combined. In the eye, for example, the cornea and the eye's lens work together to focus an image. Mirrors and lenses can be combined with each other, as they are in an overhead projector. Many of the most powerful and complex optical tools are based on different combinations of mirrors and lenses.

Microscopes

Microscopes are used to see objects that are too small to see well with the naked eye. An ordinary microscope works by combining convex lenses. The lens closer to the object is called the objective. The object is between one and two focal lengths from this lens, so the lens focuses an enlarged image of the object inside the microscope.

The other microscope lens—the one you look through—is called the eyepiece. You use this lens to look at the image formed by the objective. Like a magnifying glass, the eyepiece lens forms an enlarged image of the first image.

Very small objects do not reflect much light. Most microscopes use a lamp or a mirror to shine more light on the object.

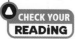 Which types of images do the lenses in a microscope form?

Telescopes

Telescopes are used to see objects that are too far away to see well with the naked eye. One type of telescope, called a refracting telescope, is made by combining lenses. Another type of telescope, called a reflecting telescope, is made by combining lenses and mirrors.

Refracting telescopes combine convex lenses, just as microscopes do. However, the objects are far away from the objective lens instead of near to it. The object is more than two focal lengths from the objective lens, so the lens focuses a reduced image of the object inside the telescope. The eyepiece of a telescope then forms an enlarged image of the first image, just as a microscope does. This second image enlarges the object.

Reflecting telescopes work in the same way that refracting telescopes do. However, there is no objective lens where light enters the telescope. Instead, a concave mirror at the opposite end focuses an image of the object. A small flat mirror redirects the image to the side of the telescope. With this arrangement, the eyepiece does not interfere with light on its way to the concave mirror. The eyepiece then forms an enlarged image of the first image.

Both refracting and reflecting telescopes must adjust for the small amount of light received from distant objects. The amount of light gathered can be increased by increasing the diameter of the objective lens or mirror. Large mirrors are easier and less expensive to make than large lenses. So reflecting telescopes can produce brighter images more cheaply than refracting telescopes.

 How is a reflecting telescope different from a refracting telescope?

RESOURCE CENTER
CLASSZONE.COM

Find out more about microscopes and telescopes.

Microscopes and Telescopes

eyepiece lens

objective lens

stage

lamp

object

Microscope

Light from an object passes through a convex lens called an objective. The objective lens focuses the light to form an enlarged image. The eyepiece lens enlarges the image even more. The one-celled algae at right, called diatoms, appear 400 times their normal size.

diatoms

Refracting Telescope

surface of the Moon

The objective lens gathers and focuses light from a distant object to form an image of the object. The eyepiece enlarges the image. The telescope image of the Moon at left shows fine details of the lunar surface.

objective lens

light

eyepiece lens

Reflecting Telescope

A concave mirror gathers light through a wide opening and focuses it to form an image of the object. The eyepiece lens enlarges the image. The flat mirror redirects the light so that the eyepiece can be out of the way. The telescope image of Saturn at right shows details of the planet's rings.

the planet Saturn

light

flat mirror

concave mirror

READING VISUALS Which type of telescope is similar in construction to a microscope?

INVESTIGATE Optical Tools

How can you make a simple telescope?

Use what you have learned about how a telescope works to build one. Figure out how far apart the two lenses need to be and use that information to construct a working model.

PROCEDURE

1. Decide how the lenses should be positioned in relation to an object you select to view.

2. Adjust the lenses until you get a clear image.

3. Use the other materials to fix the lenses into place and to make it possible to adjust the distance between them.

WHAT DO YOU THINK?

• How did you end up positioning the lenses in relation to the object?

• Did your telescope work? Why do you think you got this result?

CHALLENGE Is your telescope image upside down or right-side up? How can you explain this observation?

Cameras

Most film cameras focus images in the same way that the eye does. The iris of a camera controls the size of the aperture, an opening for light, just as the iris of an eye controls the size of the pupil. Like an eye, a camera uses a convex lens to produce images of objects that are more than two focal lengths away. The images are reduced in size and upside down. In the eye, an image will not be focused unless it falls exactly on the retina. In a camera, an image will not be focused unless it falls exactly on the film. The camera does not change the shape of its lens as the eye does to change the focal point. Instead, the camera allows you to move the lens nearer to or farther away from the film until the object you want to photograph is in focus.

A digital camera focuses images just as a film camera does. Instead of using film, though, the digital camera uses a sensor that detects light and converts it into electrical charges. These charges are recorded by a small computer inside the camera. The computer can then reconstruct the image immediately on the camera's display screen.

READING TiP

The term *digital* is often used to describe technology involving computers. Computers process information digitally, that is, using numbers.

A camera focuses an image in the same way as an eye.

film camera

light
lens
iris
aperture
film

READING VISUALS What part of a camera corresponds to the pupil of an eye?

Eye and Camera

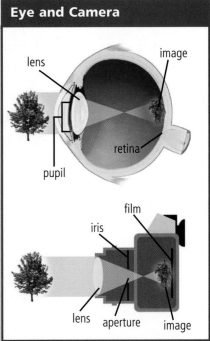

lens
image
pupil
retina

film
iris
lens
aperture
image

Digital Camera

A **digital camera** records images digitally, that is, using a computer.

Lasers use light in new ways.

A **laser** (LAY-zuhr) is a device that produces an intense, concentrated beam of light that is brighter than sunlight. The word *laser* means "light amplification by stimulated emission of radiation." Laser light has many uses. It carries a lot of energy and can be controlled precisely.

Ordinary visible light is made up of many different wavelengths. Even colored light usually contains many different wavelengths. But a laser beam is made up of light waves with a single wavelength and a pure color. In addition, the waves are in phase, which means the peaks are lined up so they match exactly.

> **REMINDER**
> The peak of a wave is where it has the greatest energy.

Visible light waves of different wavelengths

Light waves of a single wavelength

Single wavelength waves in phase

Light waves in a laser beam are highly concentrated and exactly parallel. Ordinary light spreads out, growing more faint as it gets farther from its source. Laser light spreads out very little. After traveling 1 kilometer (0.6 mi), a laser beam may have a diameter of only one meter.

Making Laser Light

RESOURCE CENTER
CLASSZONE.COM

Learn more about lasers.

A laser is made in a special tube called an optical cavity. A material that is known to give off a certain wavelength of light, such as a ruby crystal, is placed inside the tube. Next, an energy source, such as a bright flash of light, stimulates the material, causing it to emit, or give off, light waves. Both ends of the crystal are mirrored so that they reflect light back and forth between them. One end is mirrored more than the other. As the light waves pass through the crystal, they cause the material to give off more light waves—all perfectly parallel, all with the same wavelength, and all with their crests and troughs lined up. Eventually the beam becomes concentrated and strong enough to penetrate the less-mirrored end of the crystal. What comes out of the end is a laser beam.

The first laser used a cylinder of ruby crystal.

A researcher uses laser beams to study airflow in a new car design.

Visual Uses of Lasers

Lasers are used today in an amazing variety of ways. One of these ways is to create devices that do the kind of work the human eye does—detecting and interpreting light waves. For example, surveyors once used telescopes to measure distances and angles. Now lasers can be used to take these measurements more precisely. Lasers are used to read bar codes, to scan images and pages of text, and to create holograms—three-dimensional images that appear to hover in the air. Holograms, which are hard to reproduce, are sometimes used in important documents so that the documents cannot be duplicated.

Fiber Optics

Some laser applications use visible light in ways that have nothing to do with vision. One of the fastest growing technologies is fiber optics. **Fiber optics** is technology based on the use of laser light to send signals through transparent wires called optical fibers. Fiber optics makes use of a light behavior called total internal reflection. Total internal reflection occurs when all of the light inside a medium reflects off the inner surface of the medium.

When light strikes the inner surface of a transparent medium, it may pass through the surface or it may be reflected back into the medium. Which one occurs depends on the angle at which the light hits the surface. For example, if you look through the sides of an aquarium, you can see what is behind it. But if you look at the surface of the water from below, it will act like a mirror, reflecting the inside of the aquarium.

Laser light is very efficient at total internal reflection. It can travel long distances inside clear fibers of glass or other materials. Light always travels in a straight line; however, by reflecting off the sides of the fibers, laser light inside fibers can go around corners and even completely reverse direction.

optical fibers

CHECK YOUR READING What is total internal reflection? What questions do you have about this light behavior?

Fiber optics is important in communications, because it can be used to transmit information very efficiently. Optical fibers can carry more signals than a corresponding amount of electrical cable. Optical cables can be used in place of electrical wires for telephone lines, cable television, and broadband Internet connections.

This surgeon uses fiber optics to see inside a patient's body.

Fiber optics also has visual uses. For example, fiber optics is used in medicine to look inside the body. Using optical cable, doctors can examine organs and diagnose illnesses without surgery or x-rays. Optical fibers can also deliver laser light to specific points inside the body to help surgeons with delicate surgery.

Future Uses of Lasers

Research involving new uses of lasers continues at an amazing pace. Many new discoveries and developments in science and technology today are possible only because of lasers.

One area of research in which lasers have made a big impact is nanotechnology—the development of super-tiny machines and tools. Laser light can be controlled very precisely, so scientists can use it to perform extremely fine operations. For example, lasers could be used to cut out parts to make molecule-size motors. Lasers can also be used as "optical tweezers" to handle extremely small objects such as molecules. Scientists are even beginning to use lasers to change the shape of molecules. They do this by varying the laser's wavelength.

Future applications of lasers are also sure to involve new ways of transferring energy. Remember that a wave is a disturbance that transfers energy. Laser light is made up of EM waves. EM waves can move energy over great distances without losing any of it. When EM waves encounter a material medium, their energy can then be converted into other forms and put to use.

One possible future use of lasers is to supply energy to spacecraft. Scientists imagine a day when orbiting space stations will make rockets unnecessary. A cable between the ground and the station will make it possible for a "space elevator" to escape Earth's gravity by climbing up the cable. The elevator will be powered by an Earth-based laser. A device on board the elevator will convert the laser's energy into electrical power.

In this artist's illustration, a space elevator of the future draws power from a laser beam to climb to an orbiting space station.

4.4 Review

KEY CONCEPTS

1. How do refracting and reflecting telescopes use convex lenses and mirrors?

2. What is different about the way a camera focuses images from the way an eye focuses images?

3. How is laser light different from ordinary light?

CRITICAL THINKING

4. **Predict** What would happen to laser light if it passed through a prism?

5. **Analyze** What are two ways reflection is involved in fiber optics?

◢ CHALLENGE

6. **Apply** How could the speed of light and a laser beam be used to measure the distance between two satellites?

Optics in Photography

Photographers use the science of optics to help them make the best photographs possible. For example, a portrait photographer chooses the right equipment and lighting to make each person look his or her best. A photographer needs to understand how light reflects, refracts, and diffuses to achieve just the right effect.

Using Reflection

A gold-colored reflector reflects only gold-colored wavelengths of light onto the subject. Photographers use these to fill in shadows and add warmth.

without gold reflector **with gold reflector**

Using Diffusion

When light is directed toward a curved reflective surface, the light scatters in many directions. This diffused light produces a softer appearance than direct light.

direct light **diffused light**

Using Refraction

Lenses refract light in different ways. A long lens makes the subject appear closer. A wide-angle lens includes more space around the subject.

long lens

wide-angle lens

EXPLORE

1. **COMPARE** Find photos of people and compare them to the photos above. Which would have been improved by the use of a gold reflector? a long lens? diffused light?

2. **CHALLENGE** Using a disposable camera and a desk lamp, experiment with photography yourself. Try using a piece of paper as a reflector and observe its effects on the photo- graph. What happens if you use more than one reflector? What happens if you use a different color of paper?

Chapter Review

the BIG idea

Optical tools depend on the wave behavior of light.

CONTENT REVIEW
CLASSZONE.COM

◀ **KEY CONCEPTS SUMMARY**

4.1 Mirrors form images by reflecting light.

flat mirror

- Light rays obey the law of reflection.
- Mirrors work by regular reflection.
- Curved mirrors can form images that are distorted in useful ways.

VOCABULARY
optics p. 113
law of reflection p. 114
regular reflection p. 114
diffuse reflection p. 114
image p. 115
convex p. 116
concave p. 116
focal point p. 117

4.2 Lenses form images by refracting light.

ray A
focal point
focal lengths

- Lenses have curved surfaces that refract parallel light waves in different amounts.
- Convex lenses bend light inward toward a focal point.
- Concave lenses spread light out.
- Lenses form a variety of useful images.

VOCABULARY
lens p. 121
focal length p. 123

4.3 The eye is a natural optical tool.

cornea
pupil
lens
retina

- The eyes of humans and many animals use lenses to focus images on the retina.
- The retina detects images and sends information about them to the brain.

VOCABULARY
cornea p. 127
pupil p. 127
retina p. 127

4.4 Optical technology makes use of light waves.

partial mirror
full mirror
laser beam

- Many optical tools are made by combining mirrors and lenses.
- Examples of optical tools include telescopes, microscopes, cameras, and lasers.
- Lasers have a wide variety of uses.

VOCABULARY
laser p. 135
fiber optics p. 137

Reviewing Vocabulary

For each item below, fill in the blank. If the right column is blank, give a brief description or definition. If the left column is blank, give the correct term.

Term	Description
1.	shape like the inside of a bowl
2. convex	
3.	science of light, vision, and related technology
4.	picture of object formed by light rays
5. focal point	
6.	controls the amount of light entering the eye
7.	distance between mirror or lens and place where light rays meet
8. fiber optics	
9. law of reflection	
10.	concentrated, parallel light waves of a single wavelength

Reviewing Key Concepts

Multiple Choice *Choose the letter of the best answer.*

11. What shape is a mirror that reflects parallel light rays toward a focal point?

   a. convex   **c.** concave

   b. flat   **d.** regular

12. According to the law of reflection, a light ray striking a mirror

   a. continues moving through the mirror in the same direction

   b. moves into the mirror at a slightly different angle

   c. bounces off the mirror toward the direction it came from

   d. bounces off the mirror at the same angle it hits

13. Reflecting telescopes focus images using

   a. several mirrors

   b. several lenses

   c. both mirrors and lenses

   d. either a mirror or a lens, but not both

14. Ordinary light differs from laser light in that ordinary light waves

   a. all have the same wavelength

   b. tend to spread out

   c. stay parallel to one another

   d. all have their peaks lined up

15. Nearsighted vision is corrected when lenses

   a. reflect light away from the eye

   b. allow light rays to focus on the retina

   c. allow light to focus slightly past the retina

   d. help light rays reflect regularly

16. Lasers do work similar to that of human vision when they are used to

   a. perform surgery

   b. send phone signals over optical cable

   c. scan bar codes at the grocery store

   d. change the shape of molecules

Short Answer *Write a short answer to each question.*

17. Name one optical tool, describe how it works, and explain some of its uses.

18. How are the images that are produced by a convex mirror different from those produced by a concave mirror?

19. Describe what typically happens to a ray of light from the time it enters the eye until it strikes the retina.

20. How do lenses correct nearsightedness and farsightedness?

21. What does a refracting telescope have in common with a simple microscope?

22. Describe two ways the distance of an object from a lens can affect the appearance of the object's image.

Thinking Critically

INTERPRET *In the four diagrams below, light rays are shown interacting with a material medium. For the next four questions, choose the letter of the diagram that answers the question.*

A

B

C

D

23. Which diagram shows regular reflection?

24. Which diagram shows diffuse reflection?

25. Which diagram shows refraction?

26. Which diagram shows light rays converging at a focal point?

COMPARE AND CONTRAST *Copy the chart below. For each pair of terms, write down one way they are alike (compare) and one way they are different (contrast).*

Terms	Compare	Contrast
27. flat mirror, curved mirror		
28. convex lens, concave lens		
29. focal point, focal length		
30. nearsighted, farsighted		
31. simple microscope, refracting telescope		
32. regular reflection, total internal reflection		

33. **INFER** What is the approximate focal length of the eye's lens? How do you know?

34. **ANALYZE** Why is laser light used in fiber optics?

35. **APPLY** In order to increase the magnification of a magnifying glass, would you need to make the convex surfaces of the lens more or less curved?

36. **APPLY** Describe a possible use for laser light not mentioned in the chapter. What characteristics of laser light does this application make use of?

the **BIG** idea

37. **SYNTHESIZE** Using what you have learned in this chapter, describe two possible uses of an optical tool like the one shown on pages 110–111. Explain what wave behaviors of light would be involved in these uses. Then explain how these uses could benefit the person in the photo.

38. **APPLY** Make a sketch of an optical tool that would use three mirrors to make a beam of light return to its source. Your sketch should include:

- the path of light waves through the tool
- labels indicating the names of parts and how they affect the light
- several sentences describing one possible use of the tool

UNIT PROJECTS

Evaluate all the data, results, and information from your project folder. Prepare to present your project.

Interpreting Diagrams

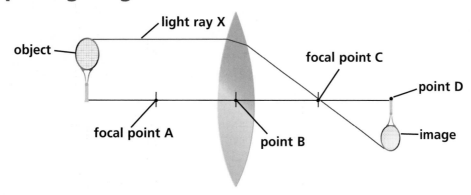

Study the diagram above and then answer the questions that follow.

1. What kind of lens is shown in the diagram?
   a. concave   **c.** flat
   b. convex   **d.** prism

2. What happens to parallel light rays passing through this type of lens?
   a. They become polarized.
   b. They form a rainbow.
   c. They bend inward.
   d. They bend outward.

3. All light rays parallel to light ray X will pass through what point?
   a. point A   **c.** point C
   b. point B   **d.** point D

4. How far is the object in the diagram from the lens?
   a. less than one focal length
   b. one focal length
   c. about two focal lengths
   d. more than three focal lengths

5. Where would you position a screen in order to see the image in focus on the screen?
   a. at point A
   b. at point B
   c. at point C
   d. at point D

Extended Response

Answer the two questions below in detail. Include some of the terms from the word box. Underline each term you use in your answer.

concave	focal point	real image
convex	refraction	virtual image
flat mirror	reflection	magnifying glass

6. What kind of mirror would you use to see what is happening over a broad area? Why?

7. Choose one of the following optical tools and explain how it uses mirrors and/or lenses to form an image: camera, telescope, periscope, microscope.

Today's Scientist at Work

© Volker Steger / Photo Researchers, Inc.

Name: James West	
Degree: PhD, Science, New Jersey Institute of Technology	
Profession: Research Scientist, The Johns Hopkins University	
Location: Baltimore, MD	

James West's parents wanted him to be a medical doctor, but he wanted to study physics. His father was convinced he'd never find a job doing physics. But Dr. West wanted to study what he loved. He studied physics and then went to work for Bell Laboratories. Today the microphone he helped develop is in almost all telephones, cell phones, and other equipment that records sound.

Dr. West's interest in the microphone started with a question on hearing. A group of scientists wanted to know how close together two sounds could be before the ear would not be able to tell them apart. However, they needed a better earphone to carry out tests. Condenser microphones and earphones require a high DC voltage for linear response. Dr. West and fellow scientist Dr. Gerhard Sessler found they could make a more sensitive microphone by using materials called "electrets" (the electrical counterpart of a permanent magnet). Like some metals can become magnetic, these materials can store an electric charge. This eliminates the need for a battery. The new microphones were cheaper, more reliable, smaller, and lighter than any microphone before them.

"Discovery is the best high I've ever had." Dr. West has said. He should know. To date, he holds more than 200 U.S. and foreign patents. Dr. West retired from Bell Laboratories in 2001 and now is a professor of engineering at the Johns Hopkins University. He has won numerous awards for his inventions including both the Silver and Gold Medals from the Acoustical Society of America. In 1999 he was inducted into the National Inventors Hall of Fame.

© Andrew Lambert Photography / Photo Researchers, Inc.

Using computers scientists can analyze sound waves.

Student Resource Handbooks

Scientific Thinking Handbook

Making Observations

An **observation** is an act of noting and recording an event, characteristic, behavior, or anything else detected with an instrument or with the senses.

Observations allow you to make informed hypotheses and to gather data for experiments. Careful observations often lead to ideas for new experiments. There are two categories of observations:

- **Quantitative observations** can be expressed in numbers and include records of time, temperature, mass, distance, and volume.

- **Qualitative observations** include descriptions of sights, sounds, smells, and textures.

EXAMPLE

A student dissolved 30 grams of Epsom salts in water, poured the solution into a dish, and let the dish sit out uncovered overnight. The next day, she made the following observations of the Epsom salt crystals that grew in the dish.

> To determine the mass, the student found the mass of the dish before and after growing the crystals and then used subtraction to find the difference.

> The student measured several crystals and calculated the mean length. (To learn how to calculate the mean of a data set, see page R36.)

Table 1. Observations of Epsom Salt Crystals

Quantitative Observations	Qualitative Observations
• mass = 30 g	• Crystals are clear.
• mean crystal length = 0.5 cm	• Crystals are long, thin, and rectangular.
• longest crystal length = 2 cm	• White crust has formed around edge of dish.

> Photographs or sketches are useful for recording qualitative observations.

 Epsom salt crystals

MORE ABOUT OBSERVING

- Make quantitative observations whenever possible. That way, others will know exactly what you observed and be able to compare their results with yours.

- It is always a good idea to make qualitative observations too. You never know when you might observe something unexpected.

Predicting and Hypothesizing

A **prediction** is an expectation of what will be observed or what will happen. A **hypothesis** is a tentative explanation for an observation or scientific problem that can be tested by further investigation.

EXAMPLE

Suppose you have made two paper airplanes and you wonder why one of them tends to glide farther than the other one.

1. Start by asking a question.

2. Make an educated guess. After examination, you notice that the wings of the airplane that flies farther are slightly larger than the wings of the other airplane.

3. Write a prediction based upon your educated guess, in the form of an "If . . . , then . . ." statement. Write the independent variable after the word *if,* and the dependent variable after the word *then.*

4. To make a hypothesis, explain why you think what you predicted will occur. Write the explanation after the word *because.*

---

1. Why does one of the paper airplanes glide farther than the other?

2. The size of an airplane's wings may affect how far the airplane will glide.

3. Prediction: If I make a paper airplane with larger wings, then the airplane will glide farther.

> To read about independent and dependent variables, see page R30.

4. Hypothesis: If I make a paper airplane with larger wings, then the airplane will glide farther, because the additional surface area of the wing will produce more lift.

> Notice that the part of the hypothesis after *because* adds an explanation of why the airplane will glide farther.

MORE ABOUT HYPOTHESES

- The results of an experiment cannot prove that a hypothesis is correct. Rather, the results either support or do not support the hypothesis.

- Valuable information is gained even when your hypothesis is not supported by your results. For example, it would be an important discovery to find that wing size is not related to how far an airplane glides.

- In science, a hypothesis is supported only after many scientists have conducted many experiments and produced consistent results.

Inferring

An **inference** is a logical conclusion drawn from the available evidence and prior knowledge. Inferences are often made from observations.

EXAMPLE

A student observing a set of acorns noticed something unexpected about one of them. He noticed a white, soft-bodied insect eating its way out of the acorn.

> The student recorded these observations.

Observations
- There is a hole in the acorn, about 0.5 cm in diameter, where the insect crawled out.
- There is a second hole, which is about the size of a pinhole, on the other side of the acorn.
- The inside of the acorn is hollow.

> Here are some inferences that can be made on the basis of the observations.

Inferences
- The insect formed from the material inside the acorn, grew to its present size, and ate its way out of the acorn.
- The insect crawled through the smaller hole, ate the inside of the acorn, grew to its present size, and ate its way out of the acorn.
- An egg was laid in the acorn through the smaller hole. The egg hatched into a larva that ate the inside of the acorn, grew to its present size, and ate its way out of the acorn.

> When you make inferences, be sure to look at all of the evidence available and combine it with what you already know.

MORE ABOUT INFERENCES

Inferences depend both on observations and on the knowledge of the people making the inferences. Ancient people who did not know that organisms are produced only by similar organisms might have made an inference like the first one. A student today might look at the same observations and make the second inference. A third student might have knowledge about this particular insect and know that it is never small enough to fit through the smaller hole, leading her to the third inference.

Identifying Cause and Effect

In a **cause-and-effect relationship,** one event or characteristic is the result of another. Usually an effect follows its cause in time.

There are many examples of cause-and-effect relationships in everyday life.

Cause	Effect
Turn off a light.	Room gets dark.
Drop a glass.	Glass breaks.
Blow a whistle.	Sound is heard.

Scientists must be careful not to infer a cause-and-effect relationship just because one event happens after another event. When one event occurs after another, you cannot infer a cause-and-effect relationship on the basis of that information alone. You also cannot conclude that one event caused another if there are alternative ways to explain the second event. A scientist must demonstrate through experimentation or continued observation that an event was truly caused by another event.

EXAMPLE

Make an Observation

Suppose you have a few plants growing outside. When the weather starts getting colder, you bring one of the plants indoors. You notice that the plant you brought indoors is growing faster than the others are growing. You cannot conclude from your observation that the change in temperature was the cause of the increased plant growth, because there are alternative explanations for the observation. Some possible explanations are given below.

- The humidity indoors caused the plant to grow faster.

- The level of sunlight indoors caused the plant to grow faster.

- The indoor plant's being noticed more often and watered more often than the outdoor plants caused it to grow faster.

- The plant that was brought indoors was healthier than the other plants to begin with.

To determine which of these factors, if any, caused the indoor plant to grow faster than the outdoor plants, you would need to design and conduct an experiment.

See pages R28–R35 for information about designing experiments.

Recognizing Bias

Television, newspapers, and the Internet are full of experts claiming to have scientific evidence to back up their claims. How do you know whether the claims are really backed up by good science?

Bias is a slanted point of view, or personal prejudice. The goal of scientists is to be as objective as possible and to base their findings on facts instead of opinions. However, bias often affects the conclusions of researchers, and it is important to learn to recognize bias.

When scientific results are reported, you should consider the source of the information as well as the information itself. It is important to critically analyze the information that you see and read.

SOURCES OF BIAS

There are several ways in which a report of scientific information may be biased. Here are some questions that you can ask yourself:

1. **Who is sponsoring the research?**

   Sometimes, the results of an investigation are biased because an organization paying for the research is looking for a specific answer. This type of bias can affect how data are gathered and interpreted.

2. **Is the research sample large enough?**

   Sometimes research does not include enough data. The larger the sample size, the more likely that the results are accurate, assuming a truly random sample.

3. **In a survey, who is answering the questions?**

   The results of a survey or poll can be biased. The people taking part in the survey may have been specifically chosen because of how they would answer. They may have the same ideas or lifestyles. A survey or poll should make use of a random sample of people.

4. **Are the people who take part in a survey biased?**

   People who take part in surveys sometimes try to answer the questions the way they think the researcher wants them to answer. Also, in surveys or polls that ask for personal information, people may be unwilling to answer questions truthfully.

SCIENTIFIC BIAS

It is also important to realize that scientists have their own biases because of the types of research they do and because of their scientific viewpoints. Two scientists may look at the same set of data and come to completely different conclusions because of these biases. However, such disagreements are not necessarily bad. In fact, a critical analysis of disagreements is often responsible for moving science forward.

Identifying Faulty Reasoning

Faulty reasoning is wrong or incorrect thinking. It leads to mistakes and to wrong conclusions. Scientists are careful not to draw unreasonable conclusions from experimental data. Without such caution, the results of scientific investigations may be misleading.

EXAMPLE

Scientists try to make generalizations based on their data to explain as much about nature as possible. If only a small sample of data is looked at, however, a conclusion may be faulty. Suppose a scientist has studied the effects of the El Niño and La Niña weather patterns on flood damage in California from 1989 to 1995. The scientist organized the data in the bar graph below.

The scientist drew the following conclusions:

1. The La Niña weather pattern has no effect on flooding in California.

2. When neither weather pattern occurs, there is almost no flood damage.

3. A weak or moderate El Niño produces a small or moderate amount of flooding.

4. A strong El Niño produces a lot of flooding.

For the six-year period of the scientist's investigation, these conclusions may seem to be reasonable. However, a six-year study of weather patterns may be too small of a sample for the conclusions to be supported. Consider the following graph, which shows information that was gathered from 1949 to 1997.

Flood and Storm Damage in California

- Weak–moderate El Niño
- Strong El Niño

Starting year of season
(July 1–June 30)

SOURCE: *Governor's Office of Emergency Services, California*

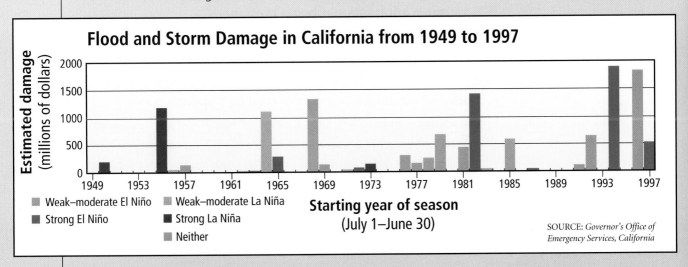

Flood and Storm Damage in California from 1949 to 1997

- Weak–moderate El Niño
- Strong El Niño
- Weak–moderate La Niña
- Strong La Niña
- Neither

Starting year of season
(July 1–June 30)

SOURCE: *Governor's Office of
Emergency Services, California*

The only one of the conclusions that all of this information supports is number 3: a weak or moderate El Niño produces a small or moderate amount of flooding. By collecting more data, scientists can be more certain of their conclusions and can avoid faulty reasoning.

Analyzing Statements

To **analyze** a statement is to examine its parts carefully. Scientific findings are often reported through media such as television or the Internet. A report that is made public often focuses on only a small part of research. As a result, it is important to question the sources of information.

Evaluate Media Claims

To **evaluate** a statement is to judge it on the basis of criteria you've established. Sometimes evaluating means deciding whether a statement is true.

Reports of scientific research and findings in the media may be misleading or incomplete. When you are exposed to this information, you should ask yourself some questions so that you can make informed judgments about the information.

1. **Does the information come from a credible source?**

   Suppose you learn about a new product and it is stated that scientific evidence proves that the product works. A report from a respected news source may be more believable than an advertisement paid for by the product's manufacturer.

2. **How much evidence supports the claim?**

   Often, it may seem that there is new evidence every day of something in the world that either causes or cures an illness. However, information that is the result of several years of work by several different scientists is more credible than an advertisement that does not even cite the subjects of the experiment.

3. **How much information is being presented?**

   Science cannot solve all questions, and scientific experiments often have flaws. A report that discusses problems in a scientific study may be more believable than a report that addresses only positive experimental findings.

4. **Is scientific evidence being presented by a specific source?**

   Sometimes scientific findings are reported by people who are called experts or leaders in a scientific field. But if their names are not given or their scientific credentials are not reported, their statements may be less credible than those of recognized experts.

Differentiate Between Fact and Opinion

Sometimes information is presented as a fact when it may be an opinion. When scientific conclusions are reported, it is important to recognize whether they are based on solid evidence. Again, you may find it helpful to ask yourself some questions.

1. **What is the difference between a fact and an opinion?**

   A **fact** is a piece of information that can be strictly defined and proved true. An **opinion** is a statement that expresses a belief, value, or feeling. An opinion cannot be proved true or false. For example, a person's age is a fact, but if someone is asked how old they feel, it is impossible to prove the person's answer to be true or false.

2. **Can opinions be measured?**

   Yes, opinions can be measured. In fact, surveys often ask for people's opinions on a topic. But there is no way to know whether or not an opinion is the truth.

HOW TO DIFFERENTIATE FACT FROM OPINION

Human Activities and the Environment

Unfortunately, human use of fossil fuels is one of the most significant developments of the past few centuries. Humans rely on fossil fuels, a non-renewable energy resource, for more than 90 percent of their energy needs.

This careless misuse of our planet's resources has resulted in pollution, global warming, and the destruction of fragile ecosystems. For example, oil pipelines carry more than one million barrels of oil each day across tundra regions. Transporting oil across such areas can only result in oil spills that poison the land for decades.

Opinions

Notice words or phrases that express beliefs or feelings. The words *unfortunately* and *careless* show that opinions are being expressed.

Opinion

Look for statements that speculate about events. These statements are opinions, because they cannot be proved.

Facts

Statements that contain statistics tend to be facts. Writers often use facts to support their opinions.

Lab Handbook

Safety Rules

Before you work in the laboratory, read these safety rules twice. Ask your teacher to explain any rules that you do not completely understand. Refer to these rules later on if you have questions about safety in the science classroom.

Directions

- Read all directions and make sure that you understand them before starting an investigation or lab activity. If you do not understand how to do a procedure or how to use a piece of equipment, ask your teacher.
- Do not begin any investigation or touch any equipment until your teacher has told you to start.
- Never experiment on your own. If you want to try a procedure that the directions do not call for, ask your teacher for permission first.
- If you are hurt or injured in any way, tell your teacher immediately.

Dress Code

goggles

apron

gloves

- Wear goggles when
  — using glassware, sharp objects, or chemicals
  — heating an object
  — working with anything that can easily fly up into the air and hurt someone's eye
- Tie back long hair or hair that hangs in front of your eyes.
- Remove any article of clothing—such as a loose sweater or a scarf—that hangs down and may touch a flame, chemical, or piece of equipment.
- Observe all safety icons calling for the wearing of eye protection, gloves, and aprons.

Heating and Fire Safety

fire safety

heating safety

- Keep your work area neat, clean, and free of extra materials.
- Never reach over a flame or heat source.
- Point objects being heated away from you and others.
- Never heat a substance or an object in a closed container.
- Never touch an object that has been heated. If you are unsure whether something is hot, treat it as though it is. Use oven mitts, clamps, tongs, or a test-tube holder.
- Know where the fire extinguisher and fire blanket are kept in your classroom.
- Do not throw hot substances into the trash. Wait for them to cool or use the container your teacher puts out for disposal.

Electrical Safety

electrical safety

- Never use lamps or other electrical equipment with frayed cords.
- Make sure no cord is lying on the floor where someone can trip over it.
- Do not let a cord hang over the side of a counter or table so that the equipment can easily be pulled or knocked to the floor.
- Never let cords hang into sinks or other places where water can be found.
- Never try to fix electrical problems. Inform your teacher of any problems immediately.
- Unplug an electrical cord by pulling on the plug, not the cord.

Chemical Safety

chemical safety

poison

fumes

- If you spill a chemical or get one on your skin or in your eyes, tell your teacher right away.
- Never touch, taste, or sniff any chemicals in the lab. If you need to determine odor, waft. Wafting consists of holding the chemical in its container 15 centimeters (6 in.) away from your nose, and using your fingers to bring fumes from the container to your nose.
- Keep lids on all chemicals you are not using.
- Never put unused chemicals back into the original containers. Throw away extra chemicals where your teacher tells you to.
- Pour chemicals over a sink or your work area, not over the floor.
- If you get a chemical in your eye, use the eyewash right away.
- Always wash your hands after handling chemicals, plants, or soil.

Wafting

Glassware and Sharp-Object Safety

sharp objects

- If you break glassware, tell your teacher right away.
- Do not use broken or chipped glassware. Give these to your teacher.
- Use knives and other cutting instruments carefully. Always wear eye protection and cut away from you.

Animal Safety

- Never hurt an animal.
- Touch animals only when necessary. Follow your teacher's instructions for handling animals.
- Always wash your hands after working with animals.

Cleanup

disposal

- Follow your teacher's instructions for throwing away or putting away supplies.
- Clean your work area and pick up anything that has dropped to the floor.
- Wash your hands.

Using Lab Equipment

Different experiments require different types of equipment. But even though experiments differ, the ways in which the equipment is used are the same.

Beakers

- Use beakers for holding and pouring liquids.
- Do not use a beaker to measure the volume of a liquid. Use a graduated cylinder instead. (See page R16.)
- Use a beaker that holds about twice as much liquid as you need. For example, if you need 100 milliliters of water, you should use a 200- or 250-milliliter beaker.

Test Tubes

- Use test tubes to hold small amounts of substances.
- Do not use a test tube to measure the volume of a liquid.
- Use a test tube when heating a substance over a flame. Aim the mouth of the tube away from yourself and other people.
- Liquids easily spill or splash from test tubes, so it is important to use only small amounts of liquids.

Test-Tube Holder

- Use a test-tube holder when heating a substance in a test tube.
- Use a test-tube holder if the substance in a test tube is dangerous to touch.
- Make sure the test-tube holder tightly grips the test tube so that the test tube will not slide out of the holder.
- Make sure that the test-tube holder is above the surface of the substance in the test tube so that you can observe the substance.

Test-Tube Rack

- Use a test-tube rack to organize test tubes before, during, and after an experiment.

- Use a test-tube rack to keep test tubes upright so that they do not fall over and spill their contents.

- Use a test-tube rack that is the correct size for the test tubes that you are using. If the rack is too small, a test tube may become stuck. If the rack is too large, a test tube may lean over, and some of its contents may spill or splash.

Forceps

- Use forceps when you need to pick up or hold a very small object that should not be touched with your hands.

- Do not use forceps to hold anything over a flame, because forceps are not long enough to keep your hand safely away from the flame. Plastic forceps will melt, and metal forceps will conduct heat and burn your hand.

Hot Plate

- Use a hot plate when a substance needs to be kept warmer than room temperature for a long period of time.

- Use a hot plate instead of a Bunsen burner or a candle when you need to carefully control temperature.

- Do not use a hot plate when a substance needs to be burned in an experiment.

- Always use "hot hands" safety mitts or oven mitts when handling anything that has been heated on a hot plate.

Microscope

Scientists use microscopes to see very small objects that cannot easily be seen with the eye alone. A microscope magnifies the image of an object so that small details may be observed. A microscope that you may use can magnify an object 400 times—the object will appear 400 times larger than its actual size.

LAB HANDBOOK

Body The body separates the lens in the eyepiece from the objective lenses below.

Nosepiece The nosepiece holds the objective lenses above the stage and rotates so that all lenses may be used.

High-Power Objective Lens This is the largest lens on the nosepiece. It magnifies an image approximately 40 times.

Stage The stage supports the object being viewed.

Diaphragm The diaphragm is used to adjust the amount of light passing through the slide and into an objective lens.

Mirror or Light Source Some microscopes use light that is reflected through the stage by a mirror. Other microscopes have their own light sources.

Eyepiece Objects are viewed through the eyepiece. The eyepiece contains a lens that commonly magnifies an image 10 times.

Coarse Adjustment This knob is used to focus the image of an object when it is viewed through the low-power lens.

Fine Adjustment This knob is used to focus the image of an object when it is viewed through the high-power lens.

Low-Power Objective Lens This is the smallest lens on the nosepiece. It magnifies an image approximately 10 times.

Arm The arm supports the body above the stage. Always carry a microscope by the arm and base.

Stage Clip The stage clip holds a slide in place on the stage.

Base The base supports the microscope.

VIEWING AN OBJECT

1. Use the coarse adjustment knob to raise the body tube.
2. Adjust the diaphragm so that you can see a bright circle of light through the eyepiece.
3. Place the object or slide on the stage. Be sure that it is centered over the hole in the stage.
4. Turn the nosepiece to click the low-power lens into place.
5. Using the coarse adjustment knob, slowly lower the lens and focus on the specimen being viewed. Be sure not to touch the slide or object with the lens.
6. When switching from the low-power lens to the high-power lens, first raise the body tube with the coarse adjustment knob so that the high-power lens will not hit the slide.
7. Turn the nosepiece to click the high-power lens into place.
8. Use the fine adjustment knob to focus on the specimen being viewed. Again, be sure not to touch the slide or object with the lens.

MAKING A SLIDE, OR WET MOUNT

1 Place the specimen in the center of a clean slide.

2 Place a drop of water on the specimen.

3 Place a cover slip on the slide. Put one edge of the cover slip into the drop of water and slowly lower it over the specimen.

4 Remove any air bubbles from under the cover slip by gently tapping the cover slip.

5 Dry any excess water before placing the slide on the microscope stage for viewing.

Spring Scale (Force Meter)

- Use a spring scale to measure a force pulling on the scale.
- Use a spring scale to measure the force of gravity exerted on an object by Earth.
- To measure a force accurately, a spring scale must be zeroed before it is used. The scale is zeroed when no weight is attached and the indicator is positioned at zero.
- Do not attach a weight that is either too heavy or too light to a spring scale. A weight that is too heavy could break the scale or exert too great a force for the scale to measure. A weight that is too light may not exert enough force to be measured accurately.

Graduated Cylinder

- Use a graduated cylinder to measure the volume of a liquid.
- Be sure that the graduated cylinder is on a flat surface so that your measurement will be accurate.
- When reading the scale on a graduated cylinder, be sure to have your eyes at the level of the surface of the liquid.
- The surface of the liquid will be curved in the graduated cylinder. Read the volume of the liquid at the bottom of the curve, or meniscus (muh-NIHS-kuhs).
- You can use a graduated cylinder to find the volume of a solid object by measuring the increase in a liquid's level after you add the object to the cylinder.

meniscus

Read the volume at the bottom of the meniscus. The volume is 96 mL.

Metric Rulers

- Use metric rulers or meter sticks to measure objects' lengths.

- Do not measure an object from the end of a metric ruler or meter stick, because the end is often imperfect. Instead, measure from the 1-centimeter mark, but remember to subtract a centimeter from the apparent measurement.

- Estimate any lengths that extend between marked units. For example, if a meter stick shows centimeters but not millimeters, you can estimate the length that an object extends between centimeter marks to measure it to the nearest millimeter.

- **Controlling Variables** If you are taking repeated measurements, always measure from the same point each time. For example, if you're measuring how high two different balls bounce when dropped from the same height, measure both bounces at the same point on the balls—either the top or the bottom. Do not measure at the top of one ball and the bottom of the other.

EXAMPLE

How to Measure a Leaf

1. Lay a ruler flat on top of the leaf so that the 1-centimeter mark lines up with one end. Make sure the ruler and the leaf do not move between the time you line them up and the time you take the measurement.

2. Look straight down on the ruler so that you can see exactly how the marks line up with the other end of the leaf.

3. Estimate the length by which the leaf extends beyond a marking. For example, the leaf below extends about halfway between the 4.2-centimeter and 4.3-centimeter marks, so the apparent measurement is about 4.25 centimeters.

4. Remember to subtract 1 centimeter from your apparent measurement, since you started at the 1-centimeter mark on the ruler and not at the end. The leaf is about 3.25 centimeters long (4.25 cm − 1 cm = 3.25 cm).

Triple-Beam Balance

This balance has a pan and three beams with sliding masses, called riders. At one end of the beams is a pointer that indicates whether the mass on the pan is equal to the masses shown on the beams.

1. Make sure the balance is zeroed before measuring the mass of an object. The balance is zeroed if the pointer is at zero when nothing is on the pan and the riders are at their zero points. Use the adjustment knob at the base of the balance to zero it.

2. Place the object to be measured on the pan.

3. Move the riders one notch at a time away from the pan. Begin with the largest rider. If moving the largest rider one notch brings the pointer below zero, begin measuring the mass of the object with the next smaller rider.

4. Change the positions of the riders until they balance the mass on the pan and the pointer is at zero. Then add the readings from the three beams to determine the mass of the object.

300 g	position of largest rider
90 g	position of middle rider
+ 3 g	position of smallest rider
393 g	mass of beaker

Double-Pan Balance

This type of balance has two pans. Between the pans is a pointer that indicates whether the masses on the pans are equal.

1. Make sure the balance is zeroed before measuring the mass of an object. The balance is zeroed if the pointer is at zero when there is nothing on either of the pans. Many double-pan balances have sliding knobs that can be used to zero them.

2. Place the object to be measured on one of the pans.

3. Begin adding standard masses to the other pan. Begin with the largest standard mass. If this adds too much mass to the balance, begin measuring the mass of the object with the next smaller standard mass.

4. Add standard masses until the masses on both pans are balanced and the pointer is at zero. Then add the standard masses together to determine the mass of the object being measured.

Never place chemicals or liquids directly on a pan. Instead, use the following procedure:

1. Determine the mass of an empty container, such as a beaker.

2. Pour the substance into the container, and measure the total mass of the substance and the container.

3. Subtract the mass of the empty container from the total mass to find the mass of the substance.

The Metric System and SI Units

Scientists use International System (SI) units for measurements of distance, volume, mass, and temperature. The International System is based on multiples of ten and the metric system of measurement.

Basic SI Units		
Property	**Name**	**Symbol**
length	meter	m
volume	liter	L
mass	kilogram	kg
temperature	kelvin	K

SI Prefixes		
Prefix	**Symbol**	**Multiple of 10**
kilo-	k	1000
hecto-	h	100
deca-	da	10
deci-	d	$0.1 \left(\frac{1}{10}\right)$
centi-	c	$0.01 \left(\frac{1}{100}\right)$
milli-	m	$0.001 \left(\frac{1}{1000}\right)$

Changing Metric Units

You can change from one unit to another in the metric system by multiplying or dividing by a power of 10.

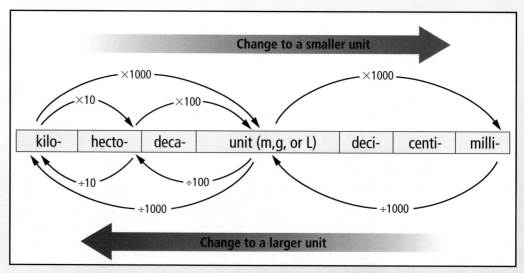

Example

Change 0.64 liters to milliliters.

(1) Decide whether to multiply or divide.

(2) Select the power of 10.

ANSWER 0.64 L = 640 mL

Change to a smaller unit by multiplying.

L ——— × 1000 ———→ mL

0.64 × 1000 = 640.

Example

Change 23.6 grams to kilograms.

(1) Decide whether to multiply or divide.

(2) Select the power of 10.

ANSWER 23.6 g = 0.0236 kg

Change to a larger unit by dividing.

kg ←——— ÷ 1000 ——— g

23.6 ÷ 1000 = 0.0236

Temperature Conversions

Even though the kelvin is the SI base unit of temperature, the degree Celsius will be the unit you use most often in your science studies. The formulas below show the relationships between temperatures in degrees Fahrenheit (°F), degrees Celsius (°C), and kelvins (K).

$$°C = \frac{5}{9}(°F - 32)$$

$$°F = \frac{9}{5}°C + 32$$

$$K = °C + 273$$

See page R42 for help with using formulas.

Examples of Temperature Conversions

Condition	Degrees Celsius	Degrees Fahrenheit
Freezing point of water	0	32
Cool day	10	50
Mild day	20	68
Warm day	30	86
Normal body temperature	37	98.6
Very hot day	40	104
Boiling point of water	100	212

Converting Between SI and U.S. Customary Units

Use the chart below when you need to convert between SI units and U.S. customary units.

SI Unit	From SI to U.S. Customary			From U.S. Customary to SI		
Length	When you know	multiply by	to find	When you know	multiply by	to find
kilometer (km) = 1000 m	kilometers	0.62	miles	miles	1.61	kilometers
meter (m) = 100 cm	meters	3.28	feet	feet	0.3048	meters
centimeter (cm) = 10 mm	centimeters	0.39	inches	inches	2.54	centimeters
millimeter (mm) = 0.1 cm	millimeters	0.04	inches	inches	25.4	millimeters
Area	When you know	multiply by	to find	When you know	multiply by	to find
square kilometer (km^2)	square kilometers	0.39	square miles	square miles	2.59	square kilometers
square meter (m^2)	square meters	1.2	square yards	square yards	0.84	square meters
square centimeter (cm^2)	square centimeters	0.155	square inches	square inches	6.45	square centimeters
Volume	When you know	multiply by	to find	When you know	multiply by	to find
liter (L) = 1000 mL	liters	1.06	quarts	quarts	0.95	liters
	liters	0.26	gallons	gallons	3.79	liters
	liters	4.23	cups	cups	0.24	liters
	liters	2.12	pints	pints	0.47	liters
milliliter (mL) = 0.001 L	milliliters	0.20	teaspoons	teaspoons	4.93	milliliters
	milliliters	0.07	tablespoons	tablespoons	14.79	milliliters
	milliliters	0.03	fluid ounces	fluid ounces	29.57	milliliters
Mass	When you know	multiply by	to find	When you know	multiply by	to find
kilogram (kg) = 1000 g	kilograms	2.2	pounds	pounds	0.45	kilograms
gram (g) = 1000 mg	grams	0.035	ounces	ounces	28.35	grams

Precision and Accuracy

When you do an experiment, it is important that your methods, observations, and data be both precise and accurate.

low precision

precision, but not accuracy

precision and accuracy

Precision

In science, **precision** is the exactness and consistency of measurements. For example, measurements made with a ruler that has both centimeter and millimeter markings would be more precise than measurements made with a ruler that has only centimeter markings. Another indicator of precision is the care taken to make sure that methods and observations are as exact and consistent as possible. Every time a particular experiment is done, the same procedure should be used. Precision is necessary because experiments are repeated several times and if the procedure changes, the results will change.

EXAMPLE

Suppose you are measuring temperatures over a two-week period. Your precision will be greater if you measure each temperature at the same place, at the same time of day, and with the same thermometer than if you change any of these factors from one day to the next.

Accuracy

In science, it is possible to be precise but not accurate. **Accuracy** depends on the difference between a measurement and an actual value. The smaller the difference, the more accurate the measurement.

EXAMPLE

Suppose you look at a stream and estimate that it is about 1 meter wide at a particular place. You decide to check your estimate by measuring the stream with a meter stick, and you determine that the stream is 1.32 meters wide. However, because it is hard to measure the width of a stream with a meter stick, it turns out that you didn't do a very good job. The stream is actually 1.14 meters wide. Therefore, even though your estimate was less precise than your measurement, your estimate was actually more accurate.

Making Data Tables and Graphs

Data tables and graphs are useful tools for both recording and communicating scientific data.

Making Data Tables

You can use a **data table** to organize and record the measurements that you make. Some examples of information that might be recorded in data tables are frequencies, times, and amounts.

EXAMPLE

Suppose you are investigating photosynthesis in two elodea plants. One sits in direct sunlight, and the other sits in a dimly lit room. You measure the rate of photosynthesis by counting the number of bubbles in the jar every ten minutes.

1. Title and number your data table.
2. Decide how you will organize the table into columns and rows.
3. Any units, such as seconds or degrees, should be included in column headings, not in the individual cells.

Table 1. Number of Bubbles from Elodea

Time (min)	Sunlight	Dim Light
0	0	0
10	15	5
20	25	8
30	32	7
40	41	10
50	47	9
60	42	9

◀ Always number and title data tables.

The data in the table above could also be organized in a different way.

Table 1. Number of Bubbles from Elodea

Light Condition	Time (min)						
	0	10	20	30	40	50	60
Sunlight	0	15	25	32	41	47	42
Dim light	0	5	8	7	10	9	9

◀ Put units in column heading.

Making Line Graphs

You can use a **line graph** to show a relationship between variables. Line graphs are particularly useful for showing changes in variables over time.

EXAMPLE

Suppose you are interested in graphing temperature data that you collected over the course of a day.

Table 1. Outside Temperature During the Day on March 7

	Time of Day						
	7:00 A.M.	9:00 A.M.	11:00 A.M.	1:00 P.M.	3:00 P.M.	5:00 P.M.	7:00 P.M.
Temp (°C)	8	9	11	14	12	10	6

1. Use the vertical axis of your line graph for the variable that you are measuring—temperature.

2. Choose scales for both the horizontal axis and the vertical axis of the graph. You should have two points more than you need on the vertical axis, and the horizontal axis should be long enough for all of the data points to fit.

3. Draw and label each axis.

4. Graph each value. First find the appropriate point on the scale of the horizontal axis. Imagine a line that rises vertically from that place on the scale. Then find the corresponding value on the vertical axis, and imagine a line that moves horizontally from that value. The point where these two imaginary lines intersect is where the value should be plotted.

5. Connect the points with straight lines.

Be sure to add a number and a title to your graph.

Figure 1. Outside Temperature During the Day on March 7

vertical axis

horizontal axis

Making Circle Graphs

You can use a **circle graph,** sometimes called a pie chart, to represent data as parts of a circle. Circle graphs are used only when the data can be expressed as percentages of a whole. The entire circle shown in a circle graph is equal to 100 percent of the data.

EXAMPLE

Suppose you identified the species of each mature tree growing in a small wooded area. You organized your data in a table, but you also want to show the data in a circle graph.

1. To begin, find the total number of mature trees.

    $56 + 34 + 22 + 10 + 28 = 150$

2. To find the degree measure for each sector of the circle, write a fraction comparing the number of each tree species with the total number of trees. Then multiply the fraction by 360°.

    Oak: $\frac{56}{150} \times 360° = 134.4°$

3. Draw a circle. Use a protractor to draw the angle for each sector of the graph.

4. Color and label each sector of the graph.

5. Give the graph a number and title.

Table 1. Tree Species in Wooded Area

Species	Number of Specimens
Oak	56
Maple	34
Birch	22
Willow	10
Pine	28

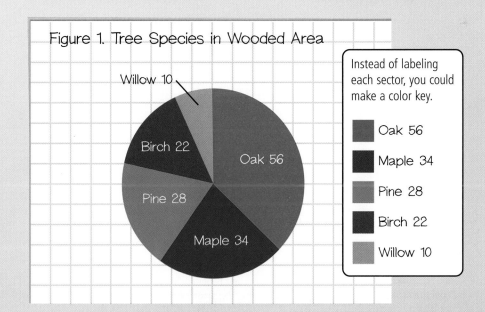

Figure 1. Tree Species in Wooded Area

Instead of labeling each sector, you could make a color key.

■ Oak 56
■ Maple 34
■ Pine 28
■ Birch 22
■ Willow 10

Bar Graph

A **bar graph** is a type of graph in which the lengths of the bars are used to represent and compare data. A numerical scale is used to determine the lengths of the bars.

EXAMPLE

To determine the effect of water on seed sprouting, three cups were filled with sand, and ten seeds were planted in each. Different amounts of water were added to each cup over a three-day period.

Table 1. Effect of Water on Seed Sprouting

Daily Amount of Water (mL)	Number of Seeds That Sprouted After 3 Days in Sand
0	1
10	4
20	8

1. Choose a numerical scale. The greatest value is 8, so the end of the scale should have a value greater than 8, such as 10. Use equal increments along the scale, such as increments of 2.

2. Draw and label the axes. Mark intervals on the vertical axis according to the scale you chose.

3. Draw a bar for each data value. Use the scale to decide how long to make each bar.

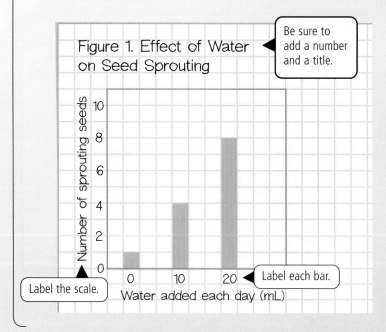

Figure 1. Effect of Water on Seed Sprouting

Be sure to add a number and a title.

Label the scale.

Label each bar.

Double Bar Graph

A **double bar graph** is a bar graph that shows two sets of data. The two bars for each measurement are drawn next to each other.

EXAMPLE

The seed-sprouting experiment was done using both sand and potting soil. The data for sand and potting soil can be plotted on one graph.

1. Draw one set of bars, using the data for sand, as shown below.

2. Draw bars for the potting-soil data next to the bars for the sand data. Shade them a different color. Add a key.

Table 2. Effect of Water and Soil on Seed Sprouting

Daily Amount of Water (mL)	Number of Seeds That Sprouted After 3 Days in Sand	Number of Seeds That Sprouted After 3 Days in Potting Soil
0	1	2
10	4	5
20	8	9

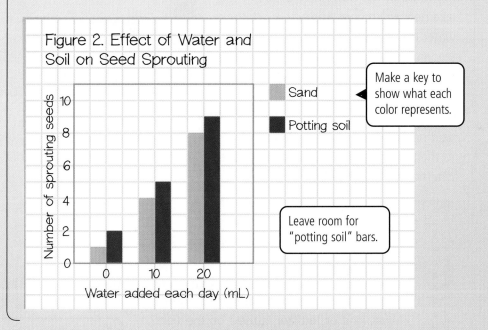

Figure 2. Effect of Water and Soil on Seed Sprouting

Make a key to show what each color represents.

Leave room for "potting soil" bars.

Designing an Experiment

Use this section when designing or conducting an experiment.

Determining a Purpose

You can find a purpose for an experiment by doing research, by examining the results of a previous experiment, or by observing the world around you. An **experiment** is an organized procedure to study something under controlled conditions.

1. Write the purpose of your experiment as a question or problem that you want to investigate.

2. Write down research questions and begin searching for information that will help you design an experiment. Consult the library, the Internet, and other people as you conduct your research.

> Don't forget to learn as much as possible about your topic before you begin.

EXAMPLE

Middle school students observed an odor near the lake by their school. They also noticed that the water on the side of the lake near the school was greener than the water on the other side of the lake. The students did some research to learn more about their observations. They discovered that the odor and green color in the lake

came from algae. They also discovered that a new fertilizer was being used on a field nearby. The students inferred that the use of the fertilizer might be related to the presence of the algae and designed a controlled experiment to find out whether they were right.

Problem

How does fertilizer affect the presence of algae in a lake?

Research Questions

- Have other experiments been done on this problem? If so, what did those experiments show?
- What kind of fertilizer is used on the field? How much?
- How do algae grow?
- How do people measure algae?
- Can fertilizer and algae be used safely in a lab? How?

> **Research**
> As you research, you may find a topic that is more interesting to you than your original topic, or learn that a procedure you wanted to use is not practical or safe. It is OK to change your purpose as you research.

Writing a Hypothesis

A **hypothesis** is a tentative explanation for an observation or scientific problem that can be tested by further investigation. You can write your hypothesis in the form of an "If . . . , then . . . , because . . ." statement.

> **Hypothesis**
>
> If the amount of fertilizer in lake water is increased, then the amount of algae will also increase, because fertilizers provide nutrients that algae need to grow.

Hypotheses
For help with hypotheses, refer to page R3.

Determining Materials

Make a list of all the materials you will need to do your experiment. Be specific, especially if someone else is helping you obtain the materials. Try to think of everything you will need.

> **Materials**
> - 1 large jar or container
> - 4 identical smaller containers
> - rubber gloves that also cover the arms
> - sample of fertilizer-and-water solution
> - eyedropper
> - clear plastic wrap
> - scissors
> - masking tape
> - marker
> - ruler

Determining Variables and Constants

EXPERIMENTAL GROUP AND CONTROL GROUP

An experiment to determine how two factors are related always has two groups—a control group and an experimental group.

1. Design an experimental group. Include as many trials as possible in the experimental group in order to obtain reliable results.

2. Design a control group that is the same as the experimental group in every way possible, except for the factor you wish to test.

Experimental Group: two containers of lake water with one drop of fertilizer solution added to each

Control Group: two containers of lake water with no fertilizer solution added

> Go back to your materials list and make sure you have enough items listed to cover both your experimental group and your control group.

VARIABLES AND CONSTANTS

Identify the variables and constants in your experiment. In a controlled experiment, a **variable** is any factor that can change. **Constants** are all of the factors that are the same in both the experimental group and the control group.

1. Read your hypothesis. The **independent variable** is the factor that you wish to test and that is manipulated or changed so that it can be tested. The independent variable is expressed in your hypothesis after the word *if*. Identify the independent variable in your laboratory report.

2. The **dependent variable** is the factor that you measure to gather results. It is expressed in your hypothesis after the word *then*. Identify the dependent variable in your laboratory report.

> **Hypothesis**
> If the amount of fertilizer in lake water is increased, then the amount of algae will also increase, because fertilizers provide nutrients that algae need to grow.

Table 1. Variables and Constants in Algae Experiment

Independent Variable	Dependent Variable	Constants
Amount of fertilizer in lake water	Amount of algae that grow	• Where the lake water is obtained • Type of container used • Light and temperature conditions where water will be stored

> Set up your experiment so that you will test only one variable.

MEASURING THE DEPENDENT VARIABLE

Before starting your experiment, you need to define how you will measure the dependent variable. An **operational definition** is a description of the one particular way in which you will measure the dependent variable.

Your operational definition is important for several reasons. First, in any experiment there are several ways in which a dependent variable can be measured. Second, the procedure of the experiment depends on how you decide to measure the dependent variable. Third, your operational definition makes it possible for other people to evaluate and build on your experiment.

EXAMPLE 1

An operational definition of a dependent variable can be qualitative. That is, your measurement of the dependent variable can simply be an observation of whether a change occurs as a result of a change in the independent variable. This type of operational definition can be thought of as a "yes or no" measurement.

Table 2. Qualitative Operational Definition of Algae Growth

Independent Variable	Dependent Variable	Operational Definition
Amount of fertilizer in lake water	Amount of algae that grow	Algae grow in lake water

A qualitative measurement of a dependent variable is often easy to make and record. However, this type of information does not provide a great deal of detail in your experimental results.

EXAMPLE 2

An operational definition of a dependent variable can be quantitative. That is, your measurement of the dependent variable can be a number that shows how much change occurs as a result of a change in the independent variable.

Table 3. Quantitative Operational Definition of Algae Growth

Independent Variable	Dependent Variable	Operational Definition
Amount of fertilizer in lake water	Amount of algae that grow	Diameter of largest algal growth (in mm)

A quantitative measurement of a dependent variable can be more difficult to make and analyze than a qualitative measurement. However, this type of data provides much more information about your experiment and is often more useful.

Writing a Procedure

Write each step of your procedure. Start each step with a verb, or action word, and keep the steps short. Your procedure should be clear enough for someone else to use as instructions for repeating your experiment.

If necessary, go back to your materials list and add any materials that you left out.

Controlling Variables
The same amount of fertilizer solution must be added to two of the four containers.

Controlling Variables
All four containers must receive the same amount of light.

Procedure

1. Put on your gloves. Use the large container to obtain a sample of lake water.

2. Divide the sample of lake water equally among the four smaller containers.

3. Use the eyedropper to add one drop of fertilizer solution to two of the containers.

4. Use the masking tape and the marker to label the containers with your initials, the date, and the identifiers "Jar 1 with Fertilizer," "Jar 2 with Fertilizer," "Jar 1 without Fertilizer," and "Jar 2 without Fertilizer."

5. Cover the containers with clear plastic wrap. Use the scissors to punch ten holes in each of the covers.

6. Place all four containers on a window ledge. Make sure that they all receive the same amount of light.

7. Observe the containers every day for one week.

8. Use the ruler to measure the diameter of the largest clump of algae in each container, and record your measurements daily.

LAB HANDBOOK

Recording Observations

Once you have obtained all of your materials and your procedure has been approved, you can begin making experimental observations. Gather both quantitative and qualitative data. If something goes wrong during your procedure, make sure you record that too.

Observations
For help with making qualitative and quantitative observations, refer to page R2.

For more examples of data tables, see page R23.

Table 4. Fertilizer and Algae Growth

Date and Time	Experimental Group		Control Group		
	Jar 1 with Fertilizer (diameter of algae in mm)	Jar 2 with Fertilizer (diameter of algae in mm)	Jar 1 without Fertilizer (diameter of algae in mm)	Jar 2 without Fertilizer (diameter of algae in mm)	Observations
5/3 4:00 P.M.	0	0	0	0	condensation in all containers
5/4 4:00 P.M.	0	3	0	0	tiny green blobs in jar 2 with fertilizer
5/5 4:15 P.M.	4	5	0	3	green blobs in jars 1 and 2 with fertilizer and jar 2 without fertilizer
5/6 4:00 P.M.	5	6	0	4	water light green in jar 2 with fertilizer
5/7 4:00 P.M.	8	10	0	6	water light green in jars 1 and 2 with fertilizer and in jar 2 without fertilizer
5/8 3:30 P.M.	10	18	0	6	cover off jar 2 with fertilizer
5/9 3:30 P.M.	14	23	0	8	drew sketches of each container

Notice that on the sixth day, the observer found that the cover was off one of the containers. It is important to record observations of unintended factors because they might affect the results of the experiment.

Use technology, such as a microscope, to help you make observations when possible.

Drawings of Samples Viewed Under Microscope on 5/9 at 100x

Jar 1 with Fertilizer

Jar 2 with Fertilizer

Jar 1 without Fertilizer

Jar 2 without Fertilizer

Summarizing Results

To summarize your data, look at all of your observations together. Look for meaningful ways to present your observations. For example, you might average your data or make a graph to look for patterns. When possible, use spreadsheet software to help you analyze and present your data. The two graphs below show the same data.

EXAMPLE 1

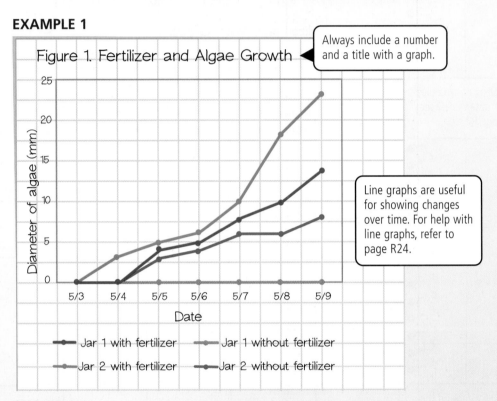

Always include a number and a title with a graph.

Line graphs are useful for showing changes over time. For help with line graphs, refer to page R24.

EXAMPLE 2

Bar graphs are useful for comparing different data sets. This bar graph has four bars for each day. Another way to present the data would be to calculate averages for the tests and the controls, and to show one test bar and one control bar for each day.

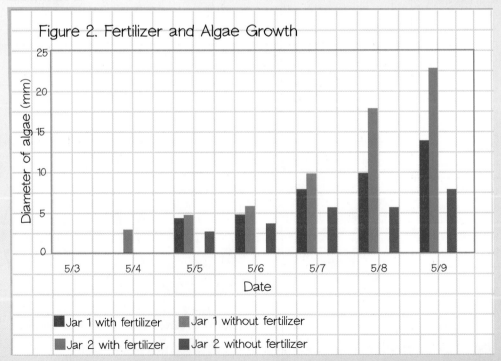

Drawing Conclusions

RESULTS AND INFERENCES

To draw conclusions from your experiment, first write your results. Then compare your results with your hypothesis. Do your results support your hypothesis? Be careful not to make inferences about factors that you did not test.

> For help with making inferences, see page R4.

Results and Inferences

The results of my experiment show that more algae grew in lake water to which fertilizer had been added than in lake water to which no fertilizer had been added. My hypothesis was supported. I infer that it is possible that the growth of algae in the lake was caused by the fertilizer used on the field.

> Notice that you cannot conclude from this experiment that the presence of algae in the lake was due only to the fertilizer.

QUESTIONS FOR FURTHER RESEARCH

Write a list of questions for further research and investigation. Your ideas may lead you to new experiments and discoveries.

Questions for Further Research

- What is the connection between the amount of fertilizer and algae growth?
- How do different brands of fertilizer affect algae growth?
- How would algae growth in the lake be affected if no fertilizer were used on the field?
- How do algae affect the lake and the other life in and around it?
- How does fertilizer affect the lake and the life in and around it?
- If fertilizer is getting into the lake, how is it getting there?

Math Handbook

Describing a Set of Data

Means, medians, modes, and ranges are important math tools for describing data sets such as the following widths of fossilized clamshells.

13 mm   25 mm   14 mm   21 mm   16 mm   23 mm   14 mm

Mean

The **mean** of a data set is the sum of the values divided by the number of values.

> **Example**
>
> To find the mean of the clamshell data, add the values and then divide the sum by the number of values.
>
> $$\frac{13 \text{ mm} + 25 \text{ mm} + 14 \text{ mm} + 21 \text{ mm} + 16 \text{ mm} + 23 \text{ mm} + 14 \text{ mm}}{7} = \frac{126 \text{ mm}}{7} = 18 \text{ mm}$$
>
> **ANSWER** The mean is 18 mm.

Median

The **median** of a data set is the middle value when the values are written in numerical order. If a data set has an even number of values, the median is the mean of the two middle values.

> **Example**
>
> To find the median of the clamshell data, arrange the values in order from least to greatest. The median is the middle value.
>
> 13 mm   14 mm   14 mm   16 mm   21 mm   23 mm   25 mm
>
> **ANSWER** The median is 16 mm.

Mode

The **mode** of a data set is the value that occurs most often.

> ### Example
>
> To find the mode of the clamshell data, arrange the values in order from least to greatest and determine the value that occurs most often.
>
> 13 mm   14 mm   14 mm   16 mm   21 mm   23 mm   25 mm
>
> **ANSWER** The mode is 14 mm.

A data set can have more than one mode or no mode. For example, the following data set has modes of 2 mm and 4 mm:

2 mm   2 mm   3 mm   4 mm   4 mm

The data set below has no mode, because no value occurs more often than any other.

2 mm   3 mm   4 mm   5 mm

Range

The **range** of a data set is the difference between the greatest value and the least value.

> ### Example
>
> To find the range of the clamshell data, arrange the values in order from least to greatest.
>
> 13 mm   14 mm   14 mm   16 mm   21 mm   23 mm   25 mm
>
> Subtract the least value from the greatest value.
>
> 13 mm is the least value.
> 25 mm is the greatest value.
>
> 25 mm − 13 mm = 12 mm
>
> **ANSWER** The range is 12 mm.

Using Ratios, Rates, and Proportions

You can use ratios and rates to compare values in data sets. You can use proportions to find unknown values.

Ratios

A **ratio** uses division to compare two values. The ratio of a value a to a nonzero value b can be written as $\frac{a}{b}$.

Example

The height of one plant is 8 centimeters. The height of another plant is 6 centimeters. To find the ratio of the height of the first plant to the height of the second plant, write a fraction and simplify it.

$$\frac{8 \text{ cm}}{6 \text{ cm}} = \frac{4 \times \overset{1}{\cancel{2}}}{3 \times \underset{1}{\cancel{2}}} = \frac{4}{3}$$

ANSWER The ratio of the plant heights is $\frac{4}{3}$.

You can also write the ratio $\frac{a}{b}$ as "a to b" or as $a:b$. For example, you can write the ratio of the plant heights as "4 to 3" or as 4:3.

Rates

A **rate** is a ratio of two values expressed in different units. A unit rate is a rate with a denominator of 1 unit.

Example

A plant grew 6 centimeters in 2 days. The plant's rate of growth was $\frac{6 \text{ cm}}{2 \text{ days}}$. To describe the plant's growth in centimeters per day, write a unit rate.

Divide numerator and denominator by 2: $\quad \frac{6 \text{ cm}}{2 \text{ days}} = \frac{6 \text{ cm} \div 2}{2 \text{ days} \div 2}$

You divide 2 days by 2 to get 1 day, so divide 6 cm by 2 also.

Simplify: $\quad = \frac{3 \text{ cm}}{1 \text{ day}}$

ANSWER The plant's rate of growth is 3 centimeters per day.

Proportions

A **proportion** is an equation stating that two ratios are equivalent. To solve for an unknown value in a proportion, you can use cross products.

Example

If a plant grew 6 centimeters in 2 days, how many centimeters would it grow in 3 days (if its rate of growth is constant)?

Write a proportion:	$\dfrac{6 \text{ cm}}{2 \text{ days}} = \dfrac{x}{3 \text{ days}}$
Set cross products:	$6 \text{ cm} \cdot 3 = 2x$
Multiply 6 and 3:	$18 \text{ cm} = 2x$
Divide each side by 2:	$\dfrac{18 \text{ cm}}{2} = \dfrac{2x}{2}$
Simplify:	$9 \text{ cm} = x$

ANSWER The plant would grow 9 centimeters in 3 days.

Using Decimals, Fractions, and Percents

Decimals, fractions, and percentages are all ways of recording and representing data.

Decimals

A **decimal** is a number that is written in the base-ten place value system, in which a decimal point separates the ones and tenths digits. The values of each place is ten times that of the place to its right.

Example

A caterpillar traveled from point *A* to point *C* along the path shown.

A   **36.9 cm**   B   **52.4 cm**   C

ADDING DECIMALS To find the total distance traveled by the caterpillar, add the distance from *A* to *B* and the distance from *B* to *C*. Begin by lining up the decimal points. Then add the figures as you would whole numbers and bring down the decimal point.

```
  36.9 cm
+ 52.4 cm
  89.3 cm
```

ANSWER The caterpillar traveled a total distance of 89.3 centimeters.

Example *continued*

SUBTRACTING DECIMALS To find how much farther the caterpillar traveled on the second leg of the journey, subtract the distance from *A* to *B* from the distance from *B* to *C*.

$$\begin{array}{r} 52.4 \text{ cm} \\ - \ 36.9 \text{ cm} \\ \hline 15.5 \text{ cm} \end{array}$$

ANSWER The caterpillar traveled 15.5 centimeters farther on the second leg of the journey.

Example

A caterpillar is traveling from point *D* to point *F* along the path shown. The caterpillar travels at a speed of 9.6 centimeters per minute.

MULTIPLYING DECIMALS You can multiply decimals as you would whole numbers. The number of decimal places in the product is equal to the sum of the number of decimal places in the factors.

For instance, suppose it takes the caterpillar 1.5 minutes to go from *D* to *E*. To find the distance from *D* to *E*, multiply the caterpillar's speed by the time it took.

9.6	1 decimal place
× 1.5	+ 1 decimal place
480	
96	
14.40	2 decimal places

> Align as shown.

ANSWER The distance from *D* to *E* is 14.4 centimeters.

DIVIDING DECIMALS When you divide by a decimal, move the decimal points the same number of places in the divisor and the dividend to make the divisor a whole number.

For instance, to find the time it will take the caterpillar to travel from *E* to *F*, divide the distance from *E* to *F* by the caterpillar's speed.

$$9.6\,\overline{)33.6}$$

> Move each decimal point one place to the right.

$$\begin{array}{r} 3.5 \\ 96\,\overline{)336.} \\ \underline{288} \\ 480 \\ \underline{480} \\ 0 \end{array}$$

> Line up decimal points.

ANSWER The caterpillar will travel from *E* to *F* in 3.5 minutes.

Fractions

A **fraction** is a number in the form $\frac{a}{b}$, where b is not equal to 0. A fraction is in **simplest form** if its numerator and denominator have a greatest common factor (GCF) of 1. To simplify a fraction, divide its numerator and denominator by their GCF.

Example

A caterpillar is 40 millimeters long. The head of the caterpillar is 6 millimeters long. To compare the length of the caterpillar's head with the caterpillar's total length, you can write and simplify a fraction that expresses the ratio of the two lengths.

Write the ratio of the two lengths: $\quad \dfrac{\text{Length of head}}{\text{Total length}} = \dfrac{6 \text{ mm}}{40 \text{ mm}}$

Write numerator and denominator as products of numbers and the GCF: $\quad = \dfrac{3 \times 2}{20 \times 2}$

Divide numerator and denominator by the GCF: $\quad = \dfrac{3 \times \overset{1}{\cancel{2}}}{20 \times \underset{1}{\cancel{2}}}$

Simplify: $\quad = \dfrac{3}{20}$

ANSWER In simplest form, the ratio of the lengths is $\frac{3}{20}$.

Percents

A **percent** is a ratio that compares a number to 100. The word *percent* means "per hundred" or "out of 100." The symbol for *percent* is %.

For instance, suppose 43 out of 100 caterpillars are female. You can represent this ratio as a percent, a decimal, or a fraction.

Percent	Decimal	Fraction
43%	0.43	$\frac{43}{100}$

Example

In the preceding example, the ratio of the length of the caterpillar's head to the caterpillar's total length is $\frac{3}{20}$. To write this ratio as a percent, write an equivalent fraction that has a denominator of 100.

Multiply numerator and denominator by 5: $\quad \dfrac{3}{20} = \dfrac{3 \times 5}{20 \times 5}$

$\quad = \dfrac{15}{100}$

Write as a percent: $\quad = 15\%$

ANSWER The caterpillar's head represents 15 percent of its total length.

Using Formulas

A **formula** is an equation that shows the general relationship between two or more quantities.

In science, a formula often has a word form and a symbolic form. The formula below expresses Ohm's law.

Word Form

$$Current = \frac{voltage}{resistance}$$

Symbolic Form

$$I = \frac{V}{R}$$

In this formula, I, V, and R are variables. A mathematical **variable** is a symbol or letter that is used to represent one or more numbers.

> The term *variable* is also used in science to refer to a factor that can change during an experiment.

Example

Suppose that you measure a voltage of 1.5 volts and a resistance of 15 ohms. You can use the formula for Ohm's law to find the current in amperes.

Write the formula for Ohm's law: $\quad I = \dfrac{V}{R}$

Substitute 1.5 volts for V and 15 ohms for R: $\quad I = \dfrac{1.5 \text{ volts}}{15 \text{ ohms}}$

Simplify: $\quad I = 0.1 \text{ amp}$

ANSWER The current is 0.1 ampere.

If you know the values of all variables but one in a formula, you can solve for the value of the unknown variable. For instance, Ohm's law can be used to find a voltage if you know the current and the resistance.

Example

Suppose that you know that a current is 0.2 amperes and the resistance is 18 ohms. Use the formula for Ohm's law to find the voltage in volts.

Write the formula for Ohm's law: $\quad I = \dfrac{V}{R}$

Substitute 0.2 amp for I and 18 ohms for R: $\quad 0.2 \text{ amp} = \dfrac{V}{18 \text{ ohms}}$

Multiply both sides by 18 ohms: $\quad 0.2 \text{ amp} \cdot 18 \text{ ohms} = V$

Simplify: $\quad 3.6 \text{ volts} = V$

ANSWER The voltage is 3.6 volts.

Finding Areas

The area of a figure is the amount of surface the figure covers.

Area is measured in square units, such as square meters (m²) or square centimeters (cm²). Formulas for the areas of three common geometric figures are shown below.

Area = (side length)²
$A = s^2$

Area = length × width
$A = lw$

Area = $\frac{1}{2}$ × base × height
$A = \frac{1}{2} bh$

Example

Each face of a halite crystal is a square like the one shown. You can find the area of the square by using the steps below.

Write the formula for the area of a square: $A = s^2$

Substitute 3 mm for s: $= (3 \text{ mm})^2$

Simplify: $= 9 \text{ mm}^2$

3 mm

3 mm

ANSWER The area of the square is 9 square millimeters.

Finding Volumes

The volume of a solid is the amount of space contained by the solid.

Volume is measured in cubic units, such as cubic meters (m³) or cubic centimeters (cm³). The volume of a rectangular prism is given by the formula shown below.

Volume = length × width × height
$V = lwh$

Example

A topaz crystal is a rectangular prism like the one shown. You can find the volume of the prism by using the steps below.

Write the formula for the volume of a rectangular prism: $V = lwh$

Substitute dimensions: $= 20 \text{ mm} \times 12 \text{ mm} \times 10 \text{ mm}$

Simplify: $= 2400 \text{ mm}^3$

10 mm

12 mm

20 mm

ANSWER The volume of the rectangular prism is 2400 cubic millimeters.

Using Significant Figures

The **significant figures** in a decimal are the digits that are warranted by the accuracy of a measuring device.

When you perform a calculation with measurements, the number of significant figures to include in the result depends in part on the number of significant figures in the measurements. When you multiply or divide measurements, your answer should have only as many significant figures as the measurement with the fewest significant figures.

Example

Using a balance and a graduated cylinder filled with water, you determined that a marble has a mass of 8.0 grams and a volume of 3.5 cubic centimeters. To calculate the density of the marble, divide the mass by the volume.

Write the formula for density: $\text{Density} = \dfrac{\text{mass}}{\text{Volume}}$

Substitute measurements: $= \dfrac{8.0 \text{ g}}{3.5 \text{ cm}^3}$

Use a calculator to divide: $\approx 2.285714286 \text{ g/cm}^3$

ANSWER Because the mass and the volume have two significant figures each, give the density to two significant figures. The marble has a density of 2.3 grams per cubic centimeter.

Using Scientific Notation

Scientific notation is a shorthand way to write very large or very small numbers. For example, 73,500,000,000,000,000,000,000 kg is the mass of the Moon. In scientific notation, it is 7.35×10^{22} kg.

Example

You can convert from standard form to scientific notation.

Standard Form	Scientific Notation
720,000	7.2×10^5
5 decimal places left	Exponent is 5.
0.000291	2.91×10^{-4}
4 decimal places right	Exponent is -4.

You can convert from scientific notation to standard form.

Scientific Notation	Standard Form
4.63×10^7	46,300,000
Exponent is 7.	7 decimal places right
1.08×10^{-6}	0.00000108
Exponent is -6.	6 decimal places left

Note-Taking Handbook

Note-Taking Strategies

Taking notes as you read helps you understand the information. The notes you take can also be used as a study guide for later review. This handbook presents several ways to organize your notes.

Content Frame

1. Make a chart in which each column represents a category.
2. Give each column a heading.
3. Write details under the headings.

NAME	GROUP	CHARACTERISTICS	DRAWING
snail	mollusks	mantle, shell	
ant	arthropods	six legs, exoskeleton	
earthworm	segmented worms	segmented body, circulatory and digestive systems	
heartworm	roundworms	digestive system	
sea star	echinoderms	spiny skin, tube feet	
jellyfish	cnidarians	stinging cells	

categories

details

Combination Notes

1. For each new idea or concept, write an informal outline of the information.
2. Make a sketch to illustrate the concept, and label it.

NOTES

Types of forces
- contact force
- gravity
- friction

informal outline

forces on a box being pushed

sketch with labels

contact force

gravity

friction

Make flash cards to help you study for a test. Write a concept on one side of each card and draw the sketch that goes with it on the other side. Use the cards to review concepts with a friend.

Main Idea and Detail Notes

1. In the left-hand column of a two-column chart, list main ideas. The blue headings express main ideas throughout this textbook.

2. In the right-hand column, write details that expand on each main idea.

You can shorten the headings in your chart. Be sure to use the most important words.

When studying for tests, cover up the detail notes column with a sheet of paper. Then use each main idea to form a question—such as "How does latitude affect climate?" Answer the question, and then uncover the detail notes column to check your answer.

MAIN IDEAS	DETAIL NOTES
1. Latitude affects climate. **main idea 1**	1. Places close to the equator are usually warmer than places close to the poles. **details about main idea 1** 1. Latitude has the same effect in both hemispheres.
2. Altitude affects climate. **main idea 2**	2. Temperature decreases with altitude. 2. Altitude can overcome the effect of latitude on temperature. **details about main idea 2**

Main Idea Web

1. Write a main idea in a box.

2. Add boxes around it with related vocabulary terms and important details.

You can find definitions near highlighted terms.

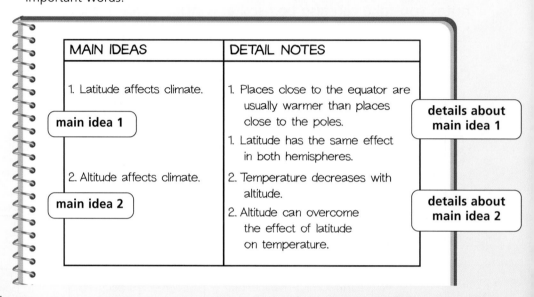

definition of *work*
Work is the use of force to move an object.

formula
Work = force · distance

main idea
Force is necessary to do work.

definition of *joule*
The joule is the unit used to measure work.

important detail
Work depends on the size of a force.

Mind Map

1. Write a main idea in the center.

2. Add details that relate to one another and to the main idea.

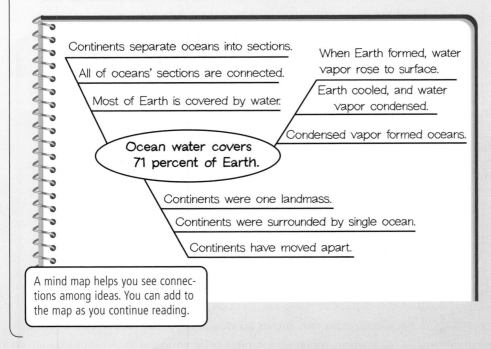

Continents separate oceans into sections.

All of oceans' sections are connected.

Most of Earth is covered by water.

When Earth formed, water vapor rose to surface.

Earth cooled, and water vapor condensed.

Condensed vapor formed oceans.

Ocean water covers 71 percent of Earth.

Continents were one landmass.

Continents were surrounded by single ocean.

Continents have moved apart.

A mind map helps you see connections among ideas. You can add to the map as you continue reading.

Supporting Main Ideas

1. Write a main idea in a box.

2. Add boxes underneath with information—such as reasons, explanations, and examples—that supports the main idea.

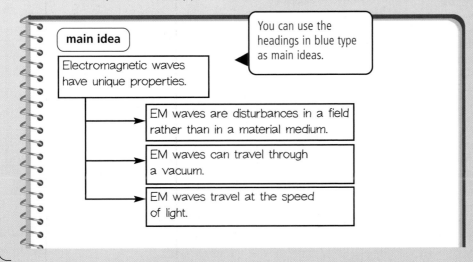

main idea

Electromagnetic waves have unique properties.

You can use the headings in blue type as main ideas.

EM waves are disturbances in a field rather than in a material medium.

EM waves can travel through a vacuum.

EM waves travel at the speed of light.

Outline

1. Copy the chapter title and headings from the book in the form of an outline.

2. Add notes that summarize in your own words what you read.

Cell Processes

1st key idea

I. Cells capture and release energy. — **1st subpoint of I**

  A. All cells need energy. — **2nd subpoint of I**

  B. Some cells capture light energy.

1st detail about B — 1. Process of photosynthesis

2nd detail about B — 2. Chloroplasts (site of photosynthesis)

     3. Carbon dioxide and water as raw materials

     4. Glucose and oxygen as products

  C. All cells release energy.

     1. Process of cellular respiration

     2. Fermentation of sugar to carbon dioxide

     3. Bacteria that carry out fermentation

II. Cells transport materials through membranes.

  A. Some materials move by diffusion.

     1. Particle movement from higher to lower concentrations

     2. Movement of water through membrane (osmosis)

  B. Some transport requires energy.

     1. Active transport

     2. Examples of active transport

Correct Outline Form
Include a title.

Arrange key ideas, subpoints, and details as shown.

Indent the divisions of the outline as shown.

Use the same grammatical form for items of the same rank. For example, if A is a sentence, B must also be a sentence.

You must have at least two main ideas or subpoints. That is, every A must be followed by a B, and every 1 must be followed by a 2.

Concept Map

1. Write an important concept in a large oval.
2. Add details related to the concept in smaller ovals.
3. Write linking words on arrows that connect the ovals.

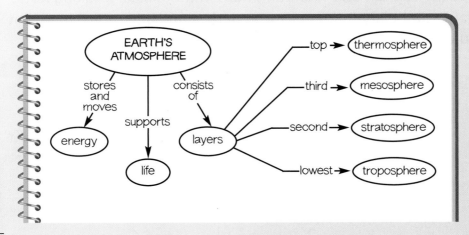

The main ideas or concepts can often be found in the blue headings. An example is "The atmosphere stores and moves energy." Use nouns from these concepts in the ovals, and use the verb or verbs on the lines.

Venn Diagram

1. Draw two overlapping circles, one for each item that you are comparing.
2. In the overlapping section, list the characteristics that are shared by both items.
3. In the outer sections, list the characteristics that are peculiar to each item.
4. Write a summary that describes the information in the Venn diagram.

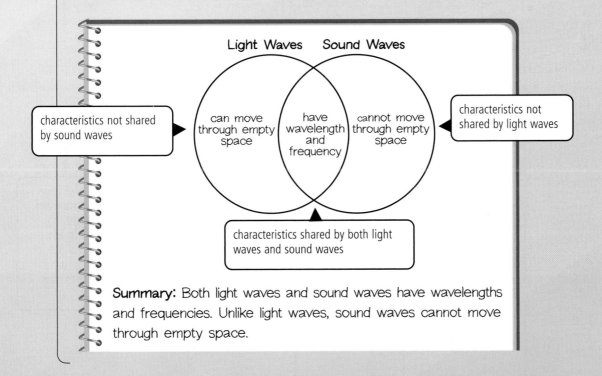

Summary: Both light waves and sound waves have wavelengths and frequencies. Unlike light waves, sound waves cannot move through empty space.

Vocabulary Strategies

Important terms are highlighted in this book. A definition of each term can be found in the sentence or paragraph where the term appears. You can also find definitions in the Glossary. Taking notes about vocabulary terms helps you understand and remember what you read.

Description Wheel

1. Write a term inside a circle.
2. Write words that describe the term on "spokes" attached to the circle.

When studying for a test with a friend, read the phrases on the spokes one at a time until your friend identifies the correct term.

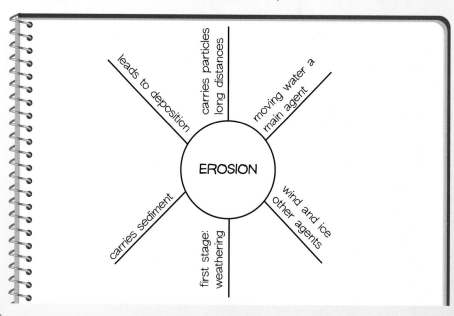

Four Square

1. Write a term in the center.
2. Write details in the four areas around the term.

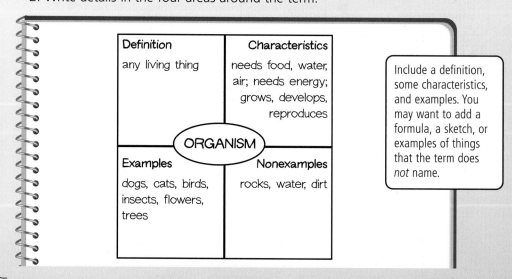

Include a definition, some characteristics, and examples. You may want to add a formula, a sketch, or examples of things that the term does *not* name.

Frame Game

1. Write a term in the center.
2. Frame the term with details.

Include examples, descriptions, sketches, or sentences that use the term in context. Change the frame to fit each new term.

Magnet Word

1. Write a term on the magnet.
2. On the lines, add details related to the term.

You can also use phrases or sentences on the lines.

Word Triangle

1. Write a term and its definition in the bottom section.
2. In the middle section, write a sentence in which the term is used correctly.
3. In the top section, draw a small picture to illustrate the term.

Glossary

A, B, C

absorption (uhb-SAWRP-shuhn)
The disappearance of a wave into a medium. When a wave is absorbed, the energy transferred by the wave is converted into another form of energy, usually thermal energy. (p. 93)

absorción La desaparición de una onda dentro de un medio. Cuando se absorbe una onda, la energía transferida por la onda se convierte a otra forma de energía, normalmente a energía térmica.

acoustics (uh-KOO-stihks)
The scientific study of sound; the behavior of sound waves inside a space. (p. 55)

acústica El estudio científico del sonido; el comportamiento de las ondas sonoras dentro de un espacio.

amplification
The strengthening of an electrical signal, often used to increase the intensity of a sound wave. (p. 55)

amplificación El fortalecimiento de una señal eléctrica, a menudo se usa para aumentar la intensidad de una onda sonora.

amplitude
The maximum distance that a disturbance causes a medium to move from its rest position; the distance between a crest or trough of a wave and line through the center of a wave. (p. 17)

amplitud La distancia máxima que se mueve un medio desde su posición de reposo debido a una perturbación; la distancia entre una cresta o valle de una onda y una línea que pasa por el centro de la onda.

atom
The smallest particle of an element that has the chemical properties of that element. (p. xv)

átomo La partícula más pequeña de un elemento que tiene las propiedades químicas de ese elemento.

bioluminescence
The production of light by living organisms. (p. 89)

bioluminiscencia La producción de luz por parte de organismos vivos.

compound
A substance made up of two or more different types of atoms bonded together.

compuesto Una sustancia formada por dos o más diferentes tipos de átomos enlazados.

concave
Curved inward toward the center, like the inside of a spoon. (p. 116)

cóncavo Dicho de una superficie con curvatura hacia dentro, como la parte interna de una cuchara.

convex
Curved outward, like the underside of a spoon. (p. 116)

convexo Dicho de una superficie con curvatura hacia afuera, como la parte externa de una cuchara.

cornea (KAWR-nee-uh)
A transparent membrane that covers the eye. (p. 127)

córnea Una membrana transparente que cubre el ojo.

crest
The highest point, or peak, of a wave. (p. 17)

cresta El punto más alto, o el pico, de una onda.

cycle
n. A series of events or actions that repeat themselves regularly; a physical and/or chemical process in which one material continually changes locations and/or forms. Examples include the water cycle, the carbon cycle, and the rock cycle.

v. To move through a repeating series of events or actions.

ciclo *s.* Una serie de eventos o acciones que se repiten regularmente; un proceso físico y/o químico en el cual un material cambia continuamente de lugar y/o forma. Ejemplos: el ciclo del agua, el ciclo del carbono y el ciclo de las rocas.

D, E, F

data
Information gathered by observation or experimentation that can be used in calculating or reasoning. *Data* is a plural word; the singular is datum.

datos Información reunida mediante observación o experimentación y que se puede usar para calcular o para razonar.

decibel dB
The unit used to measure the intensity of a sound wave. (p. 52)

decibel La unidad que se usa para medir la intensidad de una onda sonora.

density
A property of matter representing the mass per unit volume.

> **densidad** Una propiedad de la materia que representa la masa por unidad de volumen.

diffraction
The spreading out of waves as they pass through an opening or around the edges of an obstacle. (p. 26)

> **difracción** La dispersión de las ondas al pasar por una apertura o alrededor de los bordes de un obstáculo.

diffuse reflection
The reflection of parallel light rays in many different directions. (p. 114)

> **reflexión difusa** La reflexión de rayos de luz paralelos en muchas direcciones diferentes.

Doppler effect
The change in perceived pitch that occurs when the source or the one who hears the sound is moving. (p. 50)

> **efecto Doppler** El cambio en el tono percibido que ocurre cuando la fuente o el receptor de un sonido está en movimiento.

echolocation
The sending out of high-pitched sound waves and the interpretation of the returning echoes. (p. 59)

> **ecolocación** El envío de ondas sonoras de tono alto y la interpretación de los ecos que regresan.

electromagnetic spectrum EM spectrum
The range of all electromagnetic frequencies, including the following types (from lowest to highest frequency): radio waves, microwaves, infrared light, visible light, ultraviolet light, x-rays, and gamma rays. (p. 80)

> **espectro electromagnético** La escala de todas las frecuencias electromagnéticas, incluyendo los siguientes tipos (de la frecuencia más baja a la más alta): ondas de radio, microondas, luz infrarroja, luz visible, luz ultravioleta, rayos X y rayos gamma.

electromagnetic wave EM wave
A type of wave, such as a light wave or radio wave, that does not require a medium to travel; a disturbance that transfers energy through a field. (p. 73)

> **onda electromagnética** Un tipo de onda, como una onda luminosa o de radio, que no requiere un medio para propagarse; una perturbación que transfiere energía a través de un campo.

element
A substance that cannot be broken down into a simpler substance by ordinary chemical changes. An element consists of atoms of only one type. (p. xv)

> **elemento** Una sustancia que no puede descomponerse en otra sustancia más simple por medio de cambios químicos normales. Un elemento consta de átomos de un solo tipo.

energy
The ability to do work or to cause a change. For example, the energy of a moving bowling ball knocks over pins; energy from food allows animals to move and to grow; and energy from the Sun heats Earth's surface and atmosphere, which causes air to move. (p. xix)

> **energía** La capacidad para trabajar o causar un cambio. Por ejemplo, la energía de una bola de boliche en movimiento tumba los pinos; la energía proveniente de su alimento permite a los animales moverse y crecer; la energía del Sol calienta la superficie y la atmósfera de la Tierra, lo que ocasiona que el aire se mueva.

experiment
An organized procedure to study something under controlled conditions. (p. xxiv)

> **experimento** Un procedimiento organizado para estudiar algo bajo condiciones controladas.

fiber optics
Technology based on the use of laser light to send signals through transparent wires called optical fibers. This technology is often used in communications. (p. 137)

> **fibra óptica** Tecnología basada en el uso de luz de láser para mandar señales por alambres transparentes llamados fibras ópticas. Esta tecnología se usa a menudo en comunicaciones.

field
An area around an object where the object can apply a force—such as gravitational force, magnetic force, or electrical force—on another object without touching it.

> **campo** Un área alrededor de un objeto donde el objeto puede aplicar una fuerza, como fuerza gravitacional, fuerza magnética o fuerza eléctrica, sobre otro objeto sin tocarlo.

fluorescence (flu-REHS-uhns)
A phenomenon in which a material absorbs electromagnetic radiation of one wavelength and gives off electromagnetic radiation of a different wavelength. (p. 91)

> **fluorescencia** Un fenómeno en el cual un material absorbe radiación electromagnética de una longitud de onda y emite radiación electromagnética de longitud de onda diferente.

focal length
The distance from the center of a convex lens to its focal point. (p. 123)

> **distancia focal** La distancia del centro de un lente convexo a su punto focal.

focal point
The point at which parallel light rays reflected from a concave mirror come together; the point at which parallel light rays refracted by a convex lens come together. (p. 117)

> **punto focal** El punto en el cual se unen los rayos paralelos de luz reflejados por un espejo cóncavo; el punto en el cual se unen los rayos paralelos de luz refractados por un lente convexo.

force
A push or a pull; something that changes the motion of an object. (p. xxi)

> **fuerza** Un empuje o un jalón; algo que cambia el movimiento de un objeto.

friction
A force that resists the motion between two surfaces in contact. (p. xxi)

> **fricción** Una fuerza que resiste el movimiento entre dos superficies en contacto.

frequency
The number of waves that pass a fixed point in a given amount of time, usually one second; the number of cycles per unit time. (p. 17)

> **frecuencia** El número de ondas que pasan un punto fijo en un período de tiempo determinado, normal-mente un segundo; el número de ciclos por unidad de tiempo.

G, H, I

gamma rays
Part of the electromagnetic spectrum that consists of waves with the highest frequencies; electromagnetic waves with frequencies ranging from more than 10^{19} hertz to more than 10^{24} hertz. (p. 86)

> **rayos gamma** Parte del espectro electromagnético que consiste de ondas con las frecuencias más altas; las ondas electromagnéticas con frecuencias de más de 10^{19} hertzios hasta más de 10^{24} hertzios.

gravity
The force that objects exert on each other because of their mass. (p. xxi)

> **gravedad** La fuerza que los objetos ejercen entre sí debido a su masa.

hertz Hz
The unit used to measure frequency. One hertz is equal to one complete cycle per second. (p. 46)

> **hercio** La unidad usada para medir frecuencia, un hercio es igual a un ciclo completa por segundo.

hypothesis
A tentative explanation for an observation or phenomenon. A hypothesis is used to make testable predictions. (p. xxiv)

> **hipótesis** Una explicación provisional de una observación o de un fenómeno. Una hipótesis se usa para hacer predicciones que se pueden probar.

image
A picture of an object formed by rays of light. (p. 115)

> **imagen** Reproducción de la figura de un objeto formada por rayos de luz.

incandescence (IHN-kuhn-DEHS-uhns)
1. The production of light by materials having high temperatures. (p. 89) 2. Light produced by an incandescent object.

> **incandescencia** 1. La producción de luz por parte de materiales a altas temperaturas. 2. La luz producida por un objeto incandescente.

infrared light
Part of the electromagnetic spectrum that consists of waves with frequencies between those of microwaves and visible light. (p. 84)

> **luz infrarroja** Parte del espectro electromagnético que consiste de ondas con frecuencias entre las de las microondas y las de la luz visible.

intensity
The amount of energy of a wave, per wavelength. Intensity is associated with the amplitude of a sound wave and with the quality of loudness produced by the sound wave. (p. 52)

> **intensidad** La cantidad de energía de una onda sonora, por longitud de onda. La intensidad está asociada con la amplitud de una onda sonora y con la calidad del volumen producido por la onda sonora.

interference
The meeting and combining of waves; the adding or subtracting of wave amplitudes that occurs as waves overlap. (p. 27)

> **interferencia** El encuentro y la combinación de ondas; la suma o la resta de amplitudes de onda que ocurre cuando las ondas se traslapan.

J, K, L

kinetic energy
The energy of motion. A moving object has the most kinetic energy at the point where it moves the fastest.

> **energía cinética** La energía del movimiento. Un objeto que se mueve tiene su mayor energía cinética en el punto en el cual se mueve con mayor rapidez.

laser (LAY-zuhr)
A device that produces an intense, concentrated beam of light that can be brighter than sunlight. Lasers are often used in medicine and communications. (p. 135)

láser Un aparato que produce un intenso rayo de luz concentrado que es más brillante que la luz del Sol. Los láseres se usan a menudo en la medicina y las comunicaciones.

law
In science, a rule or principle describing a physical relationship that always works in the same way under the same conditions. The law of conservation of energy is an example.

ley En las ciencias, una regla o un principio que describe una relación física que siempre funciona de la misma manera bajo las mismas condiciones. La ley de la conservación de la energía es un ejemplo.

law of conservation of energy
A law stating that no matter how energy is transferred or transformed, it continues to exist in one form or another. (p. xix)

ley de la conservación de la energía Una ley que establece que no importa cómo se transfiere o transforma la energía, toda la energía sigue presente en alguna forma u otra.

law of reflection
A law of physics stating that the angle at which light strikes a surface (the angle of incidence) equals the angle at which it reflects off the surface (the angle of reflection). (p. 114)

ley de la reflexión Una ley de la física que establece que el ángulo al cual la luz incide sobre una superficie (el ángulo de incidencia) es igual al ángulo al cual se refleja (ángulo de reflexión) de la superficie.

lens
A transparent optical tool that refracts light. (p. 121)

lente Una herramienta óptica transparente que refracta la luz.

longitudinal wave (LAHN-jih-TOOD-uhn-uhl)
A type of wave in which the disturbance moves in the same direction that the wave travels. (p. 14)

onda longitudinal Un tipo de onda en la cual la perturbación se mueve en la misma dirección en la que viaja la onda.

luminescence
The production of light without the high temperatures needed for incandescence. (p. 89)

luminiscencia La producción de luz sin las altas temperaturas necesarias para la incandescencia.

M, N, O

mass
A measure of how much matter an object is made of. (p. xv)

masa Una medida de la cantidad de materia de la que está compuesto un objeto.

matter
Anything that has mass and volume. Matter exists ordinarily as a solid, a liquid, or a gas. (p. xv)

materia Todo lo que tiene masa y volumen. Generalmente la materia existe como sólido, líquido o gas.

mechanical wave
A wave, such as a sound wave or a seismic wave, that transfers kinetic energy through matter. (p. 11)

onda mecánica Una onda, como una onda sonora o una onda sísmica, que transfiere energía cinética a través de la materia.

medium
A substance through which a wave moves. (p. 11)

medio Una sustancia a través de la cual se mueve una onda.

microwaves
Part of the electromagnetic spectrum that consists of waves with higher frequencies than radio waves, but lower frequencies than infrared waves. (p. 83)

microondas Parte del espectro electromagnético que consiste de ondas con frecuencias mayores a las ondas de radio, pero menores a las de las ondas infrarrojas.

molecule
A group of atoms that are held together by covalent bonds so that they move as a single unit. (p. xv)

molécula Un grupo de átomos que están unidos mediante enlaces covalentes de tal manera que se mueven como una sola unidad.

optics (AHP-tihks)
The study of light, vision, and related technology. (p. 113)

óptica El estudio de la luz, la visión y la tecnología relacionada a ellas.

P, Q, R

pitch
The quality of highness or lowness of a sound. Pitch is associated with the frequency of a sound wave—the higher the frequency, the higher the pitch. (p. 45)

tono La cualidad de un sonido de ser alto o bajo. El tono está asociado con la frecuencia de una onda sonora: entre más alta sea la frecuencia, más alto es el tono.

polarization (POH-luhr-ih-ZAY-shuhn)
A way of filtering light so that all of the waves vibrate in the same direction. (p. 96)

> **polarización** Una manera de filtrar la luz para que todas las ondas vibren en la misma dirección.

primary colors
Three colors of light—red, green, and blue—that can be mixed to produce all possible colors. (p. 98)

> **colores primarios** Tres colores de luz, rojo, verde y azul, que se pueden mezclar para producir todos los colores posibles.

primary pigments
Three colors of substances—cyan, yellow, and magenta—that can be mixed to produce all possible colors. (p. 99)

> **pigmentos primarios** Tres colores de sustancias, cian, amarillo y magenta, que se pueden mezclar para producir todos los colores posibles.

prism
An optical tool that uses refraction to separate the different wavelengths that make up white light. (p. 97)

> **prisma** Una herramienta óptica que usa la refracción para separar las diferentes longitudes de onda que componen la luz blanca.

pupil
The circular opening in the iris of the eye that controls how much light enters the eye. (p. 127)

> **pupila** La apertura circular en el iris del ojo que controla cuánta luz entra al ojo.

radiation (RAY-dee-AY-shuhn)
Energy that travels across distances in the form of electromagnetic waves. (p. 75)

> **radiación** Energía que viaja a través de la distancia en forma de ondas electromagnéticas.

radio waves
The part of the electromagnetic spectrum that consists of waves with the lowest frequencies. (p. 82)

> **ondas de radio** La parte del espectro electromagnético que consiste de las ondas con las frecuencias más bajas.

reflection
The bouncing back of a wave after it strikes a barrier. (p. 25)

> **reflexión** El rebote de una onda después de que incide sobre una barrera.

refraction
The bending of a wave as it crosses the boundary between two mediums at an angle other than 90 degrees. (p. 25)

> **refracción** El doblamiento de una onda a medida que cruza el límite entre dos medios a un ángulo distinto a 90 grados.

regular reflection
The reflection of parallel light rays in the same direction. (p. 114)

> **reflexión especular** La reflexión de rayos de luz paralelos en la misma dirección.

resonance
The strengthening of a sound wave when it combines with an object's natural vibration. (p. 48)

> **resonancia** El fortalecimiento de una onda sonora cuando se combina con la vibración natural de un objeto.

retina (REHT-uhn-uh)
A light-sensitive membrane at the back of the inside of the eye. (p. 127)

> **retina** Una membrana sensible a la luz en la parte trasera del interior del ojo.

S, T, U

scattering
The spreading out of light rays in all directions as particles reflect and absorb the light. (p. 95)

> **dispersión** La disipación de los rayos de luz en todas las direcciones a medida que las partículas reflejan y absorben la luz.

sonar
Instruments that use echolocation to locate objects underwater; acronym for "sound navigation and ranging." (p. 59)

> **sonar** Instrumentos que usan la ecolocación para localizar objetos bajo agua; acrónimo en inglés para "navegación y determinación de distancias por sonido".

sound
A type of wave that is produced by a vibrating object and that travels through matter. (p. 37)

> **sonido** Un tipo de onda que es producida por un objeto que vibra y que viaja a través de la materia.

system
A group of objects or phenomena that interact. A system can be as simple as a rope, a pulley, and a mass. It also can be as complex as the interaction of energy and matter in the four spheres of the Earth system.

> **sistema** Un grupo de objetos o fenómenos que interactúan. Un sistema puede ser algo tan sencillo como una cuerda, una polea y una masa. También puede ser algo tan complejo como la interacción de la energía y la materia en las cuatro esferas del sistema de la Tierra.

technology
The use of scientific knowledge to solve problems or engineer new products, tools, or processes.

tecnología El uso de conocimientos científicos para resolver problemas o para diseñar nuevos productos, herramientas o procesos.

theory
In science, a set of widely accepted explanations of observations and phenomena. A theory is a well-tested explanation that is consistent with all available evidence.

teoría En las ciencias, un conjunto de explicaciones de observaciones y fenómenos que es ampliamente aceptado. Una teoría es una explicación bien probada que es consecuente con la evidencia disponible.

transmission (trans-MIHSH-uhn)
The passage of a wave through a medium. (p. 93)

transmisión El paso de una onda a través de un medio.

transverse wave
A type of wave in which the disturbance moves at right angles, or perpendicular, to the direction in which the wave travels. (p. 13)

onda transversal Un tipo de onda en el cual la perturbación se mueve en ángulo recto, o perpendicularmente, a la dirección en la cual viaja la onda.

trough (trawf)
The lowest point, or valley, of a wave (p. 17)

valle El punto más bajo de una onda.

ultrasound
Sound waves with frequencies above 20,000 hertz, the upper limit of typical hearing levels in humans, used for medical purposes, among other things. (p. 46)

ultrasonido Ondas sonoras con frecuencias superiores a 20,000 hertzios, el límite superior de los niveles auditivos típicos de los humanos. Estas ondas tienen usos médicos, entre otros.

ultraviolet light
The part of the electromagnetic spectrum that consists of waves with frequencies higher than those of visible light and lower than those of x-rays. (p. 85)

luz ultravioleta La parte del espectro electromagnético que consiste de ondas con frecuencias superiores a las de luz visible y menores a las de los rayos X.

V, W

vacuum
A space containing few or no particles of matter. (p. 41)

vacío Un espacio que no contiene partículas de materia o bien contiene muy pocas.

variable
Any factor that can change in a controlled experiment, observation, or model. (p. R30)

variable Cualquier factor que puede cambiar en un experimento controlado, en una observación o en un modelo.

vibration
A rapid, back-and-forth motion. (p. 37)

vibración Un movimiento rápido hacia delante y hacia atrás.

visible light
The part of the electromagnetic spectrum that consists of waves detectable by the human eye. (p. 84)

luz visible La parte del espectro electromagnético que consiste de ondas detectables por el ojo humano.

volume
An amount of three-dimensional space, often used to describe the space that an object takes up. (p. xv)

volumen Una cantidad de espacio tridimensional; a menudo se usa este término para describir el espacio que ocupa un objeto.

wave
A disturbance that transfers energy from one place to another without requiring matter to move the entire distance. (p. 9)

onda Una perturbación que transfiere energía de un lugar a otro sin que sea necesario que la materia se mueva toda la distancia.

wavelength
The distance from one wave crest to the next crest; the distance from any part of one wave to the identical part of the next wave. (p. 17)

longitud de onda La distancia de una cresta de onda a la siguiente cresta; la distancia de cualquier parte de una onda a la parte idéntica de la siguiente onda.

X, Y, Z

x-rays
The part of the electromagnetic spectrum that consists of waves with high frequencies and high energies; electromagnetic waves with frequencies ranging from more than 10^{16} hertz to more than 10^{21} hertz. (p. 86)

rayos X La parte del espectro electromagnético que consiste de las ondas con altas frecuencias y altas energías; las ondas electromagnéticas con frecuencias de más de 10^{16} hertzios hasta más de 10^{21} hertzios.

Index

Page numbers for definitions are printed in **boldface** type.
Page numbers for illustrations, maps, and charts are printed in *italics.*

E

ear, 39, *39*
ear canal, 39
eardrum, 39, *39*
earthquakes, 10, *10*, 11, *11*
echolocation, *59*, **59**
Edison, Thomas, 62, 63
electric field, 73–74, *74*
electromagnetic (EM) waves, 70–101, **73**
   See also laser, light
   artificial light, 90–92
   as a disturbance, 73–74
   formation of, 74, *74*
   frequencies, 78, 79, 81
   gamma rays, 81, *81*, **86**
   infrared light, 80, *80*, **84**, 84–85, *85*
   Internet activity, 71
   laser light and, 138
   light waves and materials, 93–99, 102
   measuring, 81
   microwaves, 77, *77*, 80, *80*, *83*, **83**
   radio waves, 79, 80, *80*, *82*, **82**
   sources of, 74
   spectrum, 80–81
   sunlight, 88–89, 102
   traits, 73–77, 102
   travel of, 75
   ultraviolet light, 81, *81*, *85*, **85**
   uses of, 79–86, 102
   visible light, 81, *81*, **84**
   x-rays, 81, *81*, *86*, **86**
electromagnetic spectrum, *80–81*, **80–81**
elements, xv
energy, xviii, **xix**
   chemical, xviii
   conservation of, **xix**
   electrical, xviii
   forms, of, xviii
   kinetic, 11
   sources of, xix
energy transfer, 9–12
   EM waves, 76, 77
   laser, 138
   sound, 37, 41
evaluating, **R8**
   media claims, R8
evidence, collection of, xxiv
experimental group, R30
experiments, **xxiv**. *See also* lab
   conclusions, drawing, R35
   constants, determining, R30
   controlled, **R28**, R30
   designing, R28–R35
   hypothesis, writing, R29
   materials, determining, R29
   observations, recording, R33
   procedure, writing, R32

   purpose, determining, R28
   results, summarizing, R34
   variables, R30–R31, R32
exponents, 78, **R44**
eye. *See* human eye
eyepiece lens, 132, *133*
eyesight. *See* vision

F

fact, **R9**
   different from opinion, R9
farsightedness, 129, *129*, 130
faulty reasoning, **R7**
fiber optics, **137**, *137*
field, 73–74
filament, 91, *91*
fluorescence, **91**
fluorescent light bulbs, *91*, 91–92
FM waves, 82, *82*
focal length, *122*, **123**
focal point, *116*, **117**, *121*, *122*
forces, **xxi**
   contact, xxi
   electrical, xxi
   friction, **xxi**
   gravity, **xxi**
   magnetic, xxi
   physical, xx–xxi
   waves and, 10
formulas, **R42**
   wave speed, 20–21
fractions, **R41**
frequency, 16, *17*, **17**, 18, 30, 66
   Doppler effect and, 51
   electromagnetic, 78, 79
   natural, 48
   of sound waves, 45–51, *46*
   wavelength and, 18, *18*, 46
   fundamental tone, 49
friction, **xxi**
fuel cell, hydrogen, xxvii, *xxvii*

G, H

gamma rays, 80, *81*, **86**
graphs
   bar, R26, R31
   circle, R25
   double bar, R27
   line, R24, R34
   using, 57
   wave properties, 18, *19*
gravity, **xxi**, xxiv
hair cells, ear, 39, *39*, 56, *56*
halogen light bulbs, 91, *91*
hammer, 39, *39*

Acknowledgments

Photography

Cover © David Pu'u/Corbis; **i** © David Pu'u/Corbis; **iii** *left (top to bottom)* Photograph of James Trefil by Evan Cantwell; Photograph of Rita Ann Calvo by Joseph Calvo; Photograph of Linda Carnine by Amilcar Cifuentes; Photograph of Sam Miller by Samuel Miller; *right (top to bottom)* Photograph of Kenneth Cutler by Kenneth A. Cutler; Photograph of Donald Steely by Marni Stamm; Photograph of Vicky Vachon by Redfern Photographics; **vi** © Chip Simons/Getty Images; **vii** © Alan Kearney/Getty Images; **ix** Photographs by Sharon Hoogstraten; **xiv–xv** © Larry Hamill/age fotostock america, inc.; **xvi–xvii** © Fritz Poelking/age fotostock america, inc.; **xviii–xix** © Galen Rowell/Corbis; **xx–xxi** © Jack Affleck/SuperStock; **xxii** AP/Wide World Photos; **xxiii** © David Parker/IMI/University of Birmingham High, TC Consortium/Photo Researchers; **xxiv** *left* AP/Wide World Photos; *right Washington University Record;* **xxv** *top* © Kim Steele/Getty Images; *bottom* Reprinted with permission from S. Zhou et al., *SCIENCE* 291:1944–47. Copyright 2001 AAAS; **xxvi–xxvii** © Mike Fiala/Getty Images; **xxvii** *left* © Derek Trask/Corbis; *right* AP/Wide World Photos; **xxxii** © The Chedd-Angier Production Company; **2–3** © Paul Kuroda/SuperStock; **3** *left* © B. Benoit/Photo Researchers; *right* © Powerstock/SuperStock; **4** *top* © Stephen Frink/Corbis; *bottom* © The Chedd-Angier Production Company; **5** © George Stetten, M.D., Ph.D; **6–7** © Peter Sterling/Getty Images; **7, 9** Photographs by Sharon Hoogstraten; **11** Photograph courtesy of Earthquake Engineering Research Institute Reconnaissance Team; **12** © Michael Krasowitz/Getty Images; **13** Photograph by Sharon Hoogstraten; **15** © John Lund/Getty Images; **16** © Greg Huglin/Superstock; **17** © Arnulf Husmo/Getty Images; **19** Richard Olsenius/National Geographic Image Collection; **20** Photograph by Sharon Hoogstraten; **22** *top* © 1990 Robert Mathena/Fundamental Photographs, NYC; *bottom* Photographs by Sharon Hoogstraten; **23, 24** Photographs by Sharon Hoogstraten; **25** © 2001 Richard Megna/Fundamental Photographs, NYC; **26** *top* © 1972 FP/Fundamental Photographs, NYC; *bottom* Photograph by Sharon Hoogstraten; **27** © 1998 Richard Megna/Fundamental Photographs, NYC; **28** © Hiroshi Hara/Photonica; **29** Takaaki Uda, Public Works Research Institute, Japan/NOAA; **30** *bottom center* © 2001 Richard Megna/Fundamental Photographs, NYC; *bottom right* © 1972 FP/Fundamental Photographs, NYC; **34–35** © Chip Simons/Getty Images; **35, 37** Photographs by Sharon Hoogstraten; **39** © Susumu Nishinaga/Photo Researchers; **41** Photographs by Sharon Hoogstraten; **42** © Jeff Rotman/Getty Images; **43** © John Terence Turner/Getty Images; **44** *left* © Reuters NewMedia Inc./Corbis; *background* © Jason Hindley/Getty Images; **45** Photograph by Sharon Hoogstraten; **47** *left (top to bottom)* © Will Crocker/Getty Images; © Dorling Kindersley; © Photodisc/Getty Images; © Dorling Kindersley; © Photodisc/Getty Images; © Stephen Dalton/Animals Animals; © Steve Bloom/Getty Images; *top right* © Don Smetzer/Getty Images; *bottom right* Brian Gordon Green/National Geographic Image Collection; **48** Photograph by Sharon Hoogstraten; **49** © Dorling Kindersley; **50** © Michael Melford/Getty Images; **52** © Tom Main/Getty Images; **53** Photograph by Sharon Hoogstraten; **55** *left* © Roger Ressmeyer/Corbis; *right* Symphony Center, Home of the Chicago Symphony Orchestra; **56** © Yehoash Raphael, Kresge Hearing Research Institute, The University of Michigan; **57** © Chris Shinn/Getty Images; **58** Photograph by Sharon Hoogstraten; **59** *top left* © Stephen Dalton/OSF/Animals Animals; *top right* © Paulo de Oliveira/Getty Images; *bottom left* © AFP/Corbis; *bottom right* U.S. Navy photo by Photographer's Mate 3rd Class Lawrence Braxton/Department of Defense; **60** *Fetal Fotos;* **63** © Andrew Syred/Photo Researchers; **64** *top left* © Reuters NewMedia Inc./Corbis; *bottom* Photographs by Sharon Hoogstraten; **65** Photograph by Sharon Hoogstraten; **66** *bottom left* © Stephen Dalton/OSF/Animals Animals; *bottom right* © Paulo de Oliveira/Getty Images; **68** © Photodisc/Getty Images; **70–71** © Alan Kearney/Getty Images; **71** *top, center* Photographs by Sharon Hoogstraten; *bottom* The EIT Consortium/NASA; **73** Photograph by Sharon Hoogstraten; **75** NASA, The Hubble Heritage Team, STScI, AURA; **76** Photograph by Sharon Hoogstraten; **78** *top* Palomar Observatory/Caltech; *center* NASA/MSFC/SAO; *bottom* NASA/CXC/ASU/J. Hester et al; *background* NASA/JHU/AUI/R. Giacconi et al.; **79** Photograph by Sharon Hoogstraten; **80** *left* © China Tourism Press/Getty Images; *center* © David Nunuk/Photo Researchers; *right* © Dr. Arthur Tucker/Photo Researchers; **81** *left to right* © Jeremy Woodhouse/Getty Images; © Sinclair Stammers/Photo Researchers; © Hugh Turvey/Photo Researchers; © Alfred Pasieka/Photo Researchers; **84** Photograph by Sharon Hoogstraten; **85** *top* © Dr. Arthur Tucker/Photo Researchers; *bottom* © Thomas Eisner, Cornell University; **86** © Martin Spinks; **87** © Photodisc/Getty Images; *inset* © David Young-Wolff/Getty Images; **88** Robert F. Sisson/National Geographic Image Collection; **89** © George D. Lepp/Corbis; **90** *top* © Raymond Blythe/OSF/Animals Animals; *bottom* Photograph by Sharon Hoogstraten; **92** © Traffic Technologies; **93** Photograph by Sharon Hoogstraten; **94** © Jeff Greenberg/Visuals Unlimited; **95** © Raymond Gehman/Corbis; **96** © Charles Swedlund; **97** *top* © Ace Photo Agency/Phototake; *bottom* © Dorling Kindersley; **98** Photograph by Sharon Hoogstraten; **100** *top* © Michael Newman/PhotoEdit; *bottom* Photographs by Sharon Hoogstraten; **101** Photographs by Sharon Hoogstraten; **102** *center right* Robert F. Sisson/National Geographic Image Collection; *bottom* © Ace Photo Agency/Phototake; **106** *top* The Granger Collection, New York; **107** *top* The Granger Collection, New York; *center left* Diagram of the eye from the *Opticae thesaurus. Alhazeni Arabis libri septem, nunc primum editi* by Ibn al-Haytham (Alhazen). Edited by Federico Risnero (Basleae, 1572), p. 6. Private collection, London; *center right* Courtesy of NASA/JPL/Caltech; *bottom* © Royal Greenwich Observatory/Photo Researchers; **108** *top* © Stock Connection/Alamy; *center* © Florian Marquardt; *bottom* © Museum of Holography, Chicago; **109** *top left* © Bettmann/Corbis; *top right* © Bettmann/Corbis; *bottom* © Bob Masini/Phototake; **110–111** © Tom Raymond/Getty Images; **111** *top, center* Photographs by Sharon Hoogstraten; *bottom* © Philippe Plaily/Photo Researchers; **112** Photograph by Sharon Hoogstraten; **114** © Laura Dwight/Corbis; **115** Photograph by Sharon Hoogstraten; **116** © Michael Newman/PhotoEdit; **117** Photographs by Sharon Hoogstraten; **118** Peter McBride/Aurora; **119** Photograph by Sharon Hoogstraten; **120** © Richard H. Johnston/Getty Images; **122** © Kim Heacox/Getty Images; *background* © Photodisc/Getty Images; **123** © T. R. Tharp/Corbis; **124** © Ruddy Gold/age photostock america, inc.; *bottom* Photograph by Sharon Hoogstraten; **125** Photographs by Sharon Hoogstraten; **126** © CMCD, 1994; **128** Photograph by Sharon Hoogstraten; **130** © Argentum/Photo Researchers; **131** Photograph by Sharon Hoogstraten; **133** *top* © Andrew Syred/Photo Researchers; *center* Lunar and Planetary Institute, CIRS/Library; *bottom* NASA; **134** Photograph by Sharon Hoogstraten; **135** Use of Canon Powershot S45 courtesy of Canon USA; **136** © Philippe Psaila/Photo Researchers; **137** *top* © Photodisc/Getty Images; *bottom* © Tom Stewart/corbisstockmarket.com; **138** Bradley C. Edwards, Ph.D.; **139** *top* © Photodisc/Getty Images; *center* © PhotoFlex.com; *bottom* © Michael Goldman/Photis/PictureQuest; **140** © Michael Newman/PhotoEdit; **R28** © Photodisc/Getty Images.

Illustrations

Accurate Art, Inc. **33**; Ampersand Design Group **139**; Argosy **10, 13, 14, 18, 19, 25, 30, 55, 61**; Eric Chadwick **98, 99**; Steve Cowden **12, 51, 54, 82**; Dan Stuckenschneider **62, 77, 91, 102, 133, 135, 136, 140, R11-R19, R22, R32**; Bart Vallecoccia **38, 39, 126, 127, 129, 135, 140.**